Psychodynamic Supervision

Psychodynamic Supervision

Perspectives of the Supervisor and the Supervisee

Edited by
Martin H. Rock, Ph.D.

JASON ARONSON INC.
Northvale, New Jersey
London

Director of Editorial Production: Robert D. Hack

This book was set in 10pt. New Century Schoolbook by Alabama Book Composition of Deatsville, Alabama and printed and bound by Book-mart Press of North Bergen, New Jersey.

Library of Congress Cataloging-in-Publication Data

Psychodynamic supervision : perspectives of the supervisor and the
    supervisee / [edited] by Martin H. Rock.
        p.   cm.
    Includes bibliographical references and index.
    ISBN 1-56821-693-9 (hardcover : alk. paper)
    1. Psychoanalysis—Study and teaching.   2. Psychotherapists—
Supervision of.   3. Psychodynamic psychotherapy—Study and
teaching.   I. Rock, Martin H.
    [DNLM: 1. Psychoanalysis—education.   2. Internship, Nonmedical.
3. Mentors.   WM 18 P97854 1996]
    RC502.P744   1996
    616.89'17—dc20
    DNLM/DLC
    for Library of Congress   96-5634

Manufactured in the United States of America. Jason Aronson Inc. offers books and cassettes. For information and catalog write to Jason Aronson Inc., 230 Livingston Street, Northvale, New Jersey 07647.

Contributors

Emanuel Berman, Ph.D. is an associate professor of psychology at the University of Haifa and supervising analyst at the Israel Psychoanalytic Institute; a clinical professor, New York University Postdoctoral Program in Psychoanalysis and Psychotherapy; and international editor of *Psychoanalytic Dialogues.*

Patrick J. Casement, M.A. is a training and supervising analyst, British Psycho-Analytical Society.

Nina Coltart, M.D. recently retired as a psychoanalyst and psychotherapist. She was a training analyst at the British Psycho-Analytical Society where she was also Chair of the Board and Council and Vice President. In retirement she tends to her garden, is a volunteer at Woburn Abbey, the local Stately Home, and has been made a governor at a local primary school.

Michael Eigen, Ph.D. is an associate clinical professor at the New York University Postdoctoral Program in Psychoanalysis and Psychotherapy; and a control, training analyst, and faculty member at The National Psychological Association for Psychoanalysis.

Sue N. Elkind, Ph.D. is dean of candidates, Psychoanalytic Institute of Northern California; and faculty member and supervisor, Psychotherapy Institute, Berkeley, California.

Lawrence Epstein, Ph.D. is a fellow, training, and supervising analyst at the William Alanson White Institute; and a clinical

professor of psychology in the Postdoctoral Program in Psychotherapy and Psychoanalysis, Adelphi University.

John Fiscalini, Ph.D. is a fellow, training, and supervising
analyst at the William Alanson White Institute; director of
clinical training, faculty member and supervisor, Manhattan
Institute for Psychoanalysis; faculty member and supervisor,
Institute for Contemporary Psychotherapy; and a clinical as-
sistant professor of psychology, New York University Postdoctoral Program in Psychoanalysis and Psychotherapy.

James L. Fosshage, Ph.D. is a co-founder, board director, and
faculty member, National Institute for the Psychotherapies;
faculty member and supervisor, Institute for the Psychoanalytic Study of Subjectivity; and a clinical professor, New York
University Postdoctoral Program in Psychoanalysis and Psychotherapy.

Mary Gail Frawley-O'Dea, Ph.D. is a faculty member and
supervisor at the Derner Institute of Advanced Psychological
Studies, Adelphi University.

Irwin Hirsch, Ph.D. is a faculty member and supervisor at the
Manhattan Institute for Psychoanalysis; a clinical professor
of psychology and supervisor in the Postdoctoral Program in
Psychotherapy and Psychoanalysis, Adelphi University; and a
member of the editorial board of *Psychoanalytic Dialogues.*

Robert J. Marshall, Ph.D. is a training analyst and supervisor
at the Center for Modern Psychoanalytic Studies; an associate
clinical professor at the Derner Institute of Advanced Psychological Studies, Adelphi University; and served 6 years as Chair
of the Publication Committee of Division of Psychoanalysis,
American Psychological Association.

Martin H. Rock, Ph.D. is an associate professor at the Ferkauf Graduate School of Psychology, Yeshiva University; supervisor, Institute for Contemporary Psychotherapy; supervisor and faculty member of the Supervisory Training Program, National Institute for the Psychotherapies; faculty member, Manhattan Institute for Psychoanalysis supervision training program; supervisor, Psychoanalytic Psychotherapy Study Center; and executive editor, *Contemporary Psychotherapy Review*.

Thomas Rosbrow, Ph.D. is a faculty member at the Psychoanalytic Institute of Northern California; a faculty member, San Francisco School of Psychology; a supervisor at the Mt. Zion Medical Center; and a member of the San Francisco Psychotherapy Research Group.

Benjamin Wolstein, Ph.D. is a clinical professor emeritus of psychology, Adelphi University; clinical professor of psychology, New York University Postdoctoral Program in Psychoanalysis and Psychotherapy; and supervising analyst and faculty member, William Alanson White Institute.

To Linda, Amelia, and Andrew,
and to the memory of my parents
Mildred S. and Robert G. Rock.

Contents

Acknowledgments

The first book I read on the topic of supervision, Ekstein and Wallerstein's *The Teaching and Learning of Psychotherapy*, was left to me by my aunt, Ann S. Quint, a clinical social worker who was the first person to encourage my interest in psychotherapy and psychoanalysis. I like to think of this gift as an impetus for my later interest in and exploration of the supervisory process.

I would like to express my gratitude to my wife, Linda Corman, for her forebearance, support, and considerable editorial help. Larry Epstein heartily encouraged this project, while the other authors responded enthusiastically to the suggestion that they contribute. Barbara Gerson and Ron Taffel egged me on, read my manuscripts and offered me very valuable editorial advice.

I would also like to acknowledge my students, supervisees, supervisors, the members of my peer supervision group, my patients, and fellow contributors to the book. They have taught me a great deal.

Acknowledgments

I

INTRODUCTION

Introduction

Psychodynamic Supervision: Perspectives of the Supervisor and the Supervisee

MARTIN H. ROCK, PH.D.

Supervision is central to training and professional development in all of the mental health disciplines. For therapists working in clinics and hospitals, as well as those who conduct private practices, supervision is a crucial resource long past formal training. In supervision, the recipient learns anew, keeps abreast, renews interest, restores confidence, and maintains hope in what Freud termed "the impossible profession" (Freud 1937). However, in spite of its importance, remarkably little attention has been devoted to discussions of the nature of the process and the factors which contribute to its effectiveness or ineffectiveness. In addition, there have been too few efforts to bring conceptualizations of supervision in line with the developments in psychoanalytic theory over the past decades (viz. Gill 1995). For many years there have been calls for specialized training in supervision (e.g. Grinberg 1970) over and above graduate and institute training in psychotherapy and psychoanalysis, yet the literature does not adequately support a curriculum for a supervision training program.

Descriptions of supervision which recognize that both participants are fully involved and that they mutually influence one another in the supervisory process are rarely found in the literature. In addition, most of this literature is devoid of first-hand accounts of the experience. Reports from supervisees about their personal experience in supervision are few and far between (Barnat 1980, Crick 1991, Fiscalini 1985, Gaoni and Neuman 1974, and Rosiello 1989, are among the few good examples) while reports from supervisors about their private experience of the work as opposed to their prescriptions and proscriptions, observations and formulations are even harder to find. Searles' early papers on supervision (1955, 1962) are remarkable exceptions to this observation in that they demonstrate the great value to the student of supervision of disclosure of the inner experience of the supervisor. In my view, people learn by experience. And in reading about clinical issues, students learn most effectively when writing evokes for them a vivid experience, one that allows them to empathize with the participants. While the psychotherapy and psychoanalytic literature abounds with involving and interesting accounts, the literature on psychodynamically oriented supervision is anemic.

In view of these gaps in the literature on supervision—particularly in the extraordinary paucity of first person, subjective accounts of the supervisory process and the lack of formulations which recognize and integrate developments in theory—I have put together a volume which I hope will begin to fill the void. I sought noted contributors to the literature on the process of psychodynamic psychotherapy and psychoanalysis who would bring the reader into the consultation room. The chapters of this book, I believe, allow a first hand look at creative supervisors and supervisees in action. The book is addressed to therapists and analysts, supervisors and supervisees. The theoretical framework that guides these authors is psychoanalytic, but the appeal will be broad-based. My hope is that anyone who has been supervised, is in supervision, or does supervision will find these chapters to be affirming, thought provoking, and challenging.

AN HISTORICAL CONTEXT

To set the stage for a discussion of the main themes emergent in this collection, I will outline a brief history of supervision of psychoanalytic psychotherapy and psychoanalysis. Articulated conceptualizations of the supervisory process and public debates about the dilemmas and problems of the supervisory endeavor have occurred primarily in psychoanalytic forums since the 1920s.[1]

The concerns of psychoanalytic educators about supervision have been quite consistent during the past 80 years in which it has been a formal aspect of psychoanalytic training. The basic idea of supervision was stated by Grinberg (1970) in his presentation to the Pre-Congress Conference on Training of the International Psychoanalytic Congress in 1969:

> We are all aware that one of the main goals of supervision is to teach the student the necessary knowledge and skill to perform his therapeutic work as well as possible.

However, ideas about the ways in which the overriding training goals are to be achieved and the structure of the relationship in which they are to be realized have evolved considerably. A number of issues and dilemmas have been discussed

---

1. I am indebted to Fleming and Benedek (1966) for their highly informative discussion of the early years of psychoanalytic supervision.

and debated over the decades, with different resolutions in each era derived from the psychoanalysis of the time.

Terese Benedek, who was trained by the first generation of analysts—and analyzed by Ferenczi—described supervision at the earliest phase of psychoanalytic training:

> "Looking back with a critical eye," one might say that the supervisor tended to take over the case. He demonstrated more or less skillfully how *he* would deal with the material presented and he seemed to expect his student to learn by imitation (Fleming and Benedek 1966).

This was the early concept of supervision which Balint critically termed "superego training" (Balint 1948). Glover (1952) also expressed concern that "mid-Victorian pedagogy," with its "authoritarian spoon-feeding" would limit the development of candidates' ability to go beyond the theory that had been given them by their teachers. Thus there has existed a longstanding tension between the need of psychoanalysts and psychoanalytic institutions to convey their view of the theory and method of treatment, and the need of supervisees to develop an autonomous and individually created identity.

Integrally related to this dilemma is the issue of evaluation. Institutions need to establish and maintain standards of good practice. Therefore candidates have to be evaluated and their inadequacies corrected.

In the 1930's there was a longstanding debate over whether the training analyst should both analyze and supervise the candidate. The Hungarian School (Kovacs 1936) argued that the candidate could only be properly supervised if his anxieties and conflicts were known in depth. Since it was agreed that most problems trainees had with patients were countertransference problems, no one could help him more effectively than his own analyst. The opposing view was the Berlin–Viennese School (Bibring 1937; Eitingon 1936). This view was that the candidate ought to be taught as well as analyzed; supervision ought to be separate from the candidate's analysis, experienced with several different supervisors; it should be purely didactic and steer clear of analyzing countertransferences, which would be taken care of in the candidate's personal analysis.

The Berlin–Viennese position developed in the context of the growing professionalism and institutionalization of psychoanalysis. The move to separate the training analysis from formal teaching was a response to the problems encountered when the candidate's analyst might also be his teacher and mentor, the source of referrals, and his evaluator (Eitingon 1936; Fleming and Benedek 1966).

Psychoanalytic education came to be structured in a tripartite model consisting of didactic learning, personal (or training) analysis, and supervision. The student's training analysis was conceived of as the springboard from which he or she would become a self knowing and self reflective psychoanalyst. While "blind spots" and other countertransferential manifestations would be unearthed and pointed out in a didactically oriented supervision, it was in the training analysis that these personal issues would be analyzed. In the didactic supervisory approach, the candidate was discouraged from discussing personal problems and conflicts in his work with his patients; the focus was to be on understanding the patient and on learning technique. After much controversy, the didactic approach prevailed and what ensued was what Gustin (1958) characterized as "an unspoken 'Gentleman's Agreement'—a no-man's land—in which the supervisor is expected not to allude to or tamper with personal attitudes or unconscious motivations of the student and to leave such matters to the student's personal analyst. . . ." Wolstein (1984b) suggests that the model of supervision developed at this time did not adequately take countertransference into account because countertransference had not yet become a focal point of psychoanalysis.

In fact, it proved to be difficult, if not impossible, for supervisors to limit themselves to pointing out the supervisee's errors of technique and not to pursue an inquiry about the countertransference reactions that caused them. DeBell (1981) noted that this restriction of the supervisor's role limited his ability to help the supervisee become more self aware. To my knowledge, the supervisee's feelings about this limitation on what was acceptable content were not reported in the literature. This problem has been the subject of debate throughout the history of psychoanalytic education, called by DeBell (1963) the teach/treat dilemma.

In the 1950s discussions of the Program Committee of the American Psychoanalytic Association (Ekstein 1960; Keiser 1956; Sloane 1957) as well as a smattering of articles (e.g. Blitzsen and Fleming 1953; Meerloo 1952) attempted to move beyond the either/or thinking on the teach/treat dilemma by recommending that the supervisor confront the student with his countertransference *and* teach him the technique of psychoanalysis. Nevertheless, the discomfort of these analysts was revealed by their careful warnings about the necessary tact that was required (Fleming and Benedek 1966).

It was not until the late 1950s that the contribution of the personalities of the supervisor and the patient to the process of the supervision was recognized in the literature. In 1958 Ekstein and Wallerstein published their landmark study *The Teaching and Learning of Psychotherapy*, which was based on their work at the Menninger Foundation training psychiatric residents and psychology interns. Ekstein and Wallerstein presented a model of the supervisory process which took into account the complex contributions of each of the participants (patient, therapist, supervisor, and institution) and opened the way for consideration of the supervisory relationship and its problems which previously had been treated as if they were not significant. Also, Searles (1955, 1962) wrote evocatively about the powerful "reflection process" by which the supervisory interaction is influenced by the transference-countertransference processes in the analytic relationship. He demonstrated that clarification of the resultant problems in the supervision served not only to avert roadblocks to effective learning in the supervision but also to catalyze change in the therapy. Ekstein and Wallerstein also emphasized this parallel process, and they delineated the ways in which it could be used to understand the therapy process. They focused on the student's inevitable "problems about learning" (problems between the supervisor and supervisee—the supervisee's resistance to supervision) in order to shed light on the problems that existed between therapist and patient ("learning problems"). Their central concern was the character of the student as it is manifested in the work. The aim of the supervision was to facilitate learning and personal growth of the therapist. Here then was explicit focus in the supervision on the supervisee's countertransference and a compelling rationale for its inclusion. Nevertheless, considerable tension has remained for supervisors about their efforts to utilize and correct supervisees', personal contribution to the analytic process (Gorkin 1986; Issacharoff 1984; Sarnat 1992; and Wallerstein, 1981).

While the Ekstein and Wallerstein model called attention to the triadic structure of the supervisory situation and surely left room for discussion of mutual influence processes that occur among all the participants, their interest was primarily on the influence of characterological problems of the student as they impeded the therapeutic and supervisory work.

Research on the process of supervision by Fleming and Benedek (1966) supported Ekstein and Wallerstein's emphasis on "the importance of supervision as an experience which involves the whole personality of both student and teacher" (Fleming and Benedek 1966). Fleming and Benedek offered Isakower's (1957) thesis that "clarification of the analytic instrument" is an essential task of supervisory teaching. Importantly, in calling into question the value of supervision that was didactic and primarily patient centered, they articulated their view that "statements about supervision frequently do not distinguish between supervision from the position of the student and supervision from the position of the teacher." They further stated that "the fact that something is 'taught' does not guarantee it will be learned. Only the learner can accomplish this . . . [The supervisor's] activity creates only the conditions which facilitate growth, not growth itself." These authors emphasized the communication process in supervision and documented its vulnerability to derailment. Evident in these quotes is a recognition of the necessity of a perspectivistic view of dyadic supervisory interactions: Supervisors' awareness of their impact on the student is crucial. But curiously in their numerous verbatum accounts of supervisory interactions the process is often dealt with superficially: Typically their concern (and that of subsequent authors) is whether the supervisee will resist or work with or swallow whole the supervisor's instruction. They did not adequately recognize supervision as a complex negotiation between two persons with two (often very different) perspectives, in spite of their stated goals.

In addition, Fleming and Benedek (1966) contributed the concept of the "learning alliance" in supervision. This concept parallels that of the therapeutic alliance (Greenson 1966) and was seen as the basis of trust, shared learning goals, and mutual involvement on which the potentially bumpy road of supervision was grounded. Here then was a rich discussion of the intense mutual involvement of teacher and student in a relationship in which effective teaching and learning could take place.

In 1971 Doehrman completed her doctoral dissertation in which she sought to substantiate empirically the Ekstein and Wallerstein process model of supervision (Doehrman, 1976). Through her careful analysis of repeated interviews with supervisors, patients and therapists over a 6 month period, she found that the expected operation of parallel processes was clearly evident. Difficulties in the therapeutic relationship were unconsciously communicated to the supervisor via the difficulties in the supervisory relationship. Unexpectedly, however, she found that the influence of the supervisors' emotional reactions to the supervisee and to the patient were an outstanding feature of the processes observed. She did indeed find that "helping the student know the dynamics in his own struggle to use help [i.e. his problems about learning] is to know also the client's struggle." Yet beyond this, she found that the inevitable difficulties in the supervision were the product of an unconscious mutual influence process within the supervisory relationship.

Subsequent discussions of the parallel process phenomenon (e.g. Gediman and Wolkenfeld 1980) generally paid more attention to the supervisor's contribution to the dynamics of the supervisory situation, and much of the discussion has centered on the supervisor's style of working. Style has been highlighted for many years, beginning with DeBell's 1963 paper (DeBell 1963, 1981, Levenson 1982) and seems universally to be acknowledged as a significant contributing factor in the quality of the interaction and the nature of the learning that takes place in supervision.

Yet such conceptions seem typically to have omitted any pointed discussion of the supervisor's personality or of his or her susceptibility to being profoundly influenced by the supervisory process. The contributions of Searles (1955, 1962) and Grinberg (1970) are important exceptions. Searles wrote about the extraordinary emotional impact of the supervisory experience on both supervisor and supervisee, while Grinberg detailed the ways in which the personal psychopathology of both participants might derail the supervisory process. But it was not until recent years that authors explicitly dealt with the supervisor's countertransference and resistance processes in supervision. Wolstein (1984a), Issacharoff (1984), Fiscalini (1985), Teitelbaum (1990), Gorkin (1986), Caligor (1984), and

Sarnat (1992), among others, have advanced the theory of supervision in the direction of a full recognition of the 2- (or 3-) person nature of the field. What is required is a fuller understanding of supervision as operating in an intersubjective context wherein the contributions by and effects upon all the participants are acknowledged and fully utilized.

The chapters in this book articulate a contemporary psychodynamic approach from an interpersonal/relational perspective to a set of basic issues in supervision. Each of these issues has concerned psychoanalytic educators for as long as they have discussed the supervisory process. None has been or can be resolved; each attempted solution reflects the predominant therapeutic perspective of the day.

A CONTEMPORARY APPROACH TO THE DEFINING ISSUES IN THE SUPERVISORY PROCESS.

The Method of Participant Observation

Some of the chapters that I have included have previously been published (Casement 1993, Epstein 1986, Fiscalini 1985, and Wolstein 1984). All of them promote the idea that the supervisor must be carefully attuned to the nature of his or her impact on the supervisee.

John Fiscalini's essay is a rich and telling report of his experiences as a supervisee in two very different supervisory relationships. Other chapters, written for this volume, were researched according to an approach that relies upon participant observation (Sullivan 1954) and mutual inquiry. Nina Coltart and Sue N. Elkind requested of supervisees to write about what they found meaningful and influential in their supervisory and consultation experiences with the authors, while my students and I conducted questionnaire studies in which supervisees were asked to describe and evaluate their experience of supervision. The results of these inquiries lead the reader to fresh glimpses of the supervisory process. In addition, Mary Gail Frawley-O'Dae and Irwin Hirsch, in a unique pair of presentations, disclose the nature and quality of their difficult shared supervisory experience. This is truly a first-hand view from the inside, one that is unfiltered through the lens of an "objective" observer.

In the same spirit of authenticity and open disclosure, Michael Eigen presents an evocative account of his inner musings and struggles to engage in productive supervisory encounters with two supervisees who are similarly involved in struggling to make contact with patients who they find to be terribly troublesome. Eigen's profound discussion of his self-supervisory effort sheds new light on the now well-worn concept of the "learning alliance."

The Basic Issues Addressed by the Authors:

1. The nature of supervisory instruction: Coparticipation and dialogue. The classical position holds that the supervisor must use a diagnostic point of view toward the student's learning. This involves the need to diagnose what the student needs to learn and to formulate how he can best learn it. In addition, the supervisor must assess the extent to which the supervisee is "ready to learn," to engage in a learning alliance, and "brings unresolved neurotic problems" to the therapeutic and supervisory situations (Schlesinger 1981). In addition to the highly judgmental sound of such prescriptions, this stance also sets up the supervisor to be the arbiter of a considerable portion of the reality of the supervisory and therapeutic processes. The supervisor knows best (Lesser 1984) and the supervisee ought to listen.

In contrast, the contributors to this book advocate an approach

which is based on the interpersonal idea of participant observation (Sullivan 1954). Lawrence Epstein's term "active participant observation" characterizes the supervisory stance shared
by the contributors. Assessments and diagnoses are arrived at
through dialogue which is the role and responsibility of both
parties. The authors are in agreement about the need to see the
unfolding supervisory process as the shared creation of supervisor and supervisee. Thus the supervisee is viewed as substantially more aware of his or her needs and requirements
and active in the learning process. Thomas Rosbrow, in his
chapter, observes that the supervisee typically has a plan,
conscious or unconscious, for learning in supervision; it is the
job of the supervisor, then, to be "optimally responsive" to the
supervisee's learning needs. At the same time, Rosbrow points
out that the supervisor has much to gain or lose in any
supervisory relationship. His view is consistent with that of
Masud Khan (1974), who stated: "My own experience . . .
guides me to say that whenever I, as a supervisor, cannot learn
from a candidate's work, then he cannot learn from me either.
We have little to offer each other. Learning here is a mutual
and reciprocal activity" (p.118).

   In the same spirit of mutuality, the authors advise supervisors to be acutely aware of their impact, particularly of
negative effects, on the supervisee, although they recognize
that they cannot hope to be completely aware of what is being
enacted unconsciously. In his chapter, Lawrence Epstein points
out that even seemingly routine didactic interventions by the
supervisor may have powerful unintended relational consequences for the supervision and the therapy. Beyond that,
difficulties and conflicts inevitably emerge from an interactive
process with transferential and countertransferential currents
from all participants.

   The solution to such difficulties or even impasses in the
supervision is not diagnosis and interpretation of the supervisee's neurotic problems. At times the supervisor may need to

modify his technique to adjust to the supervisee's negative reaction to his intervention. At other times the solution lies in a co-participant inquiry into the subjective meaning of the interpersonal interaction between the supervisor and supervisee. In Levenson's (1991) terms the question is not: "What is the supervisee's problem?" Instead, the question is: "What's going on around here?", with the full recognition that the difficulty may be the outcome of the direct interplay of two personalities in this intense and intimate relationship, with indirect contributions from the patient. This characterization of the process represents a levelling of the (hierarchical) distance between supervisor and supervisee, minimizes the impact of blaming processes, and allows for open disclosure and exploration. The Hirsch and Frawley-O'Dea chapters present a vivid illustration and discussion of the ways in which the supervision can founder when there are unattended difficulties in the supervisory relationship. In her exciting and innovative approach to consultations for therapeutic and supervisory relationships that are stuck in impasses, Elkind illustrates the ways in which relationships mired in transference-countertransference binds can be resurrected or constructively ended. Her approach is a kind of psychoanalytically informed arbitration.

2. *Evaluation of the supervisee.* In the history of psychoanalytic supervision there has been an undermining of the hierarchy of authority of the supervisory situation reflective of larger trends in Western society. The definition of supervision has involved the investment of the supervisor with the responsibility to oversee and judge the competence of the supervisee's work. The necessary function of maintaining standards imposes severe limitations on the supervisor's ability to facilitate open discussion and the student's development. Feiner (1994) has pointed out that this is an inherent contradiction "between learning openly and being evaluated at the same time." He terms this "the recurrent contradiction between compassion

and standards." Benjamin Wolstein, in his chapter, states that the evaluation process, which by necessity interferes with the guarantee of confidentiality, always undermines the atmosphere of safety in the supervision. Similarly Coltart argues persuasively that the hierarchical structure that underlies this function of supervision excessively constricts the creative potential of learning in supervision. While Wolstein's solution is to replace the individual model of supervision with small group supervision, Coltart attempts to avoid the dilemma altogether by only conducting private supervision, outside institutional structures. She indicates that it is only in such a protected situation that she can devote herself to a meeting of students' learning needs without regard for the institutional necessities of control and judgment. Both of these authors believe that the impact of the power differential and the supervisee's experience of the dangers of exposure and censure must be diffused. Emanuel Berman, on the other hand, suggests to us that the process of evaluation can be a very constructive aspect of the learning process. It can be brought into the supervisory dialogue and used to further a process of open communication between supervisor and supervisee.

3. Supervision as a triadic relational system. What is learned in supervision is a function of the relational context in which it is learned. Of course the supervisor is expected to positively effect the supervisee and consequently the therapy under his supervisory view. However, what the supervisee learns is substantially greater than what the supervisor sets out to teach about technique and theory, precisely because supervision is an intense and fully involving relationship for the participants, with unconscious as well as conscious aspects. Patient, therapist, and supervisor may be deeply affected by, and have an effect on, any of the others.

Initial conceptualizations of the supervisory triad by Searles (1955 and 1962) and Ekstein and Wallerstein (1958) used the concept of parallel process to frame their observations about the complex processes of mutual influence that characterize supervision. Searles emphasized the "reflection process" whereby the conflict and defenses of the patient were enacted in the supervision by the unsuspecting therapist, thus making powerful relational issues available for discussion in supervision. Ekstein and Wallerstein did not assume a necessary point of origin of these issues and indicated that they could go either "up" or "down" the hierarchy. However, as Rosbrow points out, their emphasis was on the psychopathology of the therapist. His or her conflicts and defenses, his character, were the common elements in the parallel difficulties that might beset both relationships.

Ekstein and Wallerstein and subsequent authors (e.g. Gediman and Wolkenfeld 1980) specifically referred to the contribution of the supervisor in the "supervisory jams" that often occur, but they seemed to confine their observations of supervisors' errors to the overzealous applications of method. The authors in this volume, on the other hand, point to the personality of the supervisor, in addition to that of the supervisee, as a major contributing source of influence. All of them place particular emphasis on the mutuality and co-participation of supervisor and supervisee. Indeed, Berman notes that what I might term the "myth of the healthy supervisor and neurotic supervisee" has obscured the truly reciprocal structure of supervision. Interestingly, Grinberg (1970) recalled that Gitelson (1963) related that when he was excessively active with one of his earliest patients in response to "the persecutory anxiety that supervision usually awakens," his supervisor remarked: "Doctor, when there are two people in the same room and one of them is anxious or in despair, it helps a great deal if the other is not."

In contrast to this expectation that any of the participants will be completely free of difficulty (or bias), the authors emphasize that the therapeutic and supervisory interactions are structured, enriched, and limited by each person's relational patterns, vulnerabilities, defenses, sensibilities and, indeed, the whole range of his or her experience. The authors view countertransference (of the therapist and of the supervisor) in the "totalistic" sense (Epstein and Feiner, 1979). Each participant develops transference and countertransference reactions to the other. Transference and countertransference currents at any level profoundly influence the supervisory and therapeutic processes and must be seen as legitimate topics of discussion in the supervisory discourse. Robert Marshall, in his chapter, contributes a systematic schema and the other authors provide rich descriptions of the complex interactions among the participants in the supervisory triad.

It is in this context that the perennial teach/treat dilemma is discussed by the authors. They consider it impossible to exclude countertransference and countertransference resistance from supervisory discussion. The supervisee's subjectivity, including his private anxieties and troublesome relational patterns, cannot be relegated to another arena for discussion. Wolstein pointedly indicates that supervision is experiential. To draw a firm line and exclude primary data about the therapeutic or supervisory interaction from consideration in its immediate context results in automatic distancing from what is at the core of the inquiry. The question then becomes one of tact and sensitivity of the supervisor and the receptivity of the supervisee, and the willingness by both to question themselves and their assumptions. The aim is not to purify the process of the therapist's neurosis since no one is free of countertransference. The goal is rather to stimulate curiosity, self awareness, and a striving for clarity. The focus is on the learning task at hand. Personality change of the supervisee is not the goal of supervision. However, as Rosbrow points out, the supervisee may well realize change in himself as a result of experiential learning in supervision.

4. The Listening Perspective of the Supervisor and the Supervisee
The approach to supervision described by the authors is premised on an orientation toward clinical listening which centers on understanding the other's experience from within that person's subjectively construed world. This "subject-centered listening perspective," to quote James Fosshage, is basic to the therapeutic approach advanced by the authors. In the same vein, Patrick Casement aims to foster the ability of the supervisee to "trial identify" with the patient in sessions so as to understand how the patient understands what the therapist is saying. His assumption is that what the therapist intends is not necessarily what is conveyed to the patient. Both authors clearly demonstrate the ways in which the therapeutic process may be derailed by the therapist's imposition of his views or agenda on the patient. Similarly, the consensus of the contributors to this book is that these principles must inform the supervisory process. The authors consistently emphasize the observation that students "do what I do and not what I say": They treat themselves and their patients in ways that are modeled by their supervisors.

Gardner (1994) delineates as a primary paradox of teaching that the good teacher is one who teaches "with furor"—that is with commitment, passion, and the sense that what he has to teach is indispensable for the student to know—and yet he or she must guard against the impetus to inculcate or convert. Similarly, Fosshage and Casement, as well as the other contributors, demonstrate the principle embodied in Gardner's quote of A. Bronson Alcott, *Orphic Sayings*, that "the true teacher defends his pupil against his own influence." (Gardner 1994). What the authors hope to foster is autonomy in the supervisee and what Alfred North Whitehead (1972) characterized as "the connection between knowledge and the zest of life . . ." (p. 93).

REFERENCES

Balint, M. (1948). On the psychoanalytic training system.
   International Journal of Psycho-Analysis 29: 163–173.
Barnat, B. (1980). Psychotherapy supervision and the duality
   of experience. In *Psychotherapy Supervision: Theory Re-
   search, and Practice*, A. K. Hess, ed. New York: Wiley.
Berman, E. (1988). The joint exploration of the supervisory
   relationship as an aspect of psychoanalytic supervision.
   In *New Concepts in Psychoanalytic Psychotherapy*, J.
   Ross and W. Myers eds. Washington D.C.: American
   Psychiatric Press.
Blitzsen, N. and Fleming, J. (1953). What is supervisory
   analysis? *Bulletin of the Menninger Clinic* 17: 117–129.
Caligor, L. (1984). Parallel and reciprocal processes in psycho-
   analytic supervision. In *Clinical Perspectives on the Super-
   vision of Psychoanalysis and Psychotherapy,* L. Caligor, P.
   Bromberg, and J. Meltzer, eds. New York: Plenum.
Casement, P. (1985). *On Learning from the Patient.* New York:
   Guilford.
———(1993). Towards autonomy: Some thoughts on psychoanalytic supervision. *Journal of Clinical Psychoanalysis*
   2: 389–403.
Crick, P. (1991). Good supervision: On the experience of being
   supervised. *Psychoanalytic Psychotherapy* 5: 235–245.
DeBell, D. (1963). A critical digest on the literature of psychoanalytic supervision. *Journal of the American Psychoanalytic Association* 11: 546–575.
———(1981). Supervisory styles and positions. In *Becoming a
   Psychoanalyst*, Wallerstein, R.S., ed. New York: International Universities Press.
Doehrmann, M. J. G. (1976). Parallel processes in supervision
   and psychotherapy. *Bulletin of the Menninger Clinic* 40:
   3–104.

Ekstein, R. (1960). Report of the panel on the teaching of psychoanalytic technique. *Journal of the American Psychoanalytic Association* 8: 167–174.

Ekstein, R., and Wallerstein, R. (1958). *The Teaching and Learning of Psychotherapy*. New York: International Universities Press.

Epstein, L. (1986). Collusive selective inattention to the negative impact of the supervisory interaction. *Contemporary Psychoanalysis* 22: 389–408.

Epstein, L., and Feiner, A. (1979). *Countertransference: The Therapist's Contribution to the Therapeutic Situation*. New York: Jason Aronson.

Feiner, A. (1994). Contradictions in the process of supervision. *Contemporary Psychoanalysis* 21: 591–607.

Fiscalini, J. (1985). On supervisory parataxis and dialogue. *Contemporary Psychoanalysis* 21: 591–608.

Fleming J., and Benedek, T. (1966). *Psychoanalytic Supervision*. New York: Grune and Stratton.

Freud, S. (1937). Analysis terminable and interminable. *Standard Edition* 23: 209–253.

Gabbard, G., and Wilkinson, S. (1994). *Management of Countertransference with Borderline Patients*. Washington D.C.: American Psychiatric Press.

Gaoni, B., and Neuman, M. (1974). Supervision from the point of view of the supervisee. *American Journal of Psychotherapy* 28: 108–114.

Gardner, M. R. (1994). *On Trying To Teach: The Mind in Correspondence*. Hillsdale, New Jersey: Analytic Press.

Gediman, H., and Wolkenfeld, F. (1980). The parallelism phenomenon in psychoanalysis: Its reconsideration as a triadic system. *Psychoanalytic Quarterly* 49: 234–55.

Gill, M. M. (1995). *Psychoanalysis in Transition: A Personal View*. Hillsdale, New Jersey: Analytic Press.

Gitelson, M. (1963). Presidential address: On the present scientific and social position of psychoanalysis. *International Journal of Psycho-Analysis* 44: 521–527.

Glover, E. (1952). Research methods in psychoanalysis. *International Journal of Psycho-Analysis* 33: 403–409.

Gorkin, M. (1986). *The Uses of Countertransference*. Northvale, New Jersey: Jason Aronson.

Greenson, R. R. (1966). *The Technique and Practice of Psychoanalysis*. New York: International Universities Press.

Grinberg, L. (1970). The problems of supervision in psychoanalytic education. *International Journal of Psycho-Analysis* 51: 371–374.

Gustin, J. C. (1958). Supervision in psychotherapy. *Psychoanalysis and the Psychoanalytic Review* 45: 63–72.

Isakower, O. (1957). Problems of supervision. Report to the Curriculum Committee of the New York Psychoanalytic Institute (Unpublished).

Issacharoff, A. (1984). Countertransference in supervision. In *Clinical Perspectives on the Supervision of Psychoanalysis and Psychotherapy*. L. Caligor, P. Bromberg, J. Meltzer, eds. New York: Plenum.

Khan, M. (1974). The becoming of a psychoanalyst (1972). In *The Privacy of the Self*. New York: International Universities Press.

Keiser, S. (1956). Report of the panel on the technique of supervised analysis. *Journal of the American Psychoanalytic Association* 4: 539–549.

Lesser, R. (1984). Supervision: Illusions, anxieties, and questions. *Contemporary Psychoanalysis* 18: 1–19.

———(1982). Follow the fox. *Contemporary Psychoanalysis* 18: 1–15.

Levenson, E. (1983). *The Ambiguity of Change*. New York: Basic Books.

———(1991). *The Purloined Self*. New York: Contemporary Psychoanalysis Books.

Meerloo, J. A. M. (1952). Some psychological processes in the supervision of therapists. *American Journal of Psychotherapy* 6: 467–470.

Obermann, N. C. (1990). Supervision and the achievement of an analytic identity. In *Psychoanalytic Approaches to Supervision*, R.C. Lane, ed. New York: Brunner/Mazel.

Racker, H. (1968). *Transference and Countertransference*. New York: International Universities Press.

Rosiello, F. (1989). Affective elements in supervision and parallel process. *Contemporary Psychotherapy Review* 5: 54–70.

Sarnat, J. (1992). Supervision in relationship. *Psychoanalytic Psychology* 9: 387–403.

Schlesinger, H. J. (1981). General principles of psychoanalytic supervision. In *Becoming a Psychoanalyst*, R.S. Wallerstein, ed. New York: International Universities Press.

Searles, H. (1955). The informational value of the supervisor's emotional experience. In *Collected Papers on Schizophrenia*. New York: International Universities Press, 1965.

———(1962). Problems of psychoanalytic supervision. In *Collected papers on schizophrenia*. New York: International Universities Press, 1965.

Sloane, P. (1957). Report of the second panel on the technique of supervised analysis. *Journal of the American Psychoanalytic Association* 5: 539–554.

Sullivan, H. S. (1954). *The Psychiatric Interview*. New York: Norton.

Teitelbaum, S. H. (1990). Supertransference: The role of the supervisor's blind spots. *Psychoanalytic Psychology* 7: 243–258.

Wallerstein, R. S., ed. (1981). *Becoming a Psychoanalyst*. New York: International Universities Press.

Whitehead, A. N. (1972). *The Aims of Education*. New York: The Free Press.

Winnicott, D. W. (1958). Hate in the countertransference. *Collected Papers*. New York: Basic Books.

Wolstein, B. (1984a). A proposal to enlarge the individual model of psychoanalytic supervision. *Contemporary Psychoanalysis* 20: 131–145.

———(1984b). Reply to the Fellows. *Contemporary Psychoanalysis* 20: 148–155.

II

THE SUPERVISEE'S EXPERIENCE

1

On Supervisory Parataxis And Dialogue*,[1]

JOHN FISCALINI, PH.D.

---

*An earlier version of this paper won the Harry Stack Sullivan Society Award for 1983.

1. The term parataxis is used here in the sense of *parataxic distortion* (Sullivan 1940); i.e., as referring to the transferential dimension of human living. In Sullivan's words an

> . . . integration is *parataxic*, . . . when, besides the interpersonal situation as defined within the awareness of the speaker, there is a concomitant interpersonal situation quite different as to its principal integrating tendencies, of which the speaker is more or less completely unaware.
>
> Besides the two-group integrated of psychiatrist [i.e., object] and subject there is in the parataxic situation, also an illusory two-group integrated of psychiatrist [i.e., object]—distorted-to-accommodate-a-special-"you"-pattern and subject-reliving-an-earlier-unresolved-integration-and-manifesting-the-corresponding-special-"me"-pattern (p. 12).

Sullivan (1953) referred more broadly to parataxis as one of three modes of human experience, developmentally intermediate between prototaxic and syntaxic experience. Parataxis, in this wider sense, includes non-rational (prelogical) intuitive processes, along with irrational and distorted experience. There may be instances in this paper when both senses of the term fit. The reader is referred to Mullahy (1970), Schecter (1971), and Grey (1982) for further discussion of this concept.

The supervisory process has received considerable attention in the psychoanalytic literature recently (Bromberg 1982, Caligor 1981, Cooper and Witenberg 1983, Gediman and Wolkenfeld 1980, Issacharoff 1982, Lederman 1982, Lesser 1983, Levenson 1982, Wolstein 1984). Several writers (Bromberg 1982, Caligor 1981, Gediman and Wolkenfeld 1980, Lederman 1982) have focused on the parallel process phenomenon. Bromberg's (1982) and Caligor's (1981) studies of parallel and reciprocal processes examine, from an interpersonal and operational perspective, how transference and countertransference in the analytic relationship provoke parataxes in the supervisory dyad. Issacharoff (1982) and Lesser (1983), among others, discuss the related question of the pedagogic versus therapeutic role of the supervisor; that is, whether the supervisor should "teach or treat" with respect to the supervisee's countertransference to his or her patient. And Lesser observes caustically that Levenson's (1982) admonition that the supervisor "stay out of the supervisee's analysis" is more often adhered to in principle than in practice.

The psychoanalytic literature on countertransference in supervision has focused mainly on the student's countertransference to his or her patient, or on parallel process phenomena.

Supervisory parataxis (i.e., transference-countertransference between supervisee and supervisor) and its triadic consequences have been examined less extensively.

In addition to triadic sources of parataxis, many other issues, such as characterological differences, different analytic styles, cognitive styles, uses of language, differences in metapsychology, world view, view of the patient, and institutional pressures often provoke parataxic supervisory interaction. Thus, the question of whether the supervisor is to "teach or treat," traditionally discussed in terms of how the supervisor can deal most appropriately with the supervisee's countertransference vis-à-vis the patient, widens significantly. There remains the issue of parataxis in the supervisory situation itself, stemming from transference-countertransference of supervisor and supervisee vis-à-vis each other.

In pyramid fashion, the supervisory relationship is a relationship about a relationship about other relationships. Both supervisee and supervisor interact in an interpersonal field in which each is, in Sullivan's (1954) words, a "participant observer." In the supervisory hour, the supervisee is not merely telling a teacher about the supervisee's relationship with another person (the patient); the supervisee is constantly interacting and relating with the supervisor in the process. Irrational aspects of the supervisory relationship, when dissociated, inattended to, or inarticulated, will inevitably affect the analytic relationship by affecting the nature, use, or understanding of supervisory information about the analytic relationship.

Searles (1955), Ekstein and Wallerstein (1958), and more recently Caligor (1981) point to the diagnostic value of supervisory parataxis as a triadic source of information about transference-countertransference vicissitudes in the analytic relationship. Issacharoff (1982) further describes how judicious analytic exploration of the supervisee's contertransference within the supervisory situation can result in corrective analytic benefits. I think that it may be equally informative and corrective for supervisor and supervisee to examine directly any dialogic difficulties in supervision which arise from parataxic complication of differences in viewpoint, style, metapsychology, etc. Open review of their integration by supervisor and supervisee leading to a more candid, even creative, supervisory dialogue can correct or obviate negative triadic effects and enrich both the analytic and the supervisory experience. In other words, supervision works best when supervisor and supervisee can talk straightforwardly with one another, including talking about each other. My supervisory experience suggests that it would be ameliorative and instructive for supervisor and supervisee to review their transference and countertransference difficulties directly within the supervisory situation. The supervisory dialogue, the exchange of experiences, ideas, and opinions between supervisor and supervisee, is richest when it permits open and candid review of the supervisory as well as the analytic relationship.

Perhaps it is axiomatic to state that the dyadic relationships within the supervisory triangle of patient-analyst-supervisor may provoke triadic consequences for both. That the nature and quality of the supervisory relationship will affect and influence the analytic relationship seems self-evident. After all, the supervisory situation is arranged explicitly to have impact on the analysis and the analyst. It seems fruitful, however, to draw a distinction between the *supervisory relationship* and *supervisory information* and to examine how the former affects or shapes the latter, and hence the analytic relationship and analyst. In fact, the supervisory relationship itself, and the processes therein often, if not always, become supervisory information through conscious and unconscious modeling and identification.

I will preface further discussion of supervisory parataxis and dialogue with an illustration from my experience as a supervisee. I will briefly review two supervisory relationships and their differing impact on me, my patient, and the psycho-analytic inquiry.

CLINICAL ILLUSTRATION

Early in my psychoanalytic training, I saw an aspiring journalist in supervised analysis. The patient was a paranoid and narcissistic young man in his late twenties, who had sought treatment because he felt "stuck," unable to move forward professionally, and helplessly victimized in his intimate and work relationships. He had lost his father when he was very young and been raised as the "special" child by his depressed and self-centered mother, an insecure and overwhelmed woman who was symbioti-cally tied to her own psychotic mother.

Initially, I sympathized with the patient. I also noted his passive-dependent stance, perfectionism, his use of projection, and his defensive use of abstract language. I further noted a forlorn and "sad-sack" quality in his awkward and tense physical manner. I empathized with the patient's sense of despair and with his neediness and fragile self-esteem.

In the first several months of the analysis the patient repeatedly and angrily described how he felt taken ad-vantage of and insensitively treated by his boss, girl friend, mother, and society in general. Often glib and abstruse, he was highly intellectualized and frequently evasive in inquiry. He was unaware of how his injustice-collecting, "helplessness," and self-justification covered his lack of responsibility and desire to have others take care of him, and also masked his profound feelings of inferiority and inadequacy.

Supervision focused on my countertransferential hesi-tancy in inquiry and on my selective inattention to the fullness of the patient's arrogance and his narcissistic expectations of unconditional devotion from others, especially the masked references to me. My supervisor emphasized the importance of confronting the patient's hostile security operations and his self-centered disregard of others. In the analytic relationship, I began to attend more closely to the patient's transferential competitiveness, contempt, and hostility toward me which previously I had unconsciously parried and not confronted or inquired about. My countertransferential blindness to the patient's hostility and grandiosity stemmed in part from my countertransference wish to like him, to think paternally of him as a hurt orphan (as he thought of himself) who needed comfort and reassurance, and my wish to avoid his rage. Thus, in the analytic situation, I had often retreated from inquiry and become overly protective and excessively helpful, unconsciously feeding into his transference wish to be magically rescued. These countertransference trends were, of course, multiply rooted in my personal history, and reflected, in part, some identification with the patient. With supervision, I began to see through the patient's rationalizations and to confront him with his hostility and narcissistic demands and disregard of others. Analytically, the patient made progress. He began to see how he was self-victimizing and provocative and he became more aware of his sadism toward others.

As the analysis continued, parataxic difficulties, largely iatrogenic, began to cloud the analytic relationship and inquiry. My initial sympathy with the patient's plight and empathic feel for his anxiety were gradually submerged in a one-sided emphasis on his hostile and alienating defensive operations. Thus, for example, when the patient bitterly railed that his girl friend's wish to end their relationship was a selfish and callous desertion of him, I focused on his faultfinding, provocativeness, and insatiable demandingness: in other words, his own narcissistic inability to cooperate with, or care for her. Although these were valid analytic issues which required extensive working through, they missed the therapeutic need of the moment, the patient's terror of separation. I had compounded his fear of abandonment by actually failing him. The patient responded in the only way then available to him, with further rage and paranoia. The implication to me for a spiraling negative therapeutic interaction became clear later.

Then, I continued simply to interpret the error of the patient's narcissistic ways, and grew impatient with his rageful, self-justifying harangues. Early in the analysis, I had been in touch with his anxiety and underlying feelings of inadequacy and vulnerability; now, I mainly saw malevolence in his behavior. I had corrected my earlier timid and softgloved approach, but I had, in the process, stepped out of an empathic concern with his inner world and had unwittingly adopted an emotionally distanced and antagonistic position. The analysis did not devolve into an impasse and significant analytic work was accomplished. His insights, however were all too often suffused with rage and self-hatred.

During this phase of our work, I thought, at times, uneasily, that I was throwing the baby out with the bathwater, that I was focusing too narrowly on the darker side of the patient's psyche, perhaps even exaggerating it. I dismissed these intuitions as residuals of my earlier countertransference, that is, as indicative of my earlier analytic timidity and over-protectiveness. My actual parataxic involvement in the analysis was not clearly formulated until later. I similarly dismissed the nagging thought that the supervisor viewed the patient pejoratively. The supervisor, an impressive and admired clinician, also seemed authoritarian to me. I did not raise these questions with the supervisor for complex transferential reasons. Thus, I precluded the possibility of consensually validating my supervisory and analytic experience. My (transferential) difficulties with the supervisor, manifested in our dialogue, meant, in other words, that I was not able to confirm my intuitions or to correct them, if they were parataxic distortions in the first place.

In the second year of the analysis, I began working with a second supervisor, who soon diagnosed the parataxic difficulty between the patient and myself, helping me to see the impact of my anxiety and anger on the analytic relationship. As I became less frightened of the patient's and my own analytic hostility, I gradually began to extricate myself from our battle. My second supervisor's comments about my anxiety in the analytic relationship and in the supervisory relationship (manifested by my keeping my supervisor at arm's length psychologically) facilitated a more sensitive approach to the patient's experience and problems. I began to see his pathology from a more empathic perspective, recognizing its survival value, without ignoring or exaggerating the hostile, angry nature of his paranoid and grandiose security operations. The patient, in turn, became less defensive and felt more understood.

In the supervisory situation, the supervisor focused on my anxiety in the supervision as well as on my anxiety in the analysis. The supervisor's initiative in addressing this directly and respectfully opened the way to a more candid relationship in which I felt more free to express my thoughts and perceptions and to examine differences or disagreements with the supervisor. This more candid dialogue included a frank review of my transferential difficulties with supervisory authority, both in the previous supervisory situation and in this one. In discussions of both the analytic and the supervisory relationships, the supervisor evinced an open and nonauthoritarian attitude. The supervisor welcomed my perceptions and thoughts about the analytic (and supervisory) processes. With this focus, a more collaborative experience in the analysis and in the supervision was facilitated.

In the analytic situation, I had come full circle. Originally, I had identified with the patient's anxiety and vulnerability but bought his rationalizations. I had attempted to rescue him, ignoring his uglier behavior. Then, with supervision, I had corrected my earlier stance and confronted his paranoia and hostility, swinging too far in the opposite direction, identifying with the victims of his hostility and no longer with him. With the second supervision, I was able to do both, in a more analytically effective fashion.

As I became more secure in the analytic relationship and in supervision and grasped my parataxic participation in both, the analytic inquiry became broader and deeper. No longer adversaries, the patient and I explored collaboratively the salient analytic issues. The patient gradually saw more of his grandiosity, hostility, and deep suspiciousness, as well as his fearful masochism and inability to stand alone or to stand up for himself (i.e., his dread of adulthood and autonomy), both in the transference and in his everyday life. And, in time, the patient began to show genuine concern and sympathy for others in his life and he became better able to see them and himself realistically.

Striking in my work with this patient were my shifts in my perceptions of and integrations with him. These shifts in attitude, of course, may be understood or examined from a variety of perspectives.[2] However, I think that the swing from

---

2. For example, Levenson's (1972) notion of the patient's transformation of the analyst, or, from a different point of view, Grinberg's (1979) concept of projective counteridentification may describe dyadic processes that were operative in my relationship with the patient. Never-

a sympathetic, but narrow, concern with the patient's anxiety to an exclusive and unempathic attention to his pathology and then to an eventual appropriate concern with both may be best understood or illuminated by examining the nature of my participation in the two different supervisory relationships.

In my first supervisory experience, I dismissed my initial perceptions of the patient in my hurry to correct my oversights, and disregarded my overcorrected bias. I also suppressed my disagreement with what I thought was my supervisor's pejorative bias. This stemmed, I think, from my desire to impress my supervisor, my parataxic attitudes toward supervisory authority, and my faulty view of the supervisee's role in the supervisory situation.

In other words, my countertransference in the analysis (that aspect of it that developed during the first supervisory phase) was revealed equally in the supervisory parataxis. In the supervisory situation, I was a compliant student, rather than a collaborative participant supervisee who could discuss openly, disagree with, and eventually clarify, integrate, or resolve possibly differing viewpoints or emphases. Thus significant supervisory questions went unasked. Was my supervisor biased? Did the supervisor view the patient pessimistically? If so, on what basis? Or was this my transferential or defensive distortion? In what ways did we differ in our views of the patient and the analytic inquiry, and why? Was the supervisor authoritarian? Or did the supervisor also wish for more candid dialogue on supervisory issues? As important as the answers to these questions, are the fresh ideas and perspectives, new to both supervisor and supervisee, that such inquiry may generate.

---

theless, neither addresses the triadic issue in these particular essays, that is, the supervisory influences on the analysis. Of course, the processes they describe may have played a contributory role in the development of the supervisory parataxis.

My dialogic difficulty in the supervision was clinically similar, although dynamically different, to a situation briefly mentioned by Searles (1962). Searles remarks on how the supervisee may act out supervisory parataxis by mechanically applying or caricaturing supervisory instruction in such a manner that the patient's adverse analytic response makes a mockery of the supervisory information. Searles sees this as occurring in an authoritarian supervisory context and not as expressive of the supervisee's hostility. He thinks it follows "more fundamentally from a stubborn and healthy determination to be allowed to use his own best capacities, and to have them acknowledged as *his*" (p. 586). The situations described by Searles and by myself illustrate the triadic impact of unnoted or unexamined supervisory parataxis. These are two of the myriad ways in which supervisory parataxis may tilt the analytic relationship. Another is the reverse parallel process mentioned recently by Gediman and Wolkenfeld (1980).

It seems now, in retrospect, that explicit attention to the parataxic aspects of the supervisory relationship in the supervisory situation might well have clarified my faulty use of supervisory information (or, possibly, my faulty use of faulty supervisory information), thus correcting my parataxically inappropriate participation in the analysis.

In the second supervisory situation, my anxiety in the analysis and in the supervision was focused on early in the supervision. With a collaborative focus, a richer and more therapeutic experience was facilitated in both the analysis and the supervision.

The two different supervision experiences that I have described illustrate that it is not simply expert supervisory information which guides the analysis and teaches the supervisee, but also, and very importantly, the nature of the supervisory relationship itself adds something significantly. And in this relationship, the supervisee is not merely a studious recipient of expertise, but is rather an active participant supervisee, both informing and being informed. When this interchange of supervisory information is candid and open, both supervisor and supervisee have the opportunity not only to clarify their ideas and experiences but also to generate fresh perspectives, new to them both. When this happens, the supervision experience is characterized by a sense of aliveness and discovery.

PARATAXIS AND DIALOGUE IN SUPERVISION

My experience of parataxis in supervision, although uniquely patterned, is not uncommon. My guess is that most supervisees, if candid, would acknowledge parataxic inhibitions and disruptions in their supervisory work. My first supervision was not a bad experience; it was highly informative about analytic work and rewarding in many ways. In supervision, as in all human relationships, parataxis is inevitable. Its shape and its consequences are, of course, infinitely varied. Supervisory parataxis may be minimal and relatively insignificant; or it may be intense, pervasive, and disruptive, in some instances leading to a supervisory impasse, and crisis. The point that I wish to emphasize is that when significant parataxic aspects of the supervisory relationship are not directly addressed in that relationship, they rob the supervisory situation of its potential richness as a learning experience and adversely impact on the analysis in which the supervisee is engaged. Collaboration in supervision does not imply the absence of parataxis, but rather a commitment to dialogue, that is, an openness to candid review of their participation by both supervisor and supervisee.

The analyst's countertransference participation in the analytic situation is a central and widely recognized focus of supervisory attention. The question of how to best deal with the supervisee's countertransference to his or her patient is a matter of controversy (cf. DeBell 1963). One school of thought contends that supervision is not analysis and that the supervisee, once informed about his countertransference, should take it up with his analyst. Inarguably good advice, in any event. Others, most recently Issacharoff (1982) and Lesser (1983), suggest that direct investigation of the supervisee's analytic countertransference within the supervisory situation can prove helpful to the supervisee, and to the supervisee's personal analytic relationship, and may also contribute to a more open and fertile learning alliance in the supervision.

If judicious supervisory analysis of the supervisee's countertransference to his or her patient benefits all concerned, then it seems likely that on another level such open review and analysis of the supervisor's and supervisee's countertransference *to each other* will hold similar benefit. (And what about the supervisor's countertransference to the patient?) Lesser (1983), writing from a supervisor's perspective, stresses the importance of mutual exploration of parataxis between supervisor and supervisee when she calls for

> A collaborative analysis which . . . necessitates an in-depth inquiry into and analysis of each member's transferences and countertransferences which are directly experienced by and observable to one another. . . . In being observed, the supervisor offers the supervisee an important opportunity to experience the supervisor's willingness to be self-aware and genuinely responsive to the supervisee's observations, even in the face of potential anxieties. This may encourage the supervisee to do the same (p. 127).

In their detailed study of the supervisory process, Fleming and Benedek (1966) discuss the educative and therapeutic benefit of supervisory inquiry into the supervisory relationship. They comment that such inquiry contributes to the development of the supervisee's self-analysis and further refines his or her analytic instrument. However, the inquiry they describe is limited, and onesidedly focused on the supervisee's transference or learning problems.

A group of candidates at the Denver Psychoanalytic Institute (Martin et al. 1978) have reported on their development of a method of formally evaluating supervisors (much in the manner that class instructors or seminar leaders are now formally evaluated in psychoanalytic institutes). In their report, Martin et al. comment on the salutary benefit of supervisory discussion of supervisory processes. They maintain that there is a need to

> expand the legitimate scope of the supervisory process to include what we felt were often unconscious or hitherto unacceptable issues, such as . . . the detection and open discussion of transference dilemmas *between analyst and both patient and supervisor* (p. 413) (italics mine).

One may object to mutual inquiry into supervisory parataxis within the supervisory situation on the grounds that the supervisory situation lacks the depth or breadth to properly handle useful review of countertransferential issues, whether analytic or supervisory. The supervisory situation, as currently structured, particularly in terms of confidentiality, has limitations in this regard. Nevertheless, I think it does permit relatively in-depth mutual review of supervisory parataxis. I agree with Martin et. al. that "transference-countertransference discoveries in supervision could provide important stimuli that could lead to structural [intrapsychic] change when the candidate [or supervisor] used them in his training or self-analysis" (p. 411). In fact, my experience indicates that excluding the supervisory relationship from mutual supervisory inquiry jeopardizes the analysis as well as the supervision.

Another question about candid review of supervisory parataxis within supervision concerns it possibly introducing transference complications, such as a competing with the personal
analysis. I believe this is a valid concern, but one that pertains
to the defensive use of the supervisory dialogue and not to an
inherent property of it. A frank and open supervisory dialogue
refers to a judicious in-depth discussion of differences of viewpoint or emphasis and of parataxic processes, occurring in the
supervision or in the analysis. It does not refer to defensive
pseudo-candor, exhibitionistic and intrusive pseudo-encounter,
or defensive avoidance of other supervisory issues or one's own
analytic responsibilities. Supervisory inquiry into patterns of
supervisory parataxis can complement one's personal psychoanalysis or self-analysis; it need not compete with it.

The supervisory situation involves three dyads (or six sources
of parataxis): the patient and analyst, each with parataxic input
(i.e., transference and countertransference); the supervisee-
analyst and supervisor, each with his or her parataxic input
into this particular integration; and thirdly, the patient and
supervisor and their possible long-distance parataxic involvement via the analyst. The supervisory experience is probably
most enriched and optimally productive when there is a shifting
focus on whichever relationship (or source of parataxis) is most
urgent, striking, or disruptive of collaborative work, whether in
the analytic or supervisory situation (A. Grey, personal communication).

When supervisor and supervisee meet in the supervisory
situation to teach and to learn about psychoanalysis and
psychoanalytic inquiry, there often are, obviously, many individual differences, such as differing metapsychologies, conceptions of psychoanalytic inquiry, views of the patient, world
views, styles of analytic work, cognitive styles (e.g., methodi-
cal, intuitive), concepts of one's supervisory role, along with
characterological and personality differences, and ecological

factors (e.g., the institutional context, traditions regarding supervisory authority, etc.).

Parataxic interferences in the supervisory relationship spring not only from the personal characterological and transference difficulties of one or both participants but also from factors related to the supervisory ecology. I refer here to those aspects of the traditions and beliefs and formal institutional arrangements which tend to inhibit or distort supervisory dialogue. Particularly relevant are: (1) the tradition of the supervisor as a disinterested, objective teacher; (2) the prevalent authoritarian view that the supervisor knows best, which, along with the presumed objectivity of the supervisor, is regarded by Lesser (1983) as illusory; and (3) pressures related to the training institute context, specifically, evaluations, questions of stature and reputation among colleagues, and issues of professional future and livelihood. These variables are easily and frequently suffused with parataxic concerns, either generating or being generated by transference distortion of what is optimally a candid relationship between participants. These ecological factors play an important and uniquely patterned role in all supervisory dyads, although they vary in their significance from dyad to dyad. The complex influence of these factors varies with supervisory role and with the unique personality of each supervisee and supervisor. All of these various differences require mutual understanding and acceptance for satisfactory learning to occur. This can happen implicitly and smoothly, and supervision proceeds in relatively syntaxic fashion. Frequently, however, these differences become parataxically complicated, and anxiety and derivative self-system processes interfere with learning and teaching.

In such instances, the supervisee frequently becomes compliant or defiant, depending upon the supervisee's predominant relation to authority. The supervisee may become submissive, uncritically adopt the supervisor's way, and the supervisor ends up doing analysis by ventriloquism. The analysis may proceed well (or not necessarily so), but often not for long. In any case, this is no longer supervision, for there is no genuine supervisory dialogue. Learning, of course, becomes minimal. And as Moulton (1969) observes, "The student then fails to develop his own analytic style," which she considers "the ultimate goal of supervision" (p. 148). This situation often occurs when the supervisee strives to be what Beckett (1969) terms the "good candidate," the supervisee who strives for hyper-normality and "submerges his individuality and his inner complexity in the interest of gaining [supervisory] endorsements and acceptance" (p. 176). Keiser (1956) notes that this "unproductive imitation of the supervisor" happens with dogmatic supervisors who require submission to their authority.

Sometimes the supervisee becomes covertly or overtly defiant. The supervisee, for example, may perfunctorily agree with the supervisor, while consciously or unconsciously proceeding to do what he or she thinks is therapeutic with the patient with sometimes beneficial and sometimes detrimental effect on the analysis. Here, too, supervisory dialogue is minimal or nonexistent. At times, the supervisee and supervisor become locked in overt, angry battle and everyone—patient, analyst, and supervisor—suffers from the fallout.

All of these situations occur with varying degrees of disjunctiveness and levels of awareness. These patterns are often accompanied by statements of derogation about the particular supervisor and institute, the supervision process, psychoanalytic training, even psychoanalysis itself. These are often public and are commonly observed in informal conversation between colleagues. Far more insidious and damaging are more private patterns of disparagement and discouragement about psychoanalytic education, supervision, and therapy.

Thompson (1958) cautions that the psychoanalytic institute has many of the qualities, good and bad, of the family. The supervisory situation within the context of a training institute structurally resembles aspects of the family situation. Thus, it is highly evocative of transference-countertransference complications, particularly around issues of rivalry, dependency, power, loyalty, separation, and individuation. Searles (1962) points to the transferential intensity of the emotional processes occurring between supervisor and supervisee and to the triadic consequences of denial of such intensity when he comments that

> . . . I have recurrently found myself having to understress, partly for reasons of confidence, the true intensity of the mutual emotional involvement which characterizes psycho-analytic supervision. As yet, our relative nonacceptance of this degree of intensity as "normal" to the supervisory relationship tends towards vicarious eruption of the underlying intense affects in other arenas of the two participants' lives—above all, in the arena of the treatment itself which is being discussed in supervision (p. 603).

Structuring the supervisory situation to provide for open dialogue, including candid co-inquiry into patterns of supervisory parataxis, can correct the supervisee's tendency to confuse the authoritarian with the authoritative (or vice-versa). It can also mitigate the supervisee's tendency to idealize the supervisor as the omniscient parent or to glorify him- or herself as the omnipotent child. A common reasons underlying the supervisee's reluctance to question or challenge his or her supervisor is, I believe, the fear of exposing his or her own unconscious sense of inferiority or grandiosity.

Caligor (1981) reports that having two supervisees share supervision may diminish authority problems and encourage a more candid and collaborative supervisory experience. He finds that

. . . a three-some makes for less transference on the part
of the candidate; less probability of countertransference
to any one student by the supervisor; . . . different affective, perceptual, and cognitive grids examining the same
data tend to make for a broader perspective. Also, there
tends to be less regression than can occur in the one-to-
one, because the supervisor is perceived much less as
God, the authority, and the candidate therefore feels freer
to be critical of his contributions and to verbalize his own.
It is humbling for the supervisor when the candidate
comes forth with superior insights and recommendations,
frequently better than his own. All this makes for the
analytic ethos of equality and dialogue leading to insights
broader than available to one person . . . (p. 4) (italics
mine).

Caligor's observations point to the give-and-take and generat-
ivity that characterize open and candid supervisory dialogue,
although he does not discuss the issue of supervisory inquiry
into transference-countertransference difficulties between supervisor and supervisee. Also, it is open to question whether
shared supervision reduces parataxis or simply dilutes it by
altering its form.

RESISTANCE TO SUPERVISORY DIALOGUE

If open dialogue in psychoanalytic supervision, including frank
attention to transference and countertransference between
supervisor and supervisee, promotes learning, why then is
there resistance to it? Confidentiality seems to be the important issue. First of all, there is the confidentiality required by
the self-systems of supervisee and supervisor. As discussed
earlier, either participant may defensively prefer to avoid
direct encounter for fear of acknowledging to him-, or herself,

or to the other, certain neurotic patterns characteristic of his or her integration in the analytic situation (i.e., countertransference to the patient) or his or her integration in the supervisory situation.

One important issue is the structure of the supervisory situation itself, that is, that it is not a confidential situation as is the training or personal analysis. Thus, neither participant in supervision is guaranteed expression free from repercussion. Pertinent here are issues related to the supervisory ecology. Either supervisor or supervisee may feel that candid exploration of differences in viewpoint or emphasis or of difficulties with the other will prove personally or professionally harmful. This fear is often parataxic and defensive. However, it may not be. It may reflect a realistic appraisal of the situation. Ironically, such fears may inhibit supervisory dialogue on yet another level, the published literature on supervision. Such concerns may be reflected in Arlow's (1963) observation that "Considerations of discretion often make it most difficult to present detailed data concerning supervision in published reports" (p. 584).

The interest in peer supervisory groups and the common practice of graduate psychoanalysts seeking private supervison after completion of formal training may reflect the inhibiting properties of the institutional supervisory context. Wolstein (1984) views the problem of confidentiality in supervision as fundamental. He suggests enlarging the individual one-to-one model of psychoanalytic supervision to the one-to-many model of the small case seminar as a solution to the problem.

The idea of reviewing supervisory parataxis in the supervisory situation touches also on the question of whether one prefers to view the supervisory process as inherently different than the analytic process, that teaching psychoanalysis is not psychoanalysis. As Levenson (1982) cogently points out, citing Korzybski, one should not confuse the map with the territory. Supervision is not analysis, for the goals are different. Yet the process seems similar. The interpersonal processes that characterize the analytic relationship also occur in the supervisory situation. To extend Levenson's use of Korzybski's metaphor, if two people cannot cooperatively hold or look at the map (supervisory information), its use as a guide to the territory (the psychoanalysis under study) is handicapped. We need further to consider ways in which we can change the structure of the supervisory situation or our beliefs about it so as to bring about a more candid and genuinely psychoanalytic supervisory dialogue.

MODELING INFLUENCES OF THE SUPERVISORY RELATIONSHIP

I would like to turn briefly to the issue of modeling processes in supervision, that is, how the supervisory relationship itself becomes supervisory information. The impact of the supervisory relationship upon the supervisee and his or her patient is evidenced in the common observation that supervisees tend to identify with their supervisors. Supervisees frequently begin to work with their patients in ways similar to the ways they have been or imagine themselves as having been related to in the supervisory situation.[3] In other words, identification and modeling processes are set in motion that apply to how one is or thinks one is dealt with as supervisee as well as to how one perceives that his or her supervisor works with the patients.

One of my supervisory experiences during my psychoanalytic training was with a supervisor who had a lively and deeply

---

3. Supervisees even more frequently work with their patients in ways similar to the ways they have been or think they have been analyzed in their personal (training) analyses. The personal analytic relationship is probably the most influential model of psychoanalytic inquiry for the psychoanalyst-in-training.

respectful curiosity about patients and a similar curiosity and respect about how I went about analytic work with my patient. The supervisor never talked about this or suggested that I become more interested in or curious about my patients. Nevertheless, I found that I did become more curious about my patients, in a deeper and fuller way, more aware of gaps in information, more interested in the details of their lives and especially in what those events meant to them. This supervisor's way of being with my patient, and with me, unconsciously became an important part of my own analytic attitude. Many similar examples of modeling processes relating to a multitude of attitudes, traits, and approaches, both positive and negative, can be found, I think, in the experiences of all supervisees. I am referring here to a modeling process of selective and partial identification with one's supervisor, not to a defensive imitation of the supervisor stemming from fear of using or developing one's own psychoanalytic resources.

The supervisee who is a candidate at a pluralistic training institute and thus exposed to widely different psychoanalytic approaches often will consciously or unconsciously adopt different, and even contradictory, styles or approaches (patterned after various supervisors) in the process of finding his or her own psychoanalytic identity. This trial process often confuses both supervisee and patient, until the candidate has been able to integrate his or her different supervisory (and personal psychoanalytic) experiences and form his or her own unique analytic style.

The transformation of supervisory relationship into supervisory information via identification may be one of the major was in which the supervisee learns about psychoanalysis and eventually forms his or her own identity as a psychoanalyst. And in this process of identification, an open and candid supervisory relationship can provide an invaluable model for the development of the supervisee's capacity for analytic dialogue.

REFERENCES

Arlow, J. A. (1963). The supervisory situation. *Journal of the American Psychoanalytic Association*, 11:576–594.

Beckett, T. (1969). A candidate's reflections on the supervisory process. *Contemporary Psychoanalysis*, 5:169–179.

Bromberg, P. M. (1982). The supervisory process and parallel process in psychoanalysis. *Contemporary Psychoanalysis*, 18:92–111.

Caligor, L. (1981). Parallel and reciprocal processes in psychoanalytic supervision. *Contemporary Psychoanalysis*, 17:1–27.

Cooper, A., and Witenberg, E. G. (1983). The stimulation of curiosity in the supervisory process. *Contemporary Psychoanalysis*, 19:120–129.

DeBell, D. E. (1963). A critical digest on the literature on psychoanalytic supervision. *Journal of the American Psychoanalytic Association*, 11:546–575.

Ekstein, R., and Wallerstein, R. S. (1958). *The Teaching and Learning of Psychotherapy*. New York: International Universities Press.

Fleming, J., and Benedek, T. (1966). *Psychoanalytic Supervision*. New York: Grune & Stratton.

Gediman, H. K., and Wolkenfeld, F. (1980). The parallelism phenomenon in psychoanalysis: Its reconsideration as a triadic system. *Psychoanalytic Quarterly*, 49:234–255.

Grey, A. (1979). Countertransference and parataxis. *Contemporary Psychoanalysis*, 15:472–484.

Grinberg, L. (1979). Countertransference and projective counteridentification. *Contemporary Psychoanalysis*, 15:226–247.

Issacharoff, A. (1982). Countertransference in supervision. *Contemporary Psychoanalysis*, 18:455–472.

Keiser, S. (1956). Panel report: The technique of supervised analysis. *Journal of the American Psychoanalytic Association*. 4:539–549.

Lederman, S. (1982). A contribution to the theory and practice of supervision. *Psychoanalytic Review*, 69:423–434.

Lesser, R. M. (1983). Supervision: Illusions, anxieties, and questions. *Contemporary Psychoanalysis*. 19:120–129.

Levenson, E. A. (1972). *The Fallacy of Understanding*. New York: Basic Books.

——— (1982). Follow the fox. *Contemporary Psychoanalysis*. 18:1–15.

Martin, G. C., Mayerson, P., Olsen, H. E., and Wiberg, J. L. (1978). Candidates' evaluation of psychoanalytic supervision. *Journal of the American Psychoanalytic Association*. 26:407–424.

Moulton, R. (1969). Multiple dimensions in supervision. *Contemporary Psychoanalysis*, 5:146–150.

Mullahy, P. (1970). *Psychoanalysis and Interpersonal Psychiatry*. New York: Science House.

Schecter, D. E. (1971). Two of Sullivan's conceptions. *Contemporary Psychoanalysis*, 8:71–74.

Searles, H. F. (1955). The informational value of the supervisor's emotional experience. *Psychiatry*. 15:135–146.

——— (1962). Problems of psychoanalytic supervision. In *Collected Papers on Schizophrenia and Related Subjects*. New York: International Universities Press.

Sullivan, H. S. (1940). *Conceptions of Modern Psychiatry*. New York: Norton.

——— (1953). *The Interpersonal Theory of Psychiatry*. New York: Norton.

——— (1954). *The Psychiatric Interview*. New York: Norton.

Thompson, C. (1958). A study of the emotional climate of psychoanalytic institutes. *Psychiatry*. 21:145–51.

Wolstein, G. (1984). A proposal to enlarge the individual model of psychoanalytic supervision. *Contemporary Psychoanalysis*, 20:131–145.

III

THE
SUPERVISOR'S
EXPERIENCE

2

Being Too Good

MICHAEL EIGEN

Some difficulties therapists and patients face arise when either in the pair seems too good for the other. The painful consequences of such a situation was brought home when a therapist (Elaine) sought help with her patient's (Susan) serious suicide attempt.

Elaine was lovely, well-dressed, well-spoken, a pleasure to see and be with. She described her patient as extremely disturbed, unpleasant, ugly. Elaine felt she had done wonders with Susan. Susan was becoming a therapist, like Elaine. But she never seemed far from breakdown or suicide. She pushed herself every step of the way. What seemed to come easily to Elaine was a series of impossible hardships for Susan.

As Elaine spoke, I felt sympathy with Susan. Elaine depicted a tormented being, always near zero, somehow managing to keep going with a blind persistence that kept splattering and starting again. Susan's suffering was immense. What a sensitive, determined person she must be, to come through her difficulties, battling enormous odds. I wondered if her difficulties made her more sensitive with patients.

How taken aback I was when Elaine responded to my thoughts with emphatic negation. Elaine was exasperated with Susan's demanding anger, low self-esteem, hysterical clutching, fragmentation. She was tired of Susan incessantly drowning in a raging, bottomless pit of worthlessness. She wanted more for her patient. She felt Susan should and could be doing better, that there was a hump to get over that Susan was pulling back from. Susan was afraid to give up suffering and leap into and sustain a better existence. Elaine was angry at Susan for still being so tortured after all their work.

Elaine felt her impatience was on the side of life. She did not want to sink into the cesspool of self-loathing that sucked Susan down. Elaine's was the voice of health. She extended a hand to lift Susan out of the muck. Susan took that hand, but could hold on only for short bursts. Elaine feared my sympathy with Susan's suffering was an invitation for Susan to regress and die out. Elaine's tendency was to be actively encouraging, hoping Susan would latch on to the taste of life and not let go.

Ostensibly, Elaine seemed to have more faith in her patient than I. She appealed to Susan's strengths, while I seemed sympathetic to weakness. Elaine and I were in danger of becoming polarized against each other. We could cut her patient up and throw pieces at each other. I felt defensive. I didn't mean to succumb to weakness, so much as acknowledge how tough it was for Susan, and how courageous to persistently come through such suffering. Elaine and I quickly felt unjustly picked on by the other. She felt my sympathy with Susan as criticism of herself. She wanted me on *her* side, not her patient's. She attacked me because she felt attacked or in the cold (as she feared I felt she somehow left Susan in the cold). She came to me for help, not to be picked on.

I shut up and sat with my feelings awhile, awash in

self-doubt. I felt badly that I jumped in too quickly on the side of her patient's pain. I felt a flaw or hole in my own personality, my impatience and inability to let build. I started going down the tubes, angry at myself for messing up the consultation. Maybe there was time to recoup and start over. Maybe we could give each other another chance.

But when I opened up and tried to start from scratch, the same thing began to happen again. Elaine was beautiful and gifted, but seemed filled with herself. Again, my sympathies shifted to her suffering patient. In a few moments Elaine and I would be polarized again. She would feel left out, rejected, judged. We would not be able to work together. Couldn't I identify with both Elaine and Susan at the same time? What about Elaine's suffering and struggles? Elaine worked hard on herself and came a long way. Surely I appreciated her love of creativeness. Was I threatened by a beautiful and bright woman? Did I become hostile/defensive to cover my fear? I struggled to stay open.

Still, the more I listened to Elaine, the more the gap between Elaine and Susan grew. Susan was taxing, inaccessible, unappreciative, eternally frustrated-frustrating. Elaine was nourishing, creative, emotionally honest, present. Elaine brought the good stuff into the room and Susan the bad stuff. Susan kept falling through a hole in herself, Elaine kept bringing her back. Elaine wondered how long she could go on picking Susan up in face of the undertow.

Elaine did not seem very ruffled, scared, or worried (as I might have been). She seemed more exasperated, exhausted, as if Susan were trying the limits of endurance. She realized she was Susan's lifeline. Her resources in bringing Susan back to life (or keeping Susan in life) were being tested. Perhaps she was doing a little of what Susan did, looking for support and encouragement to get back in the ring.

My offering support and encouragement prompted Elaine to unleash her negativism against Susan, and voice her weariness fully. Would life triumph over destructiveness? Was all their work for nothing? The depths of Susan's self-hate and worthlessness consumed whatever Elaine offered. Susan felt too badly about herself to use a good relationship. Yet she did use it. Susan and Elaine kept coming back for more, even if the tie between them broke down and seemed ruined for a time. Actually, Elaine felt the tie was always there, although sometimes they couldn't find it. Perhaps all Elaine wanted from our session was a chance for faith to regenerate.

I could let it go at that, and that would be enough. But the distance between Elaine and Susan nagged me. I don't mean distance in the usual sense. Elaine was not a distant, cold person. She was easy and comfortable to be with. She kept things flowing. She always had something to say and was brimming with experience, a warmly rich and full person, optimistic, supportive, creative. Yet *I* felt left out. It gradually dawned on me that *I* was one of the sick ones, and she was one of the healthy ones. The earlier part of our session seemed thousands of years away, but now I began to get a sense of why I jumped the gun, why I had sided with Susan prematurely. Susan was *sick me*. I did not get the sense that Elaine knew in her bones who sick me was. Elaine was on the other side of the line that divided the healthy ones from the sick ones, like Susan and me. I wondered if Elaine expected sick souls to grow like healthy ones. Perhaps we sick ones have our own ways of growing. Did Elaine really expect Susan (or me) to be like her?

I needed to know if there was any way Elaine wanted to be like Susan. What in Susan did Elaine find valuable?

I usually can find something in every patient I need more of. What did Susan have that Elaine needed?

The shock waves from the earlier part of the session had died down, although not entirely. Without quite realizing it, I had been trying to keep things calm, trying to give Elaine and me a chance. Things had superficially been going better. But if shock is there, one can't keep it under the carpet indefinitely. The impact of the last part of the session was even greater than the first. I was blown away by Elaine's strong assertion that there was absolutely no way at all that she wanted to be like Susan, and absolutely nothing of Susan's that she wanted to have.

My question was foreign to her. Why on earth would she want to be like Susan, or want anything of Susan's? Susan's life was horrible. What on earth could Susan offer her? I wondered if something was wrong with me for imagining that Susan might have something to offer Elaine. What was wrong with me that I could find something to admire in Susan's struggle? The distance between Elaine and me seemed greater than ever. Instead of two professionals establishing a helpful supervisory relationship, we were inhabitants of different universes that had not yet discovered each other's signal systems.

Elaine's basic position was clear. She had something to offer Susan, but Susan had nothing to offer her. Susan could only bring her down, and she could only bring Susan up. We had gotten back to where the session started, from another route.

I was dumbfounded and wondered how to be tactful, honest, helpful. At some point I said something like, "I can't help feeling that Susan feels you're too good for her. She can never be you, or like you enough. She'll always fall short. She's another kind of person. She's the kind you can't identify with and don't want to be like. She offers you nothing of value for yourself and is forever outside your desire. She can never get in, unless she becomes like you."

Elaine and Susan could analyze this gap forever, but Susan would always drown in it because it was real and Elaine's feelings reinforced it. Susan was in the bind of getting help from a person who somehow experienced her as an untouchable. The helper was kind and caring and warm—one of the good ones. I could *feel* the problem, because Elaine's goodness made me feel like more of a pariah too. This, even though I knew Elaine liked me and wanted affirmation from me. She wanted me to affirm her together self, but in doing so, my sick self felt all the more left out. When Elaine spoke to me, I felt she was speaking to the wrong person, to her picture of creative me that fit creative her. But *I* was somewhere else, like Susan.

Susan must be baffled by this duality. She is with a dedicated therapist whose work is superior. She is with someone who wants to help her and has very real ability. Yet Susan can not locate herself in her therapist. She cannot find herself in her therapist's psyche. Her therapist does not have a Susan she values in the depths of her being, at least not yet, not consciously. For Elaine, Susan is a not-me element, an element of revulsion. There is no point of attraction or use she can find for the Susan in her soul.

I haplessly suggested Elaine try to find some way to lessen the distance between Susan and herself. Maybe she should try to meditate on Susan's virtues. Can she find something of use or value for herself in Susan's being? Must Susan be forever foreign? Elaine is honest. She could not *see* anything in Susan that is exemplary. Susan needs help. She needs to move to another level. To be Susan would be a downward spin for Elaine. What value could there be in *that*?

Our session ended without solving the problem of how

Elaine and I might communicate. I felt I failed her. She probably left feeling criticized. She wanted to feel close to me, but I needed to include sick me, sick Susan. Elaine was too good for us I feared. I don't think I'll kill myself over that, but it might be a lot of pressure for someone like Susan.

Jackie consulted me about her patient, Tina. Tina sounded a lot like Susan, except she was less suicidal. Tina periodically fell apart and could not function. She was anxious about diseases, and needed frequent reassurance that her brain or other body parts were not disintegrating. Her social life was almost nil, and she had intermittent sexual contact with an otherwise unavailable man.

Jackie, like Elaine, was picture perfect, elegantly dressed, tenaciously intact, warm, caring. She feared her patient's periods of disintegration, and felt a little guilty over the incessant reassurances she provided. Yet she did what her patient needed, and Tina improved.

Tina grappled with issues of self-respect, and her life grew. She took better care of herself and her apartment (positive identification with Jackie), got more satisfaction from work, and began experimenting with some dating. To Jackie's relief, Tina's periods of disintegration diminished in intensity and frequency. Things were going well enough.

My problem was that I felt I could not *find* Jackie. I did not *feel* any real contact with her, or any sense that I knew who she was. I could not *feel* her insides from my insides. When I inquired about this, she insisted she was easy to find. So it was *my* problem.

Things were going well with Tina. Why should I upset the applecart with *my* problem? If I became insistent, I'd become traumatizing. Things went along swimmingly. Why should I bother? As with Elaine, I felt left out

somehow. Jackie's presentations of sessions were coherent, complete, competent. Whatever I might say seemed
tangential, superfluous. I did not find vital loose ends to
pull on. Was my main function to be reassuring and
enhance Jackie's good feeling about herself and her work?

Jackie, like Elaine, was much better dressed than I.
She was more together than I, and took pride in her warm
elegance. She spoke fluently about her work. She did not
seem to have to struggle with what she felt or said, even
when she voiced difficulties. She seemed immaculately on
top of things.

The fault lines of my personality showed more than
hers. I felt more flawed than she. But perhaps the fact I
saw her as a sort of perfect jewel was *my* problem. Maybe
I was making her into something better than she meant
to be. Perhaps my self-esteem was simply lower than
hers, my personality less intact. Maybe I was feeling the
inevitable exclusion of the less socially adept person. It
wasn't her fault if she was better than I.

Yet the feeling that I could not find her nagged at me,
although I got nowhere sharing it. Then an incident
occurred that did not establish real contact between us,
but which gave me some indication that I was not
altogether crazy. Jackie came in and anxiously reported
that Tina was disintegrating again. Perhaps Jackie was
not really anxious, but simply frustrated, a bit stalled,
uncomprehending. Maybe she was angry at Tina for
disintegrating again. Jackie went over her checklist of
things Tina fell apart about, but could not figure out what
did it.

Jackie looked different to me this week. She had a
different glow and tone. I couldn't put my finger on it but
something felt different, so I asked. Jackie broke into a
big smile and said she was in love. Her life changed since
I last saw her. She seemed delighted with what was

happening with her. It was easy for me to say something like, "I guess Tina couldn't take your being in love."

"Noooo. . . . Is that it? Could it be?" Jackie said, as if a light went on. She made the connection between her changed emotional state and her patient's.

I became dramatic: "Your patient had a new therapist this week, one she never saw before." It was the first time I felt I could be of some use to Jackie. I could feel her experiencing the link between herself and her patient in a new way. At the same time, it seemed important that she had so utterly left herself out of the equation.

What a gap existed between Jackie and Tina! Tina must have experienced the change in Jackie, although neither mentioned it. Tina's loveless life seemed more acutely empty, next to Jackie's love-filled one. The gains Tina made paled by comparison with Jackie's radiance. Jackie's *more* made Tina's *less* unendurable.

It would take a little time for Tina to get used to the new Jackie, and for Jackie to get used to herself. Tina would spontaneously come back together, as soon as she realized that she and Jackie could continue contact, in spite of the latter's change of state. It was a matter of giving each other time to regroup and come through a major affective shift in the therapist.

In this case, Jackie was more bubbly and bright, so that Tina's light seemed dimmer by comparison. The distance between them need not only stimulate envy and torment, although it might if the therapist fails to recognize the real impact her changes make. If rightly handled, Jackie's movement can provide a model for the possibility of opening and change. Changes in the analyst generate changes in the patient, for better or worse.

Jackie's breakthrough triggered waves of affect that were too much, too fast for Tina. There was too much splendor in the room for Tina to take. Yet it was good for

Tina to feel such splendor was possible. It existed. Its effects were palpable. Would she be excluded from it forever? Was she banished from the kingdom? She tasted *it* in the room. Could she share some of Jackie's? Would she only get it through identifying with her therapist, or dare she get some of her own?

Many months later Jackie came in and started weeping. Something in her life had gone wrong and she was scared. She spoke about her fears and aspirations through her tears. Her life *might* be better than Tina's, but somehow *better* was irrelevant. Jackie suffered. She had her own dreads and worries, as well as joys. She may not go all the way down the tubes, like Tina. She does not disintegrate like Tina, nor feel so totally damaged. But she can identify with Tina. Tina's lows are not alien to her. They are not signals from another planet. She *can* see herself in Tina, and Tina in herself. They are very much part of the same soup, fellow travelers facing shared obstacles, one journeywoman further along than the other, but both in it together. The distance between Jackie's and Tina's lives is immense, but from Jackie's view, not alien.

What is the function of the supervisor in instances like the above? One function is to let the impact of the therapist and her presentation grow. In the cases above, the impact included a sense of discrepancy between therapist and patient. In each case, the therapist was much better off than the patient. Elaine appeared to experience Susan as more alien than Jackie experienced Tina. Nevertheless, there were moments when the differences between therapist and patient peaked, and therapist seemed too good for patient. What was possible for the therapist, was impossible for the patient.

It is important for the supervisor to hold and metabolize the difference between analyst and patient. Neither Elaine nor

Jackie fully took in the extent their better condition impacted on Susan and Tina. For some reason, they could not bear to realize that everything they worked so hard for in their own lives could increase their patient's suffering. Elaine and Jackie had made something of themselves. Now they had to deal with how their achievements might torment others, especially those they tried to help.

Another way of describing the difference between Elaine and Jackie and their patients is in terms of aliveness-deadness. Elaine and Jackie appeared to be more alive than Susan and Tina, not simply more successful, healthy, and attractive. The more one works with deprived and fragmented individuals, the more one realizes how important it is to modulate therapeutic aliveness. A too-alive therapist easily floods the patient without meaning to.

Elaine and Jackie were proud of their aliveness. Jackie worked at becoming more alive (she felt an inner deadness). Elaine flaunted her aliveness. Aliveness was her *credo* and she waved it like a banner. Both assumed their patients would be glad to have alive therapists: Susan and Tina wanted to be more alive. What Elaine and Jackie failed to take to heart was that Susan and Tina could not tolerate too much aliveness, not their own, and not their therapist's. They might want and envy it, but they could not take it. The sudden increase of aliveness Elaine and Jackie stimulated was as fragmenting, overwhelming, and depressing as it was relieving. There were moments that therapist aliveness made Susan and Tina more hopeful, but it could evoke despair and a sense of impossibility.

The double-edged effect of aliveness is something a therapist must catch on to as time goes on. With experience, one may learn to adapt one's intensity level to what the patient can use. A therapist can either be too alive or dead for a particular individual at a given time. As one grows in attunement, one finds one's psycho-organism automatically regulates emotional volume, turning it lower/higher as situations change.

It is difficult for many therapists to recognize they may be too much or not enough for their patients, and that turning oneself on-off is an important parameter. An individual who chronically numbs or deadens herself in order to survive lacks experience and resources to deal with the full range of emotional aliveness. Therapists who work with dead and fragmented patients (parts of many patients) need to develop sensitivity to the impact their own fluctuating aliveness-deadness is having.

The theme of envied aliveness, power, and goodness is ancient. Murder is part of the experience of exclusion. Biblical psychology can be cruelly honest: To those with more, more will be given; to those with less, even that will be taken away. Therapy is concerned with how to shift the balance of lives to the *more* track. More what? Aliveness? Good living? Use of capacity? Use of self? Still, there will be more, less, differences in quality, inequities.

Empathic recognition of the suffering that differences bring helps soften the outrage. Outrage and envy can be useful as motivating spurs, but in Susan's and Tina's cases, fury too often became destructive. Outrage boomeranged and increased their sense of damage, despair, inability. The carrot that therapy held out made them feel more helpless and hopeless, at the same time that therapy helped them. Elaine and Susan needed to recognize how helping someone can be galling and can increase destructiveness for the one needing and getting help.

Suppose Elaine included in her repertoire, and made a systematic part of therapy, references to how it must feel getting help from one who seems to be more alive or on top of it. Elaine *really* did feel better than Susan. I can imagine her saying something like, "It galls you being helped by someone better off than you." A remark like that may seem harsh and wounding, but there are many ways to put it that may soften the blow. Variations of the theme of being wounded by the helper must get played out and taken for granted. If the patient bites the hand that feeds, the hurtful helping hand also must be acknowledged.

My own personal suffering has been immense so it is hard to imagine placing myself above anyone else's distress. I *feel* partners in suffering with those who see me. Nevertheless, I *know* I may appear better off to some, worse off to others, and that perceptions of better-worse are vexing. It is one of the cruelties of idealization to imagine the "better" to be less tormented. In contrast with Elaine, I might have to say, "I fear your feeling that I am better than you so torments you that getting something through me makes you feel like dying." We need to find remarks that fit our subjective states. How to be helpful by being true to ourselves taxes human ability.

If Elaine really *felt* how much her goodness and aliveness hurt Susan, something in her touch might soften. A different tone or atmosphere might evolve, one in which Susan needn't feel quite so horrible about herself when she looked at Elaine, or one in which she could more readily share the horror and pain of being propelled further and further away.

Creative Elaine came to join with creative me, but sick and dead me screamed for recognition. Sick/dead me felt unwelcomed by Elaine, and Elaine felt rejected if sick me was not happy with her creative self. Elaine did not have a category for sick me linking with sick Susan. Susan and me formed a community of sick ones that Elaine did not want to join. Who excluded whom? My ability to help Elaine with Susan was taxed. My perception of Elaine's superiority made me more defensive, less available to *her*. It was my job to begin metabolizing the difference between Elaine and me, between Elaine and Susan, between creative me and sick me. Elaine did not give me time to begin metabolizing my defensiveness, so as to better work with hers and Susan's. Differences propelled us apart instead of creating possibilities for a varied relationship.

The propulsive element was an important part of what

happened between Susan and Elaine. Elaine was propelled away from me by my sickness, as Susan was propelled away from Elaine by the latter's health. The propulsion away from the excluding object, if unchecked and unmitigated, can be suicidal. What died between Elaine and me was the possibility of working together.

What happened (or failed to happen) with Elaine, Susan, and me is a good example of selective recognition processes. I could not recognize Elaine's creative self unless she recognized my sick self. My sick self was outraged by Elaine's undervaluation of the sick me in life (Susan's, mine, hers, anyone's). I would have needed time to grow around my outrage and find ways of establishing communication between the best in Elaine and the worst in Susan and me (and perhaps, Elaine?). I would have needed time to live my way into the propulsive force our differences ignited. Perhaps in time we could soften together and find ways to connect in face of seemingly unsolvable differences. Surely, something like this needs to happen between Susan and Elaine in a way that Elaine has not yet been able to recognize and suffer.

Elaine and I acted out in brief what lacerated her work with Susan over the long haul. The gap between sick self and creative self became a propulsive force with abruptly violent possibilities (our quick end). Elaine could not give me time enough. Let us hope Susan gives her time enough.

Jackie ran through a wider range of states. She had more patience with me than Elaine. Nevertheless, there was a blankness or lack of connection between us. We somehow did not really *feel* each other. I think this blankness was part of what needed to be metabolized. I don't know where it came from or what purpose it served. Jackie spoke of sealing over a horribly traumatic background, and I suspect it partly had to do with that. However, we were not fully honest with each other, at least not yet. For the time being, I tolerate our partial holding back, our testing the waters, sparring.

Jackie speaks of holding back with her patient. She fears loss of control if she is too expressive. She is afraid she will become too emotional and lose everything. Being the competent doctor protects her patient and herself. What good would showing too much of herself do her patient or herself? Thus, in spite of her warmth and good will, an emotional blank spot substitutes for expressiveness, partly out of fear. She fears her anger and tears. I hope she is not too angry at herself for the little she showed me. Perhaps next week I'll be the weepy, frightened, angry one. It's never far away.

ADDENDUM

After I wrote this chapter, I began to feel Jackie from the inside. The inner bell jar disappeared. Now she seems exquisitely expressive to me. I can feel her moment-to-moment shifts of feeling, infinite modulations of grief, fear, joy. She surely runs away from her feelings and deflects into intellectual considerations. She keeps something of a hard edge and hangs tough. But I can feel *her*, and I was not able to before. What happened?

Was she there all along? Was it me who was not there? Or did something thaw—in her, me, Tina? Did writing this chapter sensitize me to her? Was this chapter a sort of proxy attempt at metabolizing my (her, Tina's) defensiveness?

Jackie is more open to considering how her mood shifts affect her patient. She inwardly feels the connection between her joy and Tina's disintegration, and she is aware that her depressive feelings, if they are not excessive, make Tina more comfortable. The possibility opens of her and Tina traversing a wider range of states together and learning how they affect each other in a variety of ways.

How much of Jackie dare I let in now? I can feel her *feeling self*. What a quiveringly ecstatic sense! I don't know how much

I can take at a time. Life is always given in excess, more than we can use or handle. We bite little bits to chew on—enough, enough!

I can *see* Jackie opening to what happens between her and Tina. How much can she and Tina take? They are discovering there is direct transmission of feeling between them. How will the discovery of this kind of openness transform (or fail to transform) them? The flow between us is real. What will we do with it, it with us? It spreads in waves between Jackie, Tina and me, and now, also, you.

IV

THE
STRUCTURE
OF THE
SUPERVISORY
SITUATION

3

The Interactional Triad in Supervision

ROBERT J. MARSHALL, PH.D.

8

The Interactional Triad in Supervision

ROBERT J. MARSHALL, Ph.D.

The evolution of the functions of the supervisor seems to have paralleled the development of the functions of the psychoanalyst.

The analyst has moved from being a blank screen/mirror to a person who is subject to projective identifications, counter-transferences, counterresistances, and plain old human feelings that influence the patient for better or for worse. Similarly, the supervisor has moved from the position of a teacher and overseer to being an integral part of a system wherein s/he is influenced not only by the therapist, patient, and his/her own promptings, but is a prime source of feedback to the patient through the supervisee. This chapter is an attempt to conceptualize and systematize some of the major variables in the highly complex triadic system of supervisor, supervisee, and patient as they interact with their respective transferences and countertransferences.

The terms transference and countertransference are used in a totalistic sense, especially as outlined by Tower (1956), Kernberg (1984), and Marshall and Marshall (1988). The totalistic definition denotes *all* of the reactions of an individual ranging from realistic to delusional.

PATIENT AND THERAPIST

I assume that the patient develops transferences to the therapist and, in response, the therapist develops countertransference reactions. The countertransference reactions are considered to contain necessary and valuable clinical data, especially if they are "objective," as defined by Winnicott (1958). He proposed that an objective countertransference is the average expectable response of a good-enough analyst. Spotnitz (1985) introduced the polar concept of subjective countertransference which designated the personal, idiosyncratic, and conflicted reaction of the analyst to the patient's productions. I assume that the objective and subjective countertransference are on a continuum and in accord with Tansey and Burke (1989) and Springmann (1986), I postulate that objective and subjective elements exist in every countertransference reaction. Marshall and Marshall (1988) have examined the interplay between the different transferences and countertransferences in terms of the variables of awareness, source, and differentiation.

THERAPIST/SUPERVISEE AND SUPERVISOR

I assume that the supervisee develops transference reactions to the supervisor. The term transference, used in a totalistic sense, can range from a real or objective reaction merging into a response primarily determined by the unconscious conflicts of the supervisee. The supervisor, in turn, evolves countertransference reactions to the supervisee. These transferences and countertransferences were also analyzed by Marshall and Marshall (1988) in terms of their awareness, source, and differentiation.

Teitlebaum (1990) focuses on "the supervisor's unresolved conflicts, blind spots, or inappropriate expectations" and brands these reactions a "supertransference" (p. 244). Strean (1991) follows suit and warns of the supervisor colluding with the supervisee and bogging down treatment. Rather than focus on the negative, hindering reactions of the supervisor, I postulate that *the supervisor's emotional response can be helpful and facilitating to the course of supervision and therapy*, just as we believe that the transferences of the patient and the counter-transferences of the therapist can be of use. Thus, it may be more accurate to speak of a "supercountertransference" on the part of the supervisor. The foregoing words are unmercifully long and are mindful of Germanic combinations and construc-tions. However, these elongated and somewhat "psychobab-blous" words may be a better choice than having no words or evolving new words as we logically extend words of generally accepted meaning into new contexts.

Just as a distinction has been made between an objective countertransference and a subjective countertransference, a distinction can be made between an objective and subjective supercountertransference. That is, the supervisor's reaction may be that of most supervisors as compared with an idiosyn-cratic response dictated by unresolved inner conflicts. The source of the supervisor's reaction is crucial.

Spotnitz (1985) has made a useful distinction between a countertransference reaction and a countertransference resis-tance. A countertransference reaction, again, in a totalistic sense, consists of all possible thoughts, feelings, and even trial actions of a therapist. These reactions, however intense and disagreeable at times, should not be avoided by the analyst. On the other hand, a countertransference resistance is a mobili-zation of countertransference reactions into action about which the analyst has little or no awareness and which persistently and significantly interfere with the normal flow of the thera-peutic process. Thus, we apologetically introduce into the psychoanalytic lexicon another term—supercountertransference resistance—which simply means that the supervisor actively and without awareness is fouling up the supervisory/therapeutic works.

I do expect objection to the foregoing schema from supervisors who are accustomed to a hierarchy of supervisor-supervisee-patient, because the present system places everyone in a feedback circle, tends to equalize the players, and makes them subject to similar forces.

For highly intuitive therapists, the following system may have little meaning just as some people have a profound sense of direction and have no use for maps. But I liken the system to Michelin guides and road maps while touring France. *Without* them and with a sense of adventure and spontaneity, one can have a wonderful time discovering delightful chateaux, vistas, churches, shops, and restaurants. *With* the guides, one can be aware of alternatives, formulate general and specific itineraries, evaluate the information and opinions of the Michelin writers, and pretty much know where you are and where you want to go. And of course, one can create a balance of free-spiritedness and "planfulness." The interactional triad system encourages the supervisor to use intuition while providing help in gathering relevant information and organizing a more coherent and consistent picture of the patient, the supervisee and the supervisor in movement.

The following is a system of concepts and relationships which helps us think about the triadic supervisory situation. The system, consisting of patient, analyst, and supervisor (PAS), parallels Anna Freud's postulate of the analyst situating himself equidistantly from the ego, id, and superego. As an observer and participant, the supervisor is ideally situated equidistant from the supervisee, the patient, and, as participant-observer, from him/herself. All players are subject to the interactive transferences and countertransferences described above. Figure I schematically portrays the relationship between the psychoanalytic situation and the psychoanalytic supervision in terms of types of transferences and countertransferences.

FIGURE 1

RELATIONSHIP BETWEEN PSYCHOANALYTIC TREATMENT AND
PSYCHOANALYTIC SUPERVISION IN TERMS OF TRANSFERENCES AND
COUNTERTRANSFERENCES

PSYCHOANALYSIS

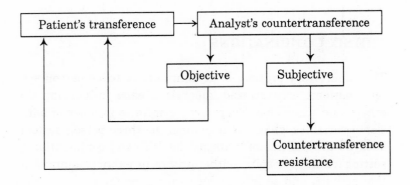

PSYCHOANALYTIC SUPERVISION

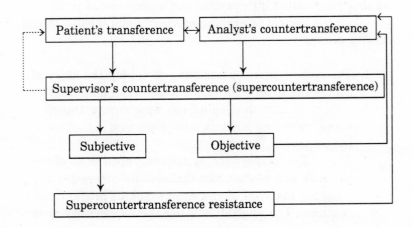

Since these models are dynamic fields and are subject to feedback principles, the reader can imagine that the analyst's countertransferences in the form of interventions can sweep back to influence the patient's transferences.

Similarly, the supervisor's countertransference impacts the supervisee's countertransference which, in turn, may affect the patient's transference. In some instances, the supervisor's countertransference may directly affect the patient's reactions.

THE SIX COMBINATIONS

The supervisory process is, at minimum, a three-person system: patient, analyst, and supervisor, each influencing the others and the whole. There are an infinite number of additional variables which impinge upon the three person system, such as the policies of managed health care, confidentiality, setting (clinic or hospital, either private or public), administrative activity, and so forth, which cannot be factored into this discourse. The present focus on a three-person closed system does violence to the real world of supervisory functioning but may help define, organize, and clarify some of the parameters of this complicated intrapsychic and interpersonal triad.

When the system is working efficiently and ideally, the following occurs:

1. The *patient* is free-associating or telling the story of his/her life in an emotionally meaningful manner. The patient is also developing the appropriate transferences, reporting dreams, and otherwise adhering to the contract.
2. The *analyst* (supervisee) is listening, open to all of the patient's and his/her own feelings. By processing the foregoing material, the analyst is making proper interventions. The analyst is using the supervisory time

recounting the therapeutic process, which includes the patient's productions, the analyst's thoughts, feelings, and actions, as well as the patient's responses to the analyst's interventions. The analyst experiences the supervisor as benign and cooperative.

3. The *supervisor* is listening in a way which opens him/herself to the experience of the patient and therapist *qua* individuals and as they interact. The supervisor is open to his/her feelings about the analyst and patient in a way that potentiates parallel process. The supervisor is attuned to the supervisee and moves into an observing role without disturbing the process. Sullivan's "participant-observer" comes to mind.

Since three variables are operating, six combinations are possible as sketched out by Marshall (1993). Let us consider each combination in this three-person interactive system.

Some of the illustrative vignettes focus on character styles interlaced with technical rituals which overpower the whole system and create stasis. Other vignettes demonstrate the mutual influence and balance of the three players which usually leads to movement from one combination to another.

1. Patient-Analyst-Supervisor *(PAS)*

In this combination, the patient initiates activity, synergizes, and potentiates the system. It is the most common and healthy system. As the patient talks, the analyst is energized, and in turn, the supervisor processes the entire interactional field, including his/her own influence. The supervisor's emotional position is similar to Daniel Stern's affective attunement, Kohut's empathy, Freud's free-floating attention and Anna Freud's identification. Caligor and colleagues (1984), Wolstein (1959), Levenson (1982), DeBell (1981), Epstein (1986), Lesser

(1984), Lane (1990), and Marshall and Marshall (1988) provide vivid descriptions of different supervisory styles. Many of the foregoing portraits focus only on the supervisor and neglect the factors introduced by supervisees and patients.

Less desirable forces can be at play. For example, the patient may control and dominate the system through threats and/or acts of violence or suicide. Treatment-destructive behavior is constantly displayed, perhaps immobilizing therapist and supervisor to such an extent that suspension or termination is advisable. As in any endeavor, "You can't win them all."

> A highly manipulative patient who had "found a home" in an institution shrewdly resisted all attempts at discharge, including assault of staff, feigned psychotic episodes and short term elopements. The hospital administration assumed a supervisory role for the patient's therapist and called for a "showdown" staff meeting with the patient in which all of the patient's tricks and resistances to discharge were to be anticipated and counteracted (shift to SPA). During the staff meeting, the staff inexorably began to bicker and disagree among themselves, until at one point the patient lit his cigar, put his feet up on the table, and contentedly surveyed the chaos that he had somehow crafted. When the staff observed the patient's smug position, the members became enraged, vindictive, and punitively arranged for a discharge which the patient negated by assaulting patients when he returned to the ward (shift to PSA).

> In another hospital setting, a severely depressed and suicidal patient passively defied the therapeutic efforts of his intern-therapist and supervisor. Unable to cope with the anxiety, depression and failure of the therapy/supervisory relations, the supervisor sought supervision from a senior staff member. After two meta-supervisory hours, the senior supervisor began to doze during the sessions. The

quality and intensity of the patient's depression seemed to filter through therapist, supervisor and the meta-supervisor, who begged off the case because he noted his own underlying depression was being mobilized.

Frequently, therapists will complain that the patient is controlling, manipulative, and trying to influence the treatment as well as the therapist's thoughts and feelings. Since we have become more aware of the power of projective identification and induced feelings, it should come as no surprise that the patient is exerting pressure on the analyst. The patient is merely doing his/her job of emotionally communicating to the therapist. The task of the therapist is to understand and use that emotional communication. The goal of the supervisor is to maintain optimum communication in the system and to help the therapist to assist the patient to put the unconscious affect into words.

The *PAS* can reflect the condition wherein the patient is attempting to supervise and/or therapize the analyst as Langs (1979) and Searles (1955) have so eloquently described. If a supervisor subscribes to Langs' and Searles' theses, several alternatives are available:

1. The supervisor can observe the corrective attempts of the patient and their effect on the analyst;
2. If the analyst is not getting the patient's message, the supervisor may work toward resolving the analyst's resistance to hearing the patients;
3. If the patient is sacrificing his/her therapy in the interest of helping the analyst, which may be reflecting a repetition, the supervisor may explore the impasse.

A patient repeatedly exhorted his analyst for "feedback." The student analyst, in a caricature of an orthodox Freudian model, maintained silence "in order not to gratify the patient." As the patient's frustration mounted and led to threats of termination, the analyst turned to interpreting a need for feeding. The patient stormed out in a rage. During the time the patient was trying to correct the therapist, we conceptualize a *PAS*. But because the analyst was not able to correctly divine the patient's request and the supervisor was immobilized by the analyst's rigid stance, the organization changed to *APS*. The analyst wanted a post-mortem about why the patient left—a shift to *ASP*. The supervisor discussed the resistances to respond to contact function, to explore requests, to accede to reasonable requests, and to give simple explanations. The supervisor suggested that the analyst call the patient—a clear shift to *SAP*. Although the supervisee was astounded at the suggestion, he telephoned the patient. The analyst was equally amazed when the patient spit forth, "It's about time you called me!" and agreed to come in to discuss the matter. Since the patient was basically a cooperative and patient person and the analyst was eager to learn, the analysis proceeded. This anecdote reflects the different shifts in power and focus along the supervisory route.

Since the literature abounds in examples of induced feelings, one vignette should suffice.

> A 35-year-old man who had been raised from infancy to take care of his depressed and affection-seeking mother eventually became a health-care worker and found himself in relationships with narcissistic women wherein he eventually felt used, depleted, and rageful. Previous attempts at treatment proved unsuccessful. In the analysis, the patient controlled the course of treatment such that the analyst found himself interested, wanting to help, but doing nothing except acknowledging and reflecting the patient's feelings. Because the analysis was the first time that the patient experienced mirroring, he enjoyed the

process and flourished in his daily life. The patient began to analyze himself. He realized that he had not only raised himself but had devoted his life to taking care of others as he had cared for his mother. Because the patient had made dramatic strides in all aspects of his life, the analyst found himself agreeing with the patient's request for fewer sessions and for termination. When the supervisor, who also had been lulled by the seeming progress, drew the analogy between the mother-child relationship, the reflective style of the analyst, and the transference-countertransference matrix, the therapist formulated a strategy that brought him into the picture and released the underlying anger (shift to *SAP*). The therapist became less reflective and more silent. He felt that he was in control of the analysis for the first time (*APS*). It was not long before the patient began accusing the analyst of laying down on the job, being a disappointment, being depressed, and so forth. He exclaimed, "You're just like my mother and all the other women in my life." The upshot of this work was that he established an exciting relationship with a woman who was much healthier and responsive than anyone he had ever met. He was back into the *PAS* configuration.

In 1922, when Bernfeld (1962) questioned Freud about Berlin's requirement to have a didactic analysis before seeing patients, Freud replied, "Nonsense. You go right ahead. You'll get in trouble. Then we will figure out what to do." Freud sent him a case in a week. When Bernfeld queried for advice, Freud responded, "Don't you know more than he? Show him as much as you can" (p. 463). In encouraging Bernfeld to start work and allow complications to develop, Freud was initially supporting a *PAS* relationship. However, Freud advocated a shift to other models, which will be explicated below.

2. Patient-Supervisor-Analyst (*PSA*)

Some patients have an uncanny sense of the advent of a supervisor or a change of supervisors. Some patients welcome the newcomer as an ally. Others dismiss the supervisor with a joke. Others experience the supervisor as an intrusion or impediment.

In the *PSA* combination, the patient and supervisor may strike up a relationship that shoves aside the analyst. The patient may know or sense that the analyst has a supervisor and that the analyst wants a relationship with that supervisor. The analyst who may appear victimized may be a player in passively accommodating to the triangulation. Some supervisors see the patient alone or in the presence of the analyst. In a slightly amplified scenario, the supervisor may develop a countertransference resistance and insinuate him/herself into the therapeutic relationship which would move the system to a Supervisor-Patient-Analyst balance (*SAP*).

> During the course of several years of analysis, a patient overcame his self-defeating patterns through an analysis of Oedipal guilt and achieved significant wealth and fame. As part of the transference resistance, the patient wanted to discharge his therapist and engage that therapist's supervisor—"Because I now deserve the best." The analyst, while intellectually acknowledging the worth of his good work, frequently felt that he should give up the patient to his superior. The supervisor felt flattered and tempted to take on a high-paying, influential patient. By not responding to these countertransference feelings, the supervisor dared to tread on therapeutic ground. He flushed out the therapist's realization that total capitulation to his father had been an old pattern which presumably had been analyzed, but which had cropped up under the patient's pressure to yield. The cooperative work

brought the patient's oedipal excesses under control and reestablished the analyst into his rightful role.

A suicidal adolescent girl developed the delusion that her therapist was a Nazi SS officer. After the girl discovered that the female supervisor had a Teutonic-sounding name, a new character crept into the patient's productions—the commandant of a concentration camp. The girl began to ask to see the commandant/supervisor, who, in reality, had been very close to the horrors of the holocaust. When denied access to the supervisor, the patient produced a series of dreams, poems, and artwork that shocked the supervisor because of this similarity to her own and her friends' experiences and the art during Hitler's regime. Although the patient was denied access to the supervisor, she was told that the supervisor would see her parents. The patient was delighted, for she imagined that the supervisor would torture and murder the parents. She was also thankful to her therapist, who seemed finally to realize how tortuous the parents were. This turn of events allowed for an analysis of the girl's repressed murderous feelings toward her parents and an alleviation of psychotic and depressive symptoms. As a consequence, the young woman became more creatively productive, made reasonable peace with her parents, and enrolled in an art college.

3. Analyst-Patient-Supervisor (APS)

In this cluster, the analyst directs the traffic, concentrates on the patient, and ignores the supervisor. This may occur in a clinic or hospital wherein the assigned supervisor is, rightly or wrongly, considered to be incompetent or iatrogenic. In concert, the supervisor may assume a laissez-faire attitude and let the full responsibility fall on the therapist. The therapist, in this triad, may have a dominating orientation or may hold authority in contempt. The therapist may be conducting creditable therapy but learning and supervision are limited.

Given a strong dependant transference, an analyst may develop a countertransference reaction wherein patient and therapist are locked into a symbiotic relationship.

> For example, a therapist under a countertransference need to "save" a patient by providing a corrective emotional experience to counteract the effects of childhood abuse and deprivation was gentle, kind, and accepting in spite of the patient's regression and provocations. The supervisor, in his supercountertransference exasperation, respectfully began to ask the supervisee about her extraordinary talent to process benignly and patiently the pathology and attacks of the patient. The therapist soon revealed a history of alcoholic parents and an alcoholic husband. She discussed the necessity of her "holding everything in to hold them together." Over the course of the supervision with similar patients, the therapist decided that she should not and could not treat children, adolescents and borderlines, but chose to specialize in the counseling of alcoholics.

There are any number of situations wherein the analyst may correctly surmise that a supervisor is not functioning appropriately. For example, a supervisee may suspect that the supervisor's erotic feelings are paramount to the goals of supervision; a supervisee finds that the supervisor regularly falls asleep during sessions; a supervisor is rigidly locked into a response mode such as lecturing and pontificating. The supervisor may not take into consideration Guest and Beutler's (1988) finding that beginning therapists like support while more advanced therapists prefer technical guidance.

Ideally, in all of the above cases, the analyst should discuss the problem with the supervisor. However, some supervisors may not be able to handle these confrontations, especially as they may relate to characterological problems, and may put the supervisee at risk by writing a negative evaluation. The supervisee may discuss the situation with other supervisees who have had experience with the troublesome supervisor and discuss the problem with a therapist. If there is some assurance that the supervisor is operating out of a supercountertransference resistance, the analyst has the option of terminating the supervision. If the problem occurs in an institutional setting wherein the therapist is stuck with a supervisor for a given amount of time, the therapist may wall off the supervisor such that the main relationship exists between patient and analyst.

4. Analyst-Supervisor-Patient (*ASP*)

This sequence may occur when the analyst develops a strong transference to the supervisor, the supervisor colludes, and the patient is neglected. The main emotional transaction occurs between analyst and supervisor at the conscious or unconscious behest of the analyst. Frequently, analyst and supervisor will conspire in the therapist's wish to be analyzed by the supervisor. The supervisor may yield out of competitive or envious feelings towards the supervisee's analyst. At the extreme end of the spectrum is the actual physical seduction of the supervisor by the analyst. The consequence is that the patient is cast to the side while the analyst and supervisor act out in unison.

Aggression rather than libido may characterize the analyst's overt relationship to the supervisor.

A young therapist was assigned to an amiable male clinic supervisor whom she disliked. Unable to change the circumstance, she chose to give the supervisor glowing reports of her interventions, with the implication that she did not need supervision. Faced with an apparent transference, the supervisor fell into a countertransference resistance of denial. Toward the end of this mutually agonizing rotation, the therapist inherited a rather disturbed borderline patient. Although the supervisor recognized that the patient was troublesome, he failed to help his trainee. He sarcastically and revengefully identified with the trainee's defense, telling her that she could cope by herself and did not need supervision. While the therapist seemed to be the provocateur, the supervisor could not rise above his feelings and help the therapist and her patients. In any event, the patient was neglected while supervisor and supervisee acted out their hateful drama.

Sometimes it is in the interest of the supervisory process to allow for a temporary shift to *ASP*.

For example, an experienced therapist who had successfully terminated her personal analysis, requested to use the couch during her supervisory session in order to discuss a personal crisis which was interfering with her therapeutic work. The supervisor agreed but with some inner reservations, for he had surmised that the supervisee had had boundary problems with her parents. After two weekly sessions on the couch, the crisis had subsided and the relationship shifted back to a normal *PAS*. From time to time, the supervisee chose to reveal personal material, but usually in the service of trying to resolve a subjective countertransference resistance. The occasional departure into an *ASP*, bordering on therapy, seemed to benefit the analyst and her therapeutic work.

A not uncommon but tactless and destructive response of a supervisor to a supervisee who begins to reveal personal feelings and conflicts is, "Take that back to your analyst." Rather than the supervisee slipping boundaries, the supervisee may be attempting to get help with a subjective countertransference. If the situation is unclear, an alternative to the foregoing off-putting blow to the supervisee is to ask tactful questions such as "Should we be discussing this in supervision?" "How does this relate to our problem with the patient?" "Is it all right with your analyst to tell me this personal material?" "I'd be pleased to get into this, but do we have your analyst's blessing?"

> In another kind of *ASP*, an analyst who had been working with an abusive borderline for several years, complained to her supervisor that he had no idea of the torture she had experienced when with the patient. Supervisor and analyst agreed that the analyst should try to infuse the supervisor with these horrible feelings. Failing to attune the supervisor, the supervisee presented to another supervisor.

When the analyst becomes too dependent on the supervisor and persists in questions such as, "What should I do?" "Did I do the right thing?", the supervisor may suggest a "consultation with the patient." (Kesten [1955]). This ploy sometimes startles the supervisee, who may sneeringly comment, "What does the patient know?" At the same time the supervisee is saying, "What does this supervisor know?" At this juncture the supervisor has several options, depending on the situation: the analyst's contempt for the patient may be explored, keeping in mind the latent representation of the supervisor and the supervisee's own self-esteem; the supervisor may choose to be educative about the patient's unconscious knowledge; or the supervisor may continue to study why there is such an imbalance in the system. That is, what is the supervisor contributing to idealization by the supervisee?

Caruth (1990) describes two types of supervisees which fit into the *ASP* configuration. One type is "immature, vulnerable, dependent, outer-directed and needy of affirmation and approval from authority figures" (p. 189). These students tend to be passive, idealize the supervisor, and "become more involved in issues in the supervisory process than in the therapy process with their patients" (p. 189). The other type is seemingly independent, aggressive, and preoccupied with autonomy and control. Competitiveness with the supervisor to the exclusion of the patient is the hallmark.

5. Supervisor-Analyst-Patient (*SAP*)

In this variation, the supervisor may develop and maintain a conscious or unconscious resistance to being a supervisor.

> In one unfortunate instance, a senior supervisor, positioning himself for retirement, reluctantly accepted an additional supervisee. They evolved a good working relationship because the young analyst enjoyed the elder statesman's reminiscences and the benefits of his vast experience while the supervisor enjoyed the adulation. However, the supervision suddenly took on a decided chill. The supervisor became critical and gratuitously didactic. Not prone to confront authority, the analyst-in-training silently condemned himself and the withdrawing supervisor. The supervisory term ground down to a civil but chilly end. Months later, the analyst put the pieces together. He realized that he had shared some of his reservations with a colleague about his elderly supervisor. That colleague, who enjoyed gossiping and creating disharmony, turned out to have been the analysand of the senior supervisor. That colleague apparently had re-

vealed and perhaps had embellished upon the criticisms of the supervisor, who could not effectively process the communication from the couch.

In a psychotherapy training clinic that had been dominated by a classical psychoanalytic orientation, a new director sought to leaven the atmosphere by hiring a young, active supervisor who was an existentialist, trained in Gestalt therapy, and experienced in working in the "here and now." Her supervisees were surprised, befuddled, and frightened by her pursuit of their feelings about their patients and about her supervision. For example, in the initial meeting she would typically pressure her interns to reveal their feelings about changing supervisors, having a woman as a supervisor, and so forth. After the students negotiated that ordeal, they found that the content of the sessions was secondary to the supervisor's focus on the therapists' emotional reactions to their patients and to the supervisor. The new supervisor's approach was a good antidote to other supervisors who were a burlesque of a classical analyst characterized by Woody Allen's dart, "My analyst only speaks to me when he raises his fee." For a considerable time, the supervisor was a prime topic of discussion among her trainees, who perhaps more profitably might have been discussing their training cases. To the supervisor's credit, she did become aware of the dramatic impact she was having on her supervisees, and she made appropriate changes in her approach which returned the field to the interaction between patient and therapist.

Gediman and Wolkenfeld (1980) describe a supervisor who was more intent on being "an authoritative guide" and using the supervisee as "an extension of himself."

A supervisor suggested to her supervisee that she get out of the field because she was using "unorthodox and unethical" methods with her institutionalized delinquent patients. The supervisor, whose theoretical system was an amalgam of classical psychoanalytic and client-centered techniques, advocated a passive, reflective, and laissez-faire orientation. The therapist found that the recommended techniques either did not work or produced regressive behavior. Being innovative, the therapist developed an approach which was more active and akin to the approach of August Aichhorn. The therapist borrowed a page of deceit out of her charges' book and did not reveal in supervisory sessions what really transpired in the therapy sessions. What started out as Supervisor-Analyst-Patient (SAP) triad, ended up as a Patient-Analyst-Supervisor (PAS) triad.

Whenever the supervisor intervenes with the analyst, the balance turns to SAP. If temporary and occasional, and when the balance returns to PAS, no problem exists.

For example, a patient had just terminated an analysis of two years because the analyst had insulted and humiliated him. Moreover, the patient refused to return to discuss the matter and said he would walk out if the present analyst contacted his previous analyst. The patient constantly talked about a verbally abusive father. In spite of the patient's provocations, the analyst was compelled to be kind and gentle as an antidote to, and a corrective emotional experience for, the traumatized man. The supervisor felt bypassed, annoyed, and anticipated that the man would leave treatment under this too-tolerant regime. The supervisor had the idea that in the context of a seemingly positive transference-countertransference, the patient needed to have the feeling that his analyst could

be like the abusive father. At some risk and with delib-
eration, the supervisor was momentarily sharp with the
analyst, confronting him with, "Why the hell do you allow
the patient to get away from cancelling at the last
moment and not paying you on time?" (Shift to *SAP*) The
surprised therapist in turn challenged the patient. While
the patient fumed and threatened to leave treatment, he
also talked less of the father and became more productive
and socially involved. Eventually the patient, with the
analyst's and supervisor's blessings, returned to his first
analyst.

6. Supervisor-Patient-Analyst (*SPA*)

SPA finds the supervisor focusing on the patient and overlooking the analyst. The supervisor has a transference and alliance
to the patient and secondarily to the analyst. *SPA* represents
an historically early model of supervision wherein the supervisor, with the analyst's acceptance, called all the shots,
provided the verbatim interventions, and otherwise treated the
patient through the analyst. When Helene Deutsch (1983)
consulted Freud about the patients he had referred to her, she
discovered that Freud offered little advice and seemed more
concerned about the referred patients than in her learning
experience.

The *SPA* arrangement sometimes occurs when the supervisor is inexperienced, insecure, or not attuned to the idea that
his primary responsibility is to the analyst, not the patient.
The supervisor, in his narcissistic, insecure state, is apt to
be overbearing, overactive, and didactic. On the other hand,
the supervisor may be passive, ungiving, and self-absorbed. If
the supervisee is relatively inexperienced, the supervisor's
attention to the patient and neglect of the therapist may go

unnoticed. More experienced analysts are more apt to engage the supervisor.

In order to salvage a deteriorated treatment situation, or when the supervisor cannot fathom a crisis, the supervisor may conduct a session with the patient and supervisee. In another variation wherein the patient cannot talk in front of the therapist, the supervisor, with the approval of the supervisee, may arrange for a consultation with the patient. These options should be used rarely and under emergency conditions and with the intent of eventually guiding the treatment situation into a *PAS* configuration.

SUMMARY

The evolution of the supervisor as a person subject to countertransference and counterresistance roughly parallels the development of the analyst as a person who originally was a blank screen but now is seen as being subject to countertransferences induced by the patient. The countertransferences of the analyst and supervisor may be a hindrance or a help. Patient, analyst, and supervisor can be seen as interacting in terms of their respective transferences and countertransferences to each other. Various alliances and relationships are set up among the players that can be conceptualized in terms of a dynamic feedback system.

In general, the normative system finds the patient initiating activity and evolving transferences that the analyst responds to with countertransference reactions in the totalistic sense. In turn, the observing and participating supervisor develops countertransference reactions which influence the system. Five other combinations may occur depending upon who is initiating action and/or controlling the system.

Supervisors may use the described system to orient themselves in a frequently confusing situation particularly when they recognize that an imbalance exists which diminishes the therapeutic endeavor. Imbalances are characterized by deviations from the Patient-Analyst-Supervisor (*PAS*) configuration. The deviations consists of: Patient-Supervisor-Analyst (*PSA*)— a collusion of patient and supervisor while bypassing the analyst; Analyst-Patient-Supervisor (*APS*)—analyst and patient relating in a way which ignores the supervisor; Analyst-Supervisor-Patient (*ASP*)—analyst establishes a relationship with supervisee which neglects the patient; Supervisor-Analyst-Patient (*SAP*)—supervisor more interested in patient than in analyst.

The process of supervision is still very much an art, learned through apprenticeships and improving over time. The system suggested tries to incorporate the supervisor as an integral part of the patient-analyst loop and may help supervisors to be more aware of and to master the bewildering factors at play.

REFERENCES

Bernfeld, S. (1962). On psychoanalytic training. *Psychoanalytic Quarterly*. 31:463.

Caligor, L., Bromberg, P.M., and Meltzer, J.D. (1984). *Clinical perspectives on the supervision of psychoanalysis and psychotherapy*. New York: Plenum.

Caruth, E. (1990). Complexities and vulnerabilities in the supervisory process. In *Psychoanalytic Approaches to Supervision*, R.C. Lane, ed. New York: Brunner/Mazel.

DeBell, D. (1981). Supervisory styles and positions. In *Becoming a Psychoanalyst*, R.S. Wallenstein, ed. New York: International Universities Press.

Deutsch, H. (1983). Control analysis. *Contemporary Psychoanalysis* 19:59–66.

Epstein, L. (1986). Collusive selective inattention to the negative impact of the supervisory interaction. *Contemporary Psychoanalysis* 22:389–408.

Gediman, H. K., and Wolkenfeld, F. (1980). The parallelism phenomenon in psychoanalysis: Its reconsideration as a triadic system. *Psychoanalytic Quarterly* 49:234–255.

Guest, P. D., and Beutler, L. E. (1988). Impact of psychotherapy supervision on therapist orientation and values. *Journal of Consulting and Clinical Psychology* 56:653–658.

Kernberg, O. (1984). Countertransference, transference regression, and the incapacity to defend. In *Between Analyst and Patient: New Dimensions in Countertransference*, H.C. Hayes, ed. Hillsdale, NJ: Analytic Press.

Kesten, J. (1955). Learning for spite. *Psychoanalysis* 4:63–67.

Lane, R. C., ed. (1990). *Psychoanalytic Approaches to Supervision*. New York: Brunner/Mazel.

Langs, R. (1979). *The Supervisory Experience*. New York: Jason Aronson.

Lesser, R. (1984). Supervision: Illusions, anxieties and questions. *Contemporary Psychoanalysis* 20:120–129.

Levenson, E. A. (1982). Follow the fox: An inquiry into the vicissitudes of psychoanalytic supervision. *Contemporary Psychoanalysis* 18:1–15.

Marshall, R. J. (1993). Perspectives on supervision: Tea or supervision. *Modern Psychoanalysis* 18:45–58.

Marshall, R. J., and Marshall, S. V. (1988). *The Transference-countertransference Matrix: The Emotional Cognitive Dialogue in Psychotherapy, Psychoanalysis, and Supervision*. New York: Columbia University Press.

Searles, H. F. (1955). The informational value of the supervisor's emotional experiences. In *Collected Papers on Schizophrenia and Related Subjects*. New York: International Universities Press.

Spotnitz, H. (1976). Trends in modern psychoanalytic supervision. *Modern Psychoanalysis* 2:201–217.

——— (1985). *Modern Psychoanalysis of the Schizophrenic Patient*. 2d ed. New York: Human Sciences Press.

Springmann, R. R. (1986). Countertransference: Clarification in supervision. *Contemporary Psychoanalysis* 22:252–277.

Strean, H. S. (1991). Colluding illusions among analytic candidates, their supervisors and their patients: A major factor in some treatment impasses. *Psychoanalytic Psychology* 8:403–414.

Tansey, M. J., and Burke, W. F. (1989). *Understanding Countertransference: From Projective Identification to Empathy*. Hillsdale, N J: Analytic Press.

Teitelbaum, S. H. (1990). Supertransference: The role of the supervisor's blindspots. *Psychoanalytic Psychology* 7:243–259.

Tower, L. E. (1956). Countertransference. *Journal of the American Psychoanalytic Association* 4:224–255.

Winnicott, D. W. (1958). Hate in the countertransference. *Collected Papers*. London: Tavistock.

Wolstein, B. (1959). *Countertransference*. New York: Grune and Stratton.

V

THE
SUPERVISORY
RELATIONSHIP

4

Effective Supervision*

MARTIN H. ROCK, PH.D.

* Portions of this paper were presented at the International Federation for Psychoanalytic Education Conference, October 30, 1993.

In this chapter I will describe what I have found to be aspects of supervision which afford highly valued and identity-enhancing experiences for the supervisee. My focus is on the role of the supervisor since I believe that close examination of this aspect of the supervisory situation has been relatively neglected in the literature. My perspective is informed by my experiences conducting individual and group supervision and by the results of several empirical studies that my students and I have conducted of trainees' subjective experiences of supervision.

SUPERVISEE'S EVALUATIONS OF THE EFFECTIVENESS OF SUPERVISION: SUPERVISEE'S LEARNING NEEDS AND SUPERVISORS' STYLES OF SUPERVISION

We found in three different surveys of a total of over 300 trainees (analysts in training and psychology graduate students) in supervision that effective supervisors are experienced as attuned to supervisees' emotional and learning needs. They are seen as committed, focused, and expert (Backman 1994, Beron 1994, Ornston 1995, Sobel 1988).

The good supervisors seem to invite their supervisees to identify with them, to take them as their mentors, and yet to encourage autonomy. They demonstrate to the supervisees how to appreciate and use their responses to the ambiguous and anxiety-provoking task of conducting psychotherapy. This learning is fostered by a relationship that is experienced by the supervisee as reciprocal, mutual, and trusting. Our surveys are supported by the results of others' studies of the supervision of graduate students conducting brief psychotherapy and counseling in a wide range of settings (Carifio and Hess 1987, Holloway and Newfeldt 1995).

In our surveys we found that supervisors who are directive, who exercise a high level of control, and who are often highly theory bound are typically experienced as critical and intrusive. The structure of this supervision is authoritarian, and as such it often leads students to conceal the interpersonal and countertransferential realities of their therapeutic work. Such supervisors are often reported to have left the supervisee with increased insecurity and an internal "harsh critic," a negative internalized supervisor who exercises an inhibitory function over the supervisee's work (Backman 1994, Beron 1994; Cohen 1992).

Supervisees faced with the dominance of what Levenson (1982) calls the "by-the-numbers" supervisor tend to avoid openness and confrontation out of a self-preservative need to maintain self esteem and a sense of identity in the face of genuine threat. Clinically I have found that supervisees who experience this diminished sense of their own competence and rightness tend to act out their unconscious response to feeling criticized and bad—they may become covertly hostile and undercutting or critical of the patient in ways that may undermine the patient and the therapeutic working relationship.

Interestingly, Strupp and his coworkers (Henry et al 1993, Najavits and Strupp 1994) have reported that attempts to train therapists to do therapy "by the book" (i.e. according to the treatment manual) lead to measurable negative effects on therapists' behavior with their patients and to poorer treatment outcomes. These researchers also found that supervisees who, to begin with, tended to be harshly self critical, were likely to become more critical in the therapeutic relationship after this training.

Alternatives to this supervision might be a "laissez faire" attitude, or what Levenson (1982) has called the "Zen" approach. Such styles, I believe, lead to confusion and even despair due to the supervisee's likely sense that he has been left alone to deal with the emotionally demanding therapeutic work himself, just when the presence of a mentor is most needed. In our surveys we have found that supervisees say that they need an active, task focused, and involved supervisor. This does not have to interfere with the supervisee's autonomy as Levenson seems to feel. In fact, active involvement by the supervisor seems to be essential for the promotion of autonomy.

Supervisees value goodness of fit—discussed by others as a good "learning alliance" (Fleming and Benedek 1966)—as much as they need the information, the insights provided by the supervisor. Supervisees value experiences that promote the development of a professional identity. I have found consistently that for supervisees, the acquisition of knowledge in supervision is inseparable from the experience of their relationship with the supervisor.

A NEW THEORETICAL CONTEXT

I believe that if we take seriously what supervisees say about what they find valuable, we will be led to a conception of supervision which incorporates a number of developments in psychoanalysis in the past 25 years.

My central point is that the profound paradigmatic shifts in the theory of psychoanalysis have been paralleled by the same changes in the theory of psychoanalytic supervision, although at a slower rate. Hoffman (1993) has succinctly characterized these developments: Psychoanalysis has moved far from a sense of the analyst as a scientific observer and facilitator of the transference and its interpretation. It came to a view of the analyst as responsive in a therapeutically corrective way to the patient's needs and deficits and to an appreciation of the usefulness of countertransference in the process. Presently, there is much discussion of the view that the analyst participates in the patient's construction of the reality of the psychoanalytic situation and of his life. The model is of an analyst who participates as "an intimate partner" in a lived encounter as the patient wrestles with conflict, develops in his identity, and makes choices in life (Hoffman 1993). In this view of analysis, the analyst is a participant observer (Sullivan 1954) and an observing participant (Hirsch 1987). Similarly, the theory of supervision has moved from a didactic and hierarchical model to a more egalitarian and relational model, with an emphasis on the mutuality of the process of influence. The influence of the supervisory relationship itself on what is learned, how it is learned, and what effect it has on the therapy being supervised has become a central focus of concern.

Just as the analyst is no longer seen as the objective observer and knowing interpreter of the psyche of the patient, so also the supervisor is no longer represented as the omniscient seer, the one who necessarily knows and sees more and imparts that information to the naive neophyte.

In this interpersonal/relational model of supervision, the focus is on co-participation and mutual engagement: Supervisee and supervisor conduct a dialogue about a field of inquiry that includes the relationship between them, although the explicit focus is, of course, the therapy being supervised.

I am also suggesting that the supervision must be a kind of analytic process in itself rather than a didactic endeavor, one that is centered on the articulation of the subjectivity and direct experience of the participants. In order to be analytic it must take itself as the subject of reflection—what occurs between the participants and how each affects and is affected by the other must be understood and, at times, subject to joint exploration (Berman 1988).

A central question with which supervisors have had to struggle has to do with how one is to work with the primary data—what is basic to what defines therapy as psychoanalytic—transference and countertransference material. Traditionally, supervisors have been wary of direct dealings with counter-transference, fearing that to do anything beyond identifying areas of difficulty for the supervisee constituted an interfer-ence with the student's analysis. The debate in the literature has been the "teach or treat" dilemma, considered by DeBell (1981) to be "perhaps one of the earliest and most persistent questions about appropriate supervisory activity" (p. 41).

The concerns expressed by various writers (e.g. Ekstein and Wallerstein 1972, Langs 1984, Levenson 1982, and Rioch 1980) were that efforts to analyze supervisee's countertransference would interfere with the supervisee's sense of autonomy and self-esteem. I agree with Sarnat (1992) that developments in analytic theory provide a new context in which to consider this dilemma, and they offer a way out.

I first want to illustrate the nature of the dilemma involved in supervisors' efforts to treat supervisees' countertransference by describing the therapeutic style of supervision. This ap-proach takes as its primary focus the countertransference of the supervisee, generally via interpretation or confrontation. Rather than advising the student to "take this up with your analyst," such as might be done in a didactic approach, the supervisor takes on the neurosis of the supervisee, often with the expectation that the student will not be able to work things out with his analyst. As Issacharoff (1984) points out, what is timely or convenient for the training process may not be consistent with the supervisee's own therapeutic needs.

The supervisor with the "therapeutic style" may well get to very significant complexes, conflicts, transferences, and countertransferences of the supervisee. Unfortunately, such supervision is also apt to induce feelings of shame. The supervisee is likely to feel intruded upon, controlled, and in danger. Spitz' comment (Fleming and Benedek 1966) that supervision is experienced by supervisees as more dangerous than analysis is well taken. The old position of "take it to your analyst" was clearly based on the attitude that the countertransference represented the psychopathology of the supervisee and thus should be subject to treatment. However, I suspect that the injunction that dictated this treatment of countertransference material was also born of empathy for the supervisee and by the realization that they were treading on dangerous ground when the supervisee's very personal conflicts were unearthed and forced into discussion with the supervisor who could neither guarantee confidentiality nor reserve judgment about the supervisee's competence (viz. Wolstein 1984). The potential for significant difficulty in such a supervision is very real and can result in disruptions, premature terminations (firing the supervisor, for example) or impasses. The supervisor's interpretations of the supervisee's conflicts can readily lead to the supervisee feeling that he or she is subject to an abuse of power.

It is in this context then that Wolstein attempts to change the structure of supervision by suggesting small groups to replace one-on-one supervision. He hopes that the group of peers can diffuse the situation, lessen the supervisee's anxiety about domination, control, and intrusion of the supervisor, and yet promote exploration of the supervisee's countertransference. In a sense the negative transference to the supervisor would be diffused to the group. While I regard group supervision as a very valuable modality, one that all analytic candi-

dates and therapists should experience, I do not believe that it
can substitute for individual supervision. Nor does it have to. I
think that if the supervisor works at establishing a facilitative
relationship, much can be learned of the supervisee's very
personal reactions to the patient while allowing the supervisee
a measure of control of what is revealed about his inner world
and personal history.

WORKING WITH COUNTERTRANSFERENCE IN SUPERVISION

How the supervisor works with the countertransference de-
pends upon his definition of it. If he holds to the narrow
definition of countertransference as the supervisee's neurotic
reactions to the patient's transference, then he will be moved to
identify it so as to neutralize or exclude it from the therapeutic
process. The goal will be to "purify" the supervisee's responses
to the patient, to render them countertransference-free. I think
that such an approach deadens the supervision and the therapy.
The problem is that work on the countertransference in this
way conveys the impression to the supervisee that there is
something wrong with him—he is thinking and (especially)
feeling the wrong way (Epstein 1985, Feiner 1994). Such a
message typically has one of several possible unfortunate
outcomes. The supervisee may identify with the supervisor and
criticize himself with the information. He is likely to feel bad,
ashamed, humiliated, guilty, angry at himself. Or it may result
in selective inattention or denial or projection of the therapist's
bad feelings on to the patient.

On the other hand, a broader definition of countertransference is more useful. In this view countertransference is the
totality of the therapist's reactions to the patient. The focus of
the supervisory inquiry is on her role-responsiveness to the

patient's transference-based role ascriptions and inductions (Sandler 1976). The emphasis, then is on the importance of encouraging open discussions of the supervisee's subjective experience and participation with the patient. It does not require a focus on the supervisee's problems, although her neurotic trends and conflicts are certainly central. An understanding of the therapist's feelings and fantasies will yield a great deal of information about the patient and the interaction. If the supervisor regards countertransference as messages from the unconsciouses of patient and therapist, as primary data rather than merely as the therapist's psychopathology, then the supervisee similarly may be able to adopt an open, curious attitude toward her often powerful, affectively charged reactions to her patients. Under the best of circumstances, shame may be replaced by awe as the supervisee finds out how much she understood about the therapeutic interaction without seeming to know it.

One scenario in which this approach is most useful often occurs. The supervisee is caught up is an intense emotional reaction to the patient—rage, humiliation, contempt, love, and so forth—and believes that her reaction is "inappropriate" and a sure sign of therapeutic incompetence and flaws in her personality. At such times she may be so overcome by the feelings evoked in the therapy sessions that she may have great difficulty thinking and reflecting rather than reacting. If she can allow herself to risk the humiliation of reporting such feelings, she and the supervisor can begin to explore them, with the notion that she may be reacting to very real inducements and provocations from the patient. Understanding the function of the patient's unconscious communications and clarifying the supervisee's reactions to them will reveal the complex interaction of patient and supervisee.

In these situations, the relative calm and detached reflectiveness of the supervisor may help to contain these powerful feelings and allow the supervisee to emulate the supervisor's reflectiveness. She may then be in a position to help contain the patient's overwhelming affects and eventually promote reflectiveness in the patient (Gabbard and Wilkinson 1994). Conveying her understanding of the patient's unconscious communications will allow the patient to feel that his therapist is in touch with even the most difficult of his feelings (Casement 1985).

With the supervisory relationship as a "potential space" in which the supervisee can express his unformulated experience of and with the patient, and with the supervisor as a co-participant in a supervisory dialogue, the material can be expanded upon and enhanced. The Winnicottian concept of "play and playfulness" is quite useful in this context. To quote Winnicott (1971): "Psychotherapy is done in the overlap of two play areas, that of the patient and that of the therapist. If the patient cannot play, then something needs to be done to enable the patient to become able to play, after which psychotherapy may begin. The reason why playing is essential is that it is in playing that the patient is being creative (p. 54)." I believe that it is a function of the supervisor to facilitate playfulness (and hence the potential for creativity) on the part of the supervisee via his own attitude of playfulness.

Ideally, the supervisor and supervisee can engage in a kind of "brainstorming" or play with their thoughts, feelings, and formulations about the therapy. Discussion of what are often unformulated reactions is particularly useful in enabling them to understand what is structuring the therapy and its movement. Their inquiry expands the data in the "outer play space" (à la Winnicott) or in the "supervisory playground" (à la Levenson 1991 and Ehrenberg 1992) with a primary aim of encouraging the development in the supervisee of the "inner play space" in which she may then rely upon herself to understand and engage the patient (Casement 1985).

THE STRUCTURE OF THE SUPERVISORY RELATIONSHIP

In the contemporary view of supervision, the supervisory relationship is less authoritarian than in didactically oriented supervision. I have suggested a notion of co-participation. Both supervisee and supervisor are participants in an exploration. Each has something to contribute to the experience of the other and each has something to learn. While the supervisor is the authority and is more knowledgeable, he is not in possession of all the relevant data. It is, after all, the supervisee who sits with the patient day in and day out. The supervisor is expert in psychoanalytic knowledge and patients in general, but he does not know the particular patient. The supervisor is well-advised to concede that first hand knowledge—the data on which therapy is based—is in possession of the supervisee.

The principle here is a basic one: The supervisee is the therapist and the therapy is his responsibility. When supervisors violate this role boundary, they will invariably produce problems in the treatment as well as compromise the supervisory process.

The value of the supervisor stems in part from the fact that he is not embedded in the therapeutic interaction. His "supervision" in this approach is more of "another vision," a different but not necessarily better perspective.

The supervisor typically sees many things that the supervisee cannot. As supervisors we would like to think that our superior understanding of the patient and of the therapy is due to long years of training and experience. Surely this is true, yet there is more. The supervisor sees more because, as Levenson (1982) points out, he is in a different, more "abstract" role. He is not embedded in the therapy situation and therefore not subject to the same anxieties that induce selective attention and other defensive processes, nor is the supervisor subject to projection processes which tend to skew his perceptions.

As I have said, my aim is to foster the development of the supervisee's autonomy. Casement (1985) has described the growth of autonomy as an outgrowth of the development of what he has called "the internal supervisor." The internal supervisor is that part of the supervisee that reflects upon and guides his therapeutic work. It includes the therapist's own personal ways of thinking and working. It is the job of the supervisor to foster the development of the supervisee's "internal supervisor" and hence of the supervisee's autonomy. "Student analysts and therapists have a particular need to be professionally held while they learn about the analytic holding that a patient needs in therapy . . . There needs to be a supervisory holding by an experienced person who believes in the student's potential to be in tune with the patient and to comment helpfully (p. 25)."

Students need to be able to develop a style of working which is compatible with their own personalities. As Casement states the issue, one of the pitfalls of being a supervisor ". . . is the danger of offering too strong a model of how to treat the patient. This can mislead students into learning by a false process, borrowing too directly from a supervisor's way of working rather than developing their own. Some students can be seriously undermined in this way, feeling as if the treatment (or even the patient) has been taken over by the supervisor (p.25)."

> For example, an experienced therapist recounts that a supervisor created a particularly difficult dilemma for him. The supervisor was a man with a passionate commitment to the British Object Relations school. Most of his formulations and interpretations seemed to be informed by this theory, and he clearly listened to what the supervisee reported to him in order to find the phenomena of interest to him (e.g. manifestations of false and true selves). The supervisee concluded, in retrospect, that

not only had he shaped what he said to the supervisor but also what he said to the patient to fit into the supervisor's frame. Eventually, he found himself talking in terms of what the supervisor needed to hear rather than in terms of what the patient needed. Indeed the supervisee's experience was a kind of false self-experience. This was conveyed to the patient in terms of subtly-expressed expectations to speak the language and report the experiences described by the theory. The supervisee's motivation was a need to please the supervisor, to be a good student, to avoid disappointing this esteemed analyst. Likewise, he felt that the patient was tailoring her presentation out of similar motivations. The alternatives for the supervisee were to rebel, which he was loathe to do, or to engage in hiding what was really going on. Discussion of the issues with the supervisor were, he felt, fruitless, due to the supervisor's tendency to interpret opposition as the supervisee's resistance to deep anxieties. In fact, the patient regressed in the treatment as she came in contact with her regressive, passive and isolated self. This was seen initially by the supervisor as constructive. However, the therapist and the patient became extremely frightened; the therapist felt that the treatment had moved too fast. Neither he nor the patient felt adequately held to be able to bear the anxiety and uncertainty. After a brief hospitalization, the patient was then sent back to her home town where she had the support of her family. She began a new therapy at that point.

Supervision which unwittingly promotes shame and guilt tends to leave the student with an image of the supervisor that is punitive. If the supervisee is to achieve a measure of autonomy in his work (and his self supervision), he will have to rid himself of or neutralize the effects of this harsh inner supervisor–critic. The supervisor who fails to be attuned to the learning needs of the supervisee will be seen as neglectful or self serving. In this sense, then, it would seem that much of the hard work of the well meaning supervisor may be for naught—he may well be "sloughed off" as an intruder.

As Epstein (1985) so clearly points out, even typical, virtually prescribed supervisory behavior of making formulations for the naive supervisee as to the dynamics of the patient or the therapeutic process can rob the supervisee of being an autonomous, valuable, significant participant in the process. If he is rendered unable to feel significant to the patient, he is simply not going to be able to be an effective therapist. Epstein states that when he sees that he is having such an effect on the therapist, he adjusts his behavior—he may keep his observations to himself, expecting that asking the good question and encouraging the supervisee to articulate his experience will eventually lead to clarification of what he felt the need to announce.

THE SUPERVISOR'S COUNTERTRANSFERENCE

I want to add particular emphasis to a consideration of the supervisor's countertransference reactions to both supervisee and patient. Until fairly recently, psychoanalytic writers stopped short of considering the supervisor's countertransference reactions. The supervisor's role seems to have been somewhat sacrosanct, as if, since "the buck stopped here," someone had to be clear, conscious, and unconflicted about what he was doing. That "healthy" one was, of course, supposed to be the supervisor. Yet experience has shown that this is impossible. Consistent with Racker's (1957) view that it is a myth that there is a sick one and a healthy one in the therapeutic dyad, we must assume that there are two personalities with values, assumptions, vulnerabilities, and idiosyncrasies in the supervision.

Teitelbaum (1990), from the point of view of someone who has the opportunity to supervise supervisors (in groups), has coined the term "supertransference" to identify the supervisors' unconscious reactions to their supervisees. Teitelbaum puts emphasis on the countertransference as a hindrance to the work and defines it as the "supervisor's blind spots." I would add to Teitelbaum's idea that countertransference also has its constructive aspect in supervision as a source of significant data about the process of the supervision and of the therapy (Epstein and Feiner 1979).

My assumption is that everyone's perception of reality is a construction determined by what that person brings into the relationship and by what is created in the interaction. It is therefore crucial that the supervisor not forget that he too has needs and goals, and that he cannot be fully aware of the nature of his participation in the supervision. He has a stake in his reputation and status in the institution; he has a need to feel esteemed, knowledgeable, and valued. It is also important that supervisors recognize that they have strengths and weaknesses. Just as therapists are not equally effective with all types of patients, so also are supervisors more or less insightful and helpful with different patients. And they too have countertransferential feelings about patients. More than one student has told me of a supervisor who seemed to have strong (generally negative) feelings about a supervisee's patient which made the supervision problematic and intruded on the therapy.

The interference of the unexamined narcissism of the supervisor and the supervisee's reactions to it are illustrated in the following example.

Dr. B, an experienced therapist in psychoanalytic training, recalled his supervision with Dr. G whom he admired as particularly astute and knowledgeable. At one point in the treatment the patient characterized his life as lacking in any relationship of trust or honesty. There was no one, he lamented, that he could confide in. The supervisor strongly felt that the patient was indirectly referring to the supervisee and that it was necessary for him to call the patient's attention to that possibility. While the supervisee recognized that the negative transference was surely there in the material, he felt that it was premature to introduce it. The supervisor persistently raised the issue and the supervisee resisted. At one point, the supervisor reached a height of frustration, and suggested that the supervision was stalemated and that perhaps it should end right there. The supervisee did not feel that he wanted to terminate the relationship. He felt that the issue did not warrant such a drastic step. While he did not agree, he decided to follow the supervisor's directive—he suggested to the patient that he had the negative feelings about the analyst, which the patient promptly and adamantly denied, adding "you are the only person I can talk to." In his own analysis the supervisee realized that he was resisting the supervisor out of resentment that he was required to support the supervisor's narcissism. He felt called upon to be "the good student who admired this wise supervisor." He decided that it was necessary to give the supervisor what he seemed to need. The result was that conflict between them ceased and the rest of their year together was uneventful. However, the supervisee felt that his learning was compromised. He gained in information, but advanced little in his sense of himself as an analyst. It was a disappointing year of work.

Just as the therapist's countertransference can be used to further therapeutic goals, so too can the supervisors' countertransference be used to further supervisory goals. The value of the diagnosis and use of parallel process has been well documented in the literature (Caligor 1984, Gediman and Wolkenfeld 1980, Searles 1955). The appearance of enactments is often signalled by the supervisor's recognition of his own affective response to the supervisee; self analysis and exploration with the supervisee will often lead to the discovery of parallel issues being enacted in the therapy. Also, articulation of the supervisor's feelings about the patient may offer an informative perspective on the therapeutic process.

Similarily, the supervisor's countertransferential reactions to the supervisee may have little to do with the patient. The supervisor may be responding to his feelings about the therapist or how he engages in the supervision with this supervisor.

PROBLEMS IN THE SUPERVISORY RELATIONSHIP

I am most impressed with the process of influence in the triad of supervisor–supervisee–patient as it works *from the top down*. Difficulties experienced in the supervisory relationship often result in significant problems in the therapy, often in therapeutic stalemates and impasses. In general one might formulate this dynamic as a "reflection" process (Searles 1955). The therapist unconsciously enacts with the patient the difficulty he is experiencing with the supervisor, often with the roles reversed. Discussion in the literature on parallel process has emphasized the upward direction of unconscious influence, even though lip service has been paid to the observation that the transferred effects may be initiated by any of the three participants (Ekstein and Wallerstein 1957, Gediman and Wolkenfeld 1980). I think it is crucial to recognize that the supervisor powerfully affects the supervisee and the treatment and not always in the intended, positive ways. Thus, for example, the supervisee may experience the supervisor as insensitive and dominating. The supervisee may become that way with the patient who may then be seen as infantile or excessively needy, and so forth. Conversely, the supervisee may experience the patient as dominating and threatening and himself as excessively needy (of the patient's time or money or associations). In either case, the patient may well react with anxiety, withdrawal or acting out, unconsciously perceiving the therapist's covert hostility.

Searles (1962) and Fiscalini (1985) have illustrated another form of unconscious enactment in the therapy of difficulties in the supervision. They describe the supervisee's seeming compliance with the supervisor in such a way that the supervisory instruction fails. These writers point out that in causing such a failure the supervisee is unconsciously asserting his "stubborn and healthy determination to be allowed to use his own best capacities, and to have them acknowledged as *his*" (Searles 1962, p. 586). The problem is not attributed to the supervisee's hostility or to the difficulty of the therapy; rather it is attributed to the authoritarian structure of the supervision. This "trickle down" dynamic provides an excellent illustration of "the triadic impact of unnoted or unexamined supervisory parataxis" (Fiscalini 1985).

MUTUAL INQUIRY INTO PROBLEMS IN THE SUPERVISORY RELATIONSHIP

Open discussion of difficulties in the supervisory relationship can lead to constructive resolution and an enhancement of the supervision and the therapy (Ornston 1995). Avoidance or collusion not to acknowledge difficulties between supervisor and supervisee may lead to constriction and attenuation of the dialogue, limit its usefulness, and negatively affect the therapy. Interestingly, it is typically the supervisee, with great trepidation, who raises the problematic issues with the supervisor (Moskowitz and Rupert 1983). The moral here is clear. If there are difficulties in the supervisory relationship, they should be addressed. To confront them is to allow for repair and growth, even for an opening up of difficulties that may be occurring in the therapy which may be the displaced repository of impasses in the supervisory relationship.

There is a modeling process that occurs. When the difficulties are jointly explored the supervisee can have the experience of confronting difficult situations directly, in the here and now (Berman 1988). If it can be done with constructive consequences with the supervisor, then the supervisee can do it with his patients. He has the opportunity to gain in courage and confidence that such forthrightness can be therapeutic. Greater trust in himself and the patient is a frequent outcome.

I am often encouraged when a supervisee disagrees with me. If I am not fixed on having to be right, or on protecting my narcissistic equilibrium, then we stand a chance of learning something from one another. Disagreement may mean that the supervisee and I are listening to two different selves or voices of the patient. Or because we have different sensibilities we are affected in very different ways by the same material. The supervisee is better able to hear me if I assume that there is no single reality, no one take on the clinical material. Ultimately it is crucial that the supervisor be able to accept the possibility that the supervisee is, at times, more insightful about the patient than is the supervisor. Hopefully the supervisee is similarly open to the observations of the supervisor.

> S., a lively and forthright candidate in supervision with me, reported a session with a handsome womanizer. He had told her, with more detail and vividness than was usual for him, of his fantasies of dominating and controlling women. Notably, while he readily evoked the interest of women he described as beautiful and sexy, he often slept with them without having sex. His interest was typically short lived and affairs often ended abruptly. At one point, the therapist felt much perturbed by the patient's fantasies about these women, so much so that

she felt her anger rising, and she confronted him by saying that these were "rape fantasies." The patient was shocked and somewhat insulted that she would understand him in this way. On hearing her report, I said I felt that what she had said was excessively harsh and would likely close off further discussion of these fantasies. She felt that I was supporting the patient, which made her very angry. She asserted that I could not know what hearing this man would mean to a woman. She was offended by what she considered to be the patient's demeaning and hostile attitude toward women. Therefore she felt bound to inform him of the implications of his fantasies, of which he was seemingly unaware.

I could not dispute her feelings, and I found it instructive to review what the patient was saying from the point of view of a woman. I was helped to see past the patient's boyishness and charm to his real impact on this woman. At the same time, I did make the point that to label his fantasies "rape" ran the risk of driving them underground, and ignored the aspect of his anxiety, guilt, and inhibition. She had made it clear that she didn't like such material, and he would likely make peace by not talking about them. I said that since he wasn't directly acting on these fantasies and wasn't likely to, it would be helpful to treat them as valuable material to be explored. She appreciated what I said, yet insisted that confrontation with his intentions and feelings was important for this patient. And, he did have a thinly disguised contempt for women. In fact, in a prior session he had revealed his expectation that the therapist would find him irresistible, but that unfortunately he did not find himself attracted to her. She replied by asking why he would assume that she would find his lack of sexual attraction to her to be a problem. Her aim was to challenge his grandiosity. Her unconscious aim, it seemed, was to counter his contempt, which I realized, continued to be a significant issue. Material from the rest of the session we were discussing, and from subsequent sessions, validated that her confrontational style did not drive this patient into hiding. But he did not stay with discussion of his fantasies of domination. In part, her effort to confront him with his contempt toward women in general was a displacement from her immediate concern in the room with him—that he was hostile and contemptuous toward her; she needed to defend herself against such a "rape." These issues were clarified as we hashed out our differences about her confrontation of the patient.

In retrospect, it also occurred to me that what was happening in the room with the patient was occurring in parallel form with me. Had I insisted that she see things my way and had I not taken seriously what she was saying to me, I think that I would have emerged dominant in our encounter, I would have symbolically raped her. Resentment and withdrawal could have been the result. Instead, I think I got my point across, and she felt free to convey to me her very strong feelings and perceptions of this patient. Our relationship remained collaborative. I believed that this issue would come up again in our supervision and in subsequent ones. We did about as much as we could, I felt, at that particular juncture.

I think it is worth noting that in Searles' (1955) seminal article on parallel process in supervision and analysis he described how he conveyed his realization that a process was occurring in which problematic aspects of the therapy relationship seemed to be enacted in the supervisory dialogue. He did not simply provide the supervisee with his insightful observations. Rather, he worked it out through a joint inquiry with the supervisee so as to free their relationship from the disruptive influence of the transferred negative elements; his effort was clearly to protect the learning alliance as well as to help the therapist work with the transference and countertransference. He states, "Thus the supervisor and the therapist are enabled to deal with the problem area therapeutically, in a here-and-now context. After a therapeutic process has been set in motion on this, so to speak, miniature scale, the therapist is in a position to carry over the therapeutic process into his relationship with the patient . . ." (p.173). I am not suggesting that the difficulty my supervisee and I had with one another represented an enactment of her difficulties with the patient. One might just as easily conjecture that our difficulties were being enacted unconsciously in the therapy. My focus in this example is on the difficulties that so often occur in the supervisory interaction because of the necessary intense emotional involvement of both parties. What was required was that we discussed our differences openly.

It also became more apparent that she and I possess different therapeutic styles, just as we are different personalities. I realized through our work together that she was more comfortable as a person and a therapist with such confrontations. Her open, authentic expression of what she thought and felt typically invited a similar and typically constructive response from her patients. I concluded that it would be very important for her to be aware of her tendency to jump to direct confrontation with difficulties rather than to feel passively helpless; at the same time her courage was admirable.

In general, research findings indicate that supervisees consider the discussion of countertransference and of issues in the supervisory relationship to be hallmarks of effective supervision (Cohn 1992, Geller and Schaffer 1988). Ornston's (1995) study found that the timely discussion of difficulties in the supervisory relationship tended to improve the quality of the supervision. Ornston also found that the longer that conflicts in the supervision were not discussed, the more negative the eventual effect on the supervisory process. Clearly, it is incumbent upon the supervisor to be sensitive to his impact on the supervisee, as well as to the supervisee's impact upon him, and to raise the issues as they arise.

Dialogue about the supervisee's feelings is not necessarily aimed at clearing up the supervisee's transferentially based distortions. Instead, discussion is aimed at restoring the sense of cooperation and supporting the supervisee's sense of control in the situation through restoring the supervisor's ability to hear and understand the experience of the supervisee.

The fact is that we can run into very knotty situations in the conduct of supervision. Problems in the therapy may make the supervisor feel that the welfare of the patient is threatened. Yet it strikes me that we have to get our priorities and roles straight: It is the supervisee who is the therapist. The supervisor is the consultant to the supervisee—or at least he is when the learning and professional development of the supervisee is of primary concern. Where administration of the clinic or other such concerns are primary, then professional development may well take a back seat. With the possible exception of extreme situations, I believe that the supervisor must work with the therapist and not through the therapist if the therapy is to be facilitated, saved, or restored. Rescue efforts that circumvent the control and which trammel the self-esteem of the supervisee may work in the short run but are probably doomed to ultimate failure. The supervision is very likely to run aground and the therapy will only be saved if the supervisory alliance is repaired or if the supervisee exits the supervision altogether.

To conclude, effective supervision is that which recognizes that the way in which the supervision is done is as important as what is taught. Indeed what is learned will be a function of the relational context in which it is learned.

REFERENCES

Backman, B. (1994). *Shame in the Process of Supervision.* Unpublished Manuscript, Yeshiva University.

Berman, E. (1988). The joint exploration of the supervisory relationship as an aspect of psychoanalytic supervision. In *New Concepts in Psychoanalytic Psychotherapy*, J. Ross and W. Myers eds. Washington D.C.: American Psychiatric Press.

Beron, E. (1994). *The supervisee's experience of "good hours" in psychoanalytic supervision.* Unpublished Manuscript, Yeshiva University.

Caligor, L. (1984). Parallel and reciprocal processes in psychoanalytic supervision. In *Clinical Perspectives on the Supervision of Psychoanalysis and Psychotherapy*, L. Caligor, P. Bromberg, and J. Meltzer eds. New York: Plenum.

Carifio, M. S., and Hess, A. K. (1987). Who is the ideal supervisor? *Professional Psychology: Research and Practice* 18(3): 244–250.

Casement, P. (1985). *Learning from the Patient.* New York: Guilford.

Cohn, O. (1992). *Analytic Candidates' Experience: Internalization and Supervisory Style.* Unpublished Ph.D. Dissertation, Yeshiva University.

DeBell, D. (1981). Supervisory styles and positions. In *Becoming a Psychoanalyst*, R. Wallerstein, ed. New York: International Universities Press.

Doehrman, M. (1976). Parallel processes in supervision and psychotherapy. *Bulletin of the Menninger Clinic* 40: 3–104.

Ehrenberg, D. B. (1992). *The Intimate Edge.* New York: Norton.

Ekstein, R., and Wallerstein, R. (1972). *The Teaching and Learning of Psychotherapy.* New York: International Universities Press.

Epstein, L. (1985). Collusive selective inattention to the negative impact of the supervisory interaction. *Contemporary Psychoanalysis* 22(3): 389-409.

Epstein, L., and Feiner, A. (1979). *Countertransference*. New York: Jason Aronson.

Feiner, A. (1994). Contradictions in the process of supervision. *Contemporary Psychoanalysis* 30(1): 57–75.

Fiscalini, J. (1985). On supervisory parataxis and dialogue. *Contemporary Psychoanalysis* 21: 591–607.

Fleming, J., and Benedek, T. (1966). *Psychoanalytic Supervision*. New York: Grune and Stratton.

Gabbard, G., and Wilkinson, S. (1994). *Management of Countertransference with Borderline Patients*. Washington D.C.: American Psychiatric Press.

Gediman, H., and Wolkenfeld, F. (1980). The parallelism phenomenon in psychoanalysis: Its reconsideration as a triadic system. *Psychoanalytic Quarterly* 49: 234–255.

Geller, J., and Schaffer, C. (1988). *Internalization of the supervisory dialogue and the development of therapeutic competence*. Paper presented at the Society for Psychotherapy Research annual meeting, Santa Fe, N.M.

Henry, W., Strupp, H., Butler, S., et al. (1993). Effects of training in time-limited dynamic psychotherapy: Mediators of therapist's responses to training. *Journal of Consulting & Clinical Psychology* 61: 434–440.

Hirsch, I. (1987) Varying modes of analytic participation. *Journal of the American Academy of Psychoanalysis* 15: 205–222.

Hoffman, I. Z. (1983). The patient as interpreter of the analyst's experience. *Contemporary Psychoanalysis* 19: 389–422.

———(1993). The intimate authority of the psychoanalyst's presence. *Psychologist Psychoanalyst* 13(2): 15–23.

Holloway, E. L. and Neufeldt, S. A. (1995). Supervision: Its contributions to treatment efficacy. *Journal of Consulting and Clinical Psychology* 63(2): 207-213.

Issacharoff, A. (1984). Countertransference in supervision: Therapeutic consequences for the supervisee. In *Clinical Perspectives on the Supervision of Psychoanalysis and Psychotherapy*, L. Caligor, P. Bromberg, and J. Meltzer eds. New York: Plenum.

Langs, R. (1984). Supervisory crises and dreams from supervisees. In *Clinical Perspectives on the Supervision of Psychoanalysis and Psychotherapy*, L. Caligor, P. Bromberg, and J. Meltzer eds. New York: Plenum.

Levenson, E. (1982). Follow the fox. *Contemporary Psychoanalysis* 18(1): 1–15.

Moskowitz, M., and Rupert, P. (1983). Conflict resolution within the supervisory relationship. *Professional Psychology: Research and Practice* 14: 633–641.

Najavits, L., and Strupp, H. (1994). Differences in the effectiveness of psychodynamic therapists: A process–outcome study. *Psychotherapy* 31(1): 114–123.

Ornston, E. (1995). *The Emergence and Resolution of Conflict in the Supervisory Relationship: The Supervisee's Experience*. Unpublished Manuscript, Yeshiva University.

Racker, H. (1968). *Transference and Countertransference*. New York: International Universities Press.

Rioch, J. (1980). The dilemmas of supervision in dynamic psychotherapy. In *Psychotherapy Supervision: Theory, Research, and Practice*. A. Hess ed. New York: Wiley.

Sandler, J. (1976). Countertransference and role responsiveness. *International Review of Psychoanalysis* 3: 43–47.

Sarnat, J. (1992). Supervision in relationship: Resolving the teach-treat controversy in psychoanalytic supervision. *Psychoanalytic Psychology* 9(3): 387–403.

Searles, H. (1955). The informational value of the supervisor's emotional experiences. In *Collected Papers on Schizophrenia and Related Subjects*. New York: International Universities Press, 1965.

————(1962). Problems of psycho-analytic supervision. In *Collected Papers on Schizophrenia and Related Subjects*. New York: International Universities Press, 1965.

Sobel, S. (1988). *The experience of therapists in supervision*. Unpublished Manuscript, Yeshiva University.

Sullivan, H. S. (1954). *The Psychiatric Interview*. New York: Norton.

Teitelbaum, S. H. (1990). Supertransference: The role of the supervisor's blind spots. *Psychoanalytic Psychology* 7(2): 243–258.

Winnicott, D. W. (1971). *Playing and Reality*. London: Tavistock.

Wolstein, B.(1984). A proposal to enlarge the individual model of psychoanalytic supervision. *Contemporary Psychoanalysis* 20: 131–145.

5

And Now for Something Completely Different: Postgraduate Supervision*

NINA COLTART

*I would like to thank "Anne" and "Mary" for their willing help in the construction of this chapter; and to add that Mary managed to get some funds together and is now in a training course with an excellent psychotherapy organization in London.

When we consider how important supervision is thought to be during the training of a psychoanalyst or psychotherapist, it is surprising how little has been written about it. A lot of weight is ascribed to the supervisors' reports during training, and yet this job, which demands high skills, may be comparatively new ground when one has clambered up the hierarchy far enough to be asked to do it. It is almost as if supervision has a special sort of privacy about it, which even experienced practitioners are reluctant to open up and write about; this is so even in the case of analysts who are perfectly prepared to write clinical papers which may be very revealing of themselves at work with patients.

I recently attended a meeting of training analysts of the British Society at which the subject under discussion, supervision, possibly threw a little light on this in the sense that writing about supervision may betray that we do, at times, exert "undue" influence on our students. A particular aspect— choice of supervisors—was discussed at length, and the problem of the extent to which the training analyst influences the choice of his/her student came up. It was suggested, discussed, and then actually proposed that the analyst should never make any sort of influential suggestion to the student but should allow absolutely free choice. This seemed to me impossibly idealistic, to a degree that is totally unrealizable. Psychoanalysts, however well-analyzed and self-aware they are, are only human, and they have their share of opinions, prejudices, likes and dislikes, rivalries, and favoritisms. In fact, in some ways I believe we are a rather disabled profession; disabled in the sense that some of our ideals—and perhaps neutrality and not being hampered by these human attributes—are so inordinately difficult to maintain. Too often, one can become aware that illusions and self-deception grow in the attempt to reach or maintain ideals. And the further up the hierarchy we go, the greater our authority in our own limited sphere and the fewer the checks and balances; truly it becomes a case of *Quis custodiet ipsos custodes*?

It was partly because I became more aware of these dangers, which subtly increase with the aging process, and partly that I was weary not only of the inbuilt constraints but also of the authoritarianism of being a long-term training analyst in a "reporting" Society, that I decided about 8 years ago to withdraw from the training structure of the British Society and henceforth only take on for supervision experienced psychotherapists who were looking for a "refresher course," and with whom I thought there would be a far greater chance of an egalitarian relationship. This turned out to be true, and supervision from then on became a different and delightful experience.

As it happened, my last spell of being a training supervisor was one which thoroughly confirmed my decision to withdraw; it was a perfectly dreadful experience and I will describe it briefly, largely as a contrast to my great enjoyment with the 2 therapists I have chosen to present as examples of postgraduate supervision. First, however, I want to refer to the notion of "giftedness" in a therapist. I believe this to be a strong concept which is widely used yet hardly ever defined, and I have never seen it written about. It is as if we all, between ourselves,

recognize the phenomenon and know what we mean by it—
someone intelligent, intuitive, skillful with words, warm, empathic, self-disciplined and capable of high levels of absorption
in the lives of others. Such people often have a sense of vocation
to the work, freely admit that they enjoy doing it, and not
infrequently describe themselves as "a round peg in a round
hole." They are, it goes without saying, psychologically minded—
another concept and one to which I have given attention in
writing (Coltart 1988, 1992). Supervision of such people, even
in training, is a pleasure. It is radically different from work
with someone who, in some fundamental and disconcerting
way, is exactly the opposite.

Such a one was the last student I supervised as part of her
training. How she had ever survived the interviews with the
Admissions Committee baffled me. She was the only student
whom I ever felt should be urged to leave and change her
career path, if only for the sake of her own happiness and
fulfillment in life. She was not unintelligent, but she was
absolutely not psychologically minded. In the way that some
people are tone deaf or completely innumerate, so she was
closed to any and all workings of the human psyche. She was
kind and practical, and at least from the point of view of future
patients I did not think she would ever be actively harmful.
She was completely unintrospective and I hesitated to imagine
what it was like to be her analyst; in fact it was her analyst
who had asked me to take her for what would be a fourth
attempt at supervising. She had lost two training patients, and
both supervisors had refused to undertake another. A third one
had actually died, one must assume for unconnected reasons.
The Training Committee had suspended her for a year but had
refused to ask her to go altogether. This was said to be because
she had already spent 9 years in analysis and 5 in the training
and the committee were increasingly reluctant *not* to qualify
her after all the time, effort, and (her) expenditure. In this way
are monstrous initial errors compounded.

There was a pathos about the situation. If she had been an idle villain, it would have been easier to expel her. But she tried so hard and was still so keen. I can only say that if devotion and care are parts of the mysterious ingredient "x" which helps to heal people (and I am sure they are), it was in this that my feeling lay that she would never do active harm. She would present an excruciating, detailed session of confused dialogue that was not like anything I had ever heard before; it was not even like conversation, which would have had its own mild value. It was a dreadful sort of psychobabble with fairly unhappy remarks from the patient (who, fortunately, was not too disturbed but who certainly did need some treatment) and almost unintelligible *non-sequitur* responses from the student. Bits of undigested theory, odd technical words, and startling and confused ideas which she had hoovered up at random during the last few years were strung together in a muddled stream which had not even the virtue of being remotely connected to what the patient had said. For example, one day the patient complained about his journey and the weather. Speedily the student intervened with what I dimly recognized as a distorted version of the Oedipus complex, which I had tried to describe to her in simple terms at our last meeting. Not surprisingly, the patient was silent for some time, and then said he didn't know what she was talking about. This, in my view, made three of us. The poor student was very easily unbalanced and was never far from desperation. She slid nearer to it at this point.

I decided that I could only try to stick to the very simplest ideas of our theory and try to convey them as often as possible. I used these ideas to reconstrue the material of these sessions insofar as I could understand it and translate it. I described transference over and over again and tended to leave out countertransference. She would listen to me and look at me with a fixed expression of hopeful bewilderment, which tended to deepen if I referred to the unconscious—as I felt bound to do.

Sometimes she would get a sudden conviction that she not only had seen, but was right about, something in the patient. Extraordinary conversations ensued between us. I hesitated to disillusion her, as her self-esteem was already low. If she *had* got hold of something, I enlarged upon it enthusiastically. Often I stressed that silence was a permissible and usually valuable quality in an analyst. I simply could not recommend qualification in my report when the time came, but neither could I commit myself strongly to an alternative. The Training Committee did recommend qualification, however, and it duly came about. The ex-student, showing a commonsense grip on reality which she had always manifested, immediately left the Society and became a General Practitioner (GP), in which field I imagine she was loved and trusted.

But now for something completely different, as the Monty Python catch-phrase went. I would like to describe 2 of the people who have come to me in recent years, when I have been available for post-graduate "refresher course" supervision. One is very experienced and has run a full psychotherapy practice for nearly 15 years as well as teaching 2 sessions of psychotherapy in the National Health Service (NHS). The other has been qualified as a counsellor for only a year but has quite a busy private practice. Counsellor trainings vary in this country; some are more "analytic" than others. Hers was about average. She had wanted to train as a psychotherapist, but she had previously been a nun in a teaching order for 15 years and money was desperately short. She took the one training for which she won a scholarship. These 2 women differed from each other in many ways, but they had one thing in common which made an immeasurable difference and was the main feature that produced such a high level of enjoyment in both their supervisions: they were both extremely gifted. With both I could thus take certain things for granted: psychological-mindedness; unceasing interest in and curiosity about the lives of others; commitment to the process; a potential for creativity.

The experienced one is Anne. With both Anne and Mary, I had long discussions about the supervision when I knew I would be writing this chapter, based on notes which I had asked each of them to make about their experience. What follows is taken from those discussions and notes with passages from their notes in quotation marks.

Anne was influenced in her work by the writings of Winnicott, on whose work she lectured widely. When I look back over her year with me, the first thing that comes to mind is the atmosphere of great good humor. We laughed for a large part of the time, although we also worked hard. I am aware that, except from certain rather esoteric philosophical angles, there is nothing intrinsically funny in our sort of work. Indeed, often it is sad or anxious, but there was something in her sense of humor and mine which met, and also something in me which responded to what she was unconsciously looking for from supervision. What this was she fully realized only when we had our discussion based on her notes.

She had in her practice 4 frantically ill and difficult patients, all of whom she had taken on about 8 to 10 years ago when her needs were different and she was simply less experienced. I am sure most analytical therapists know the state of baffled near-despair to which an exceedingly disturbed borderline patient can reduce one. Anne had wrestled alone with her four, alongside the more "normal" neurotic patients who make up a practice. The sorts of situations that can be produced, often one knows not how, are of absolute darkness when not only does progress seem to be an impossibly distant hope but the patient actually seems to be sliding rapidly downhill. Part of her laughter was simply relief at having someone deeply interested in them with her.

But most of our laughing was to do with our sense of

being truly in a "play area," and Anne realized how much she had longed for one and how much she had missed it. This is a concept of Winnicott's (Winnicott 1971). A play area is a kind of "place" or state of mind into which a child, in normal development, can withdraw from the impingement of external reality and enter upon what may be a long and complex play-fantasy or game in which he can be seen to be totally absorbed. External objects, such as toys, may be used, but as symbols of some internal reality-objects rather than as their intrinsic selves. Part of the significance of this phenomenon is that the child is not, during this time, close to, fused with, or depending on the mother, though he is likely to have his "transitional object" with him. A transitional object is another Winnicottian concept for some humble object which becomes invested with "Mother" and rarely leaves the child (Winnicott 1971). It is therefore an extremely important stage in his individuation, in which he begins to discover his "Self." It is not a solipsistic concept; Winnicott described the sort of treatment which *works* as happening at "the interface of two play-areas," and maintains that a patient will move forward into healing if patient and therapist can thus meet. It requires confidence and skill and unselfconsciousness in the therapist, and is, of course, a development of object-relations theory and not of early classical theory, in which it would have been impossible. An experienced therapist can bring this interface (or its absence or failure) from the treatment into supervision, where with luck the interface of the play areas of the therapist and supervisor will then be the meeting ground.

Anne felt that because this was the setting of our meetings, she was freed from anxiety and near-despair to value herself and her way of working again. She began to re-trust her intuitions and free associations. "It liberated

me into being my Self again—my best Self as a therapist—or perhaps I really got there for the first time." This
"playing" does not happen nearly so often or so easily
during a training supervision. The student is too anxious,
too constrained by the requirements of the training, and
has not yet approached the much more advanced state of
mind in which technique can seem so natural and unselfconscious but is based on years of hard work and is a
considerable art. Anne looked back on her training as a
sort of container into which she put parts of herself, which
were gradually learned and retrieved. But as we discussed it, she saw it as very limited, both by its demands
and her own self-limitations, by the relatively small
quantity of theory she had absorbed, and by her own
narcissism. As she said to me: "But I've made theory my
own now. Before, it was something that belonged to the
training, which was Out There." I could actually see her
moving about with ever greater ease and mobility in
theory, and in her technique it became her servant and
not her master. She enabled me to add to this through
freedom in my own ideas in our "play-area."

To link up with another concept of Winnicott's, the
play-area is also a "potential space" (Winnicott 1971,
1982). In the chapter in *Playing and Reality* entitled
"Playing: A Theoretical Statement" (pp. 44–62), Winnicott connects the ideas from the point of view of the
therapist, and describes how characteristics of the therapist's state of mind include absorption (almost a withdrawal). This is because the state of mind is dependent on
inner thought and fantasy and not on external stimuli. He
sees the potential space as a feature of the area that
cannot easily be left, so absorbing is the creative play
which happens in it. All this Anne translated in terms of
her supervision, in which she had felt absorbed, creative,

and free to wander, "ploughing my own furrow," as she phrased it.

A large part of the wandering consisted of free association to some material earlier presented from one of her borderline patients. In this I joined, and often from this shared activity there would arise, unexpectedly, rich ideas far beyond the theme of our starting point that were also enlightening to it. Anne described this experience as "Validation of one's own imaginative creativity, and how to use it in technique, but all within a disciplined framework; yet at the same time the frame is now elastic, more expansible." This was a valuable and paradoxical conjunction of ideas.

We both felt an increase in energy and alertness during and after a supervision; we agreed it had a desirable kind of excitement about it, and we also thought that if one's reserves are depleted, one is not only less likely to reach this state, but there is less potential for it. As a result, one can get into a downward spiral in which further depletion of resources is likely. On the whole, although one can have inspired peak experiences while working alone with a patient, we felt that the particular energizing and high level pleasure we enjoyed was probably a function of a particular sort of supervision, one in which an egalitarian interacting of "play" and theoretically rooted free-association was the keynote, alongside an absence of dogmatic "teaching." We also thought that this was only possible when the supervisee is already very experienced (and preferably shares a sense of humor with the supervisor!).

Anne was aware that "the supervision both conveyed and confirmed the importance of faith." By faith she meant specifically faith as I have written about it elsewhere (Coltart 1987, 1992), which is faith in oneself. This faith lends itself deeply to unselfconscious attention and faith in the therapeutic process, which it is our job to help build and sustain.

Finally, since she had had no supervision since her training, she was surprised and pleased that it was "so different," and that we could share so much so openly. It is certainly true that during the training the supervisor is inevitably experienced by the student as being—and simply *is*—in a dominant position of authority. A lot of straight teaching of basics has to be done, and furthermore, both participants know that reports are written throughout. They know that the reports finally weigh heavily in the assessment for qualification.

We moved about between her four most difficult patients, though sometimes we stayed with one for weeks on end. Predominantly we worked on one whom I call Jane. Jane was an inordinately intelligent actuary in her late twenties, an example of the sort of patient whose intelligence is largely a hindrance to the therapy. Mostly, however, she managed to stay at work, even when most disturbed. She was considered to be a great asset there, even though she was somewhat eccentric. Indeed she carved out for herself a niche in an exceedingly esoteric field of recondite finance, on which, during the course of her frantically difficult treatment, she became a world authority! She was what used to be called a "colonial" and had come to this country impelled by a need, rather than a wish, to get away from her family. She was referred by a distinguished psychiatrist, who could not reach her at all. She was also a severe asthmatic, and she had already incorporated the asthma in a deadly acting-out. She was tall, pretty, supercilious and mostly hostile to Anne. She never looked at Anne, and rarely addressed her. Indeed, she rarely spoke at all most of the time. The question of why did she come was probably answered by her blind love for her doctor, who thought therapy was the only hope for her eccentric and unhappy life, and also for better control of her chronically recurring asthma attacks.

Anne's formulation of Jane to me was that of a woman who had very little definable ego and no boundaried Self. Anne described her as almost entirely fragmented in her Self, except for the professional persona which she managed to hold together, probably through intellectual fascination with an engrossing and highly ordered external object. She appeared to be totally unsuitable for insight therapy and had no interest whatever in her internal world. Nevertheless, for some years early in therapy, a passionately strong and in-love transference to Anne was detectable, which it would have been destructive to interpret since it represented a nucleus of a developmental stage where none had been before in spite of an involved relationship which Jane still had to her possessive and disturbed mother. Out of these transference feelings, she would bring inappropriate presents for Anne—flowers and buns and a stuffed animal—"a bizarre and noxious object," in Anne's words.

Jane would appear in sessions (always punctually) in such different personality guises that Anne was bewildered, until she finally worked out that Jane's fluid, fragile ego would present in identification with whomever she had last been with. This could be a professor, a lesbian, a male heterosexual lawyer, a butcher. Jane gave no signs of even being aware of Anne; these various people would slowly disappear, but consistently they ignored Anne. When Jane spoke, it was deeply impersonal. She had a rare dream in which she indirectly signalled her awareness of Anne only through projective paradox. She was "rampaging" through Anne's house, but when Anne appeared, it was only to ignore her, Jane, completely. Anne felt "a deadly exclusion," particularly at times when

Jane acted out by deliberately distorting her medication or forgetting to carry it with her. She was also careless and destructive with her body, which seemed like an alien object to her, and her clothes were weird and ugly.

Jane manifested no moral sense, which I thought was a result of the very early disturbance and deprivation which we had to postulate in her. As far as developmental stages are concerned, she probably never got beyond the age of 2, when a moral sense begins to develop primarily through guilt and concern, of which she seemed incapable. But she was not exactly a psychopath. It seemed rather that she had no sense, moral or otherwise, that actions have consequences. (This was something I had encountered and written about before, in a patient brought up from the age of 3 as a Cinderella orphan in a boarding school (Coltart 1993).) During Jane's treatment, for example, she was tenuously linked to a hospital because of the severity of her physical illness. She agreed to take part in a long experimental study there by providing regular data. But she fed in false information with no sense of responsibility for truth or research, both of which had been fully explained and which she perfectly well understood. Another egregious example was that she had a man arrested for raping her—which, as she later said, he had not done. Much of her life was lived almost by accident or through psychotic identifications. She stopped using any medication when an uncle, wishing to end his life from cancer, stopped palliative medicine. She lived in the garden as a child, for weeks on end, occasionally fed by her sister and unsought by her mother. She also seriously planned to marry her sister.

Anne had no sense of relationship or intersubjectivity in all she was and said to Jane. Interpretations were ignored as irrelevant, yet occasionally Jane would write, or say, something which, though sounding extremely mad, also played back to Anne all that had gone before between them. Yet she did not recognize it as such and thought she might have made it up herself. Anne often said she was "awful to be with." When I asked her to give me an example, she quoted Jane as saying "I'm so sick of you and your tired optimism" in a way that was "indescribably malignant." Anne said Jane could make her feel "morally and in every way simply *beyond the pale.*" This state, after the initial flush of transference love, had gone on for years.

Anne's increased sense of freedom, aliveness and creativeness, together with her feeling less vulnerable to Jane's psychotic attacks and having a firmer foothold in the theory of psychosis, gradually, against great odds, began to affect the patient. From feeling that she did not exist, that there was no one there, even to *consider* "having relationships" with, Jane began to "become visible to the world." There was a slender increase in coherence. She had the idea, from she knew not where, that Anne was *right*, and from being violently scornful of this, she began to believe (have faith) that, since Anne seemed to continue to behave as though she and the psychotherapy could make a positive difference to her, in fact it might. The greatest gain was that Anne felt quite different, and stronger, about this extremely difficult treatment.

My other, completely contrasting experience during the same year was with a 40-year-old woman who had recently completed a 2-year training as a counsellor and was building up a private practice. She wrote me such an engaging, intelligent letter after reading my first book that I broke my intention only to accept experienced therapists and took her on. She had been a nun for the 15 years preceding her counselling course. Her order was a teaching one founded by Jesuits, and therefore rooted in the ideas and personality of St. Ignatius of Loyola. I had recently reviewed for the International Journal of Psychoanalysis a long book on St. Ignatius by the Boston psychoanalyst and Jesuit William Meissner (Meissner 1992). This added to my interest in this woman, whom I will call Mary. She too wrote a piece for me on her experience of supervision, which we discussed. It could not have been more different from my time with Anne, and yet there was this aforementioned distinct element in common; she too was very gifted, subtle and intuitive, and psychologically-minded. I have no doubt whatever that, had she trained with us, or with one of the 3 or 4 excellent psychotherapy organizations in London, I would have supervised her in exactly the way I did under her actual circumstances now. I said to her early on: "You may call yourself a counsellor, but we are turning you into a psychotherapist. I hope you don't mind!" As a matter of fact, towards the end of her year, and in her notes, she confessed that one of the most memorable things that had done the most for her was my *telling her* that I thought she was gifted. She had received an injection of confidence, affirmation, and pleasure from this that had not left her. Yet in many ways it was a radically different experience from the year with Anne.

Mary opened her written account with a memory of when she was a small child frequently visiting her grandmother. Mary would sit beside her on a stool as her grandmother taught her to knit. She came away cheerful and encouraged and feeling that she would be good at it in time. This connects directly with *my* enjoyment of the particular pedagogic role that I had with her: She was engagingly keen, hungry and willing to learn. She said she felt "welcomed" and I recalled that to welcome her and make her feel at home and confirmed in her work was certainly part of my attitude at the beginning. It was years since I had supervised a near-beginner. In fact, I had never had someone who was so psychologically minded and open, and yet at the same time such a recent explorer in a new and entrancing field. I am very sold on the idea that a good and enjoyable life means true enjoyment of one's chosen work, and indeed my second book is all about that (Coltart 1993). "Survival" means survival-with-enjoyment, not grimly hanging on. Our work can be seen as belonging to the moral order, and to do it well means an increase in genuine happiness not only for a healing patient but for ourselves. It is the old familiar idea of "be good and you'll be happy"! This line of thought was, of course, familiar to Mary and welcomed by her.

To begin with, Mary was quite anxious and she showed signs of wanting very much to please me and to appear, as she described herself, "more proficient than I was, less of a beginner than I felt." She said 3 things had got her over, or through, this. One was that I had told her a little anecdote about how my analyst, on the day I qualified, said to my rather cock-a-hoop self: "Now, in ten years you'll be an analyst." I added that it was true, and it took all that time for one's anxiety to subside and it was just the same for therapists and counsellors. The second thing she said was that I had taken her on "with all the gaps in [my] training and even though [I'm] only a counsellor." And the third, which I have already referred to, was that I said I thought she was talented. I do believe that in supervision, in therapy, and indeed in our ordinary lives, we sometimes need to remind ourselves that we can genuinely enhance the life of someone else if we put into words a considered, experienced, and positive opinion of that person rather than just thinking it. The grudging fears, often encountered in psychoanalysts, that we shall have some grim negative influence by this sort of behavior, represent one of the less-attractive aspects of psycho-analysis and are, I think, rooted in a primitive, Calvinistic sort of morality approaching superstition rather than in rational thought or even human experience.

I can probably best illustrate the character of this supervision and the many ways in which it differed enormously from the free-ranging, sophisticated and, on many occasions, hilarious work with Anne by describing briefly one of the patients she brought for our attention and the sort of issues I found myself quite clearly "teaching her" about (an experience I had rarely, if ever, had with Anne). In the nature of things, Mary tended to get a certain number of referrals connected with the Church. One was a parish priest in his fifties. He was required to be in therapy as part of a course he was doing. Mary did not really understand him beyond a superficial recognition and knowledge of a type. This was hardly surprising as, beneath a glossy and defensive veneer, he was a very disturbed man with a severe narcissistic character disorder. She had neither the theoretical knowledge nor the technique to address this, and they both felt that they were making little headway. Mary had often nearly reached the point of saying they must stop when "something would happen," there was a slight sense of breakthrough, and on they went. Mary nevertheless felt frustrated and intimidated.

The priest, whom I will call Mark, had a massive defensive armor. For one thing, he carried a heavy workload, which in itself was intrinsically stressful. For another, he had little sense of need and less insight. The training requirements of his course gave him sufficient external reason to be there. Further to that, he did externalize widely. His self-satisfied and grandiose omnipotence made it almost impossible for him to see, let alone take responsibility for, flaws in his personality. If "imperfections," as he called them, were detected, he would rapidly blame his early life and his parents. This was one of the first things that Mary and I worked on: how to get him to start looking inwards, acknowledging his part in the growth of his flawed self, and that there was only stasis to be found in constant anger towards his early environment, however imperfect it had been. Of course, he was always alert for criticism and had a general paranoid coloring to his personality. His relationships with fellow-priests and parishioners were either rivalrous or patronizing, and only with his bishop, to whom he felt special, did he acknowledge affection and admiration. All this is apart from his secret relationship with a woman in the parish, for which he had a complex system of justification.

Mark was the youngest of a large family and he grew up in an atmosphere of confusion, violence, and sexual innuendo, seeing sex as the source of unhappiness in his parents. He had an ideal vision of himself "rising above it all," especially as a celibate priest, and frequently he managed to convince himself, in his grandiosity, that he achieved this ideal in spite of some glaring evidence to the contrary.

I used the opportunity presented by this unappealing man to develop, first, the more recent work on narcissism and its disorders, and second, to put it in the context of development theory and the sorts of neurotic/psychotic disturbances which are consequent upon difficulty or trauma in the stages of childhood. I suggested some reading to Mary, mostly the appropriate Freud papers, one or two classics (e.g., by Abraham) and, since I had been influenced in recent years by the work of Kohut, a clear text on self-psychology (Lee and Cooper 1991). I found this sort of teaching, with such a responsive receiver, a most agreeable challenge, and it caused me to think I would look out for another committed and keen novice to supervise.

From Mary's notes, I extract the points which were of most use to her in the ongoing work on Mark. She felt that she finally had a real grasp on his psychopathology, one that gave her many openings for the development of further ideas and the (very difficult) subject of technique with a narcissistic patient. In addition to narcissism, we had discussed at length the characteristics and consequences of "false self" development, which she could also now summon to the aid of her thinking. She had ceased to feel stuck and intimidated and found that our work on development and disturbance was applicable to all sorts of patients, with whom the treatments began to move more easily. Rather than following the material and hoping to encounter something she could comment on, she felt capable of sustained thought and of making more focused interventions. We had done a lot of work through Mark and other patients on transference and countertransference, especially the latter, and she felt far more confident with them. For example, she felt with Mark she could now translate her feelings, which were often of anger and frustration, into interpretations rather than just sitting there stifled and seething. She got hold of the idea of the importance of having a rough treatment plan, rooted in theory. But, more importantly, she understood the apparent paradox of the value of a thought-out frame for the work hand-in-hand with trying to observe Bion's teaching on aiming to be free from memory and desire in every session. I had stayed with this with her at some length, knowing the growing value it had had for me over the years as I came to understand it better. Again, in reference to Mark, she felt there was great value in being able to listen to him more skillfully, at several levels, and therefore to formulate interpretation according to what she understood him to need rather than being pushed about into what he wanted.

One of the subjects that Mary and I discussed at considerable length, and which I feel often does not get sufficient attention, was the place of one's own moral self in the whole practice of analytic psychotherapy. She had believed, as I am sure is common to many beginners, that analytical therapists "do not make moral judgments." She had been alarmed and anxious when she noticed that she made them frequently, not in what she said but in what she thought and how she reacted to patients. She thought that this was a rare problem and was probably a hang-over from her years in religion, her degree in theology, her whole training. She was greatly relieved when we talked this out and I said she was not expected to give up, or not use, a huge part of her intrinsic self. I added that if any analyst or therapist ever said that we do not make any moral judgments, they were suffering from a grave delusion—the whole matter was more complicated than that, and involved self-knowledge, the practice of detach-ment, the unsentimental development of compassion and empathy, and the skill to translate one's countertransfer-ence into sayable language that was tough but maybe would be acceptable to the patient. Armed with this new awareness, Mary was able to stop unwillingly colluding with Mark's lack of guilt and his complacency and gran-diosity and to confront him with the wide gaps between his self-views, his opinions on his virtues, and the critical disdain he felt for people who actually were very much like him. The treatment took a dramatic leap forward— "almost as if he had been waiting for me to help him with just this"—which I thought at one level he had.

Finally, although of course it would have been entirely inappropriate to laugh in the way Anne and I had done, I certainly did not make huge efforts to suppress my sense of humor, which has noticeably played a greater part in all my work as I have got older and freer. Along with demonstrating from time to time that humor need not be dangerous, I had also put a considerable amount of effort into enabling Mary to be tougher in her approach. It is a very common weakness in the technique of younger—or new—therapists to be far too nervous of doing wrong or upsetting the patient if they harness their aggression and use it creatively in their work. The result is often that they make no impact, convey a feeling of lack of confidence, and tend towards the sentimental as a kind of reaction formation to their anxiety about being tough and clear. I was delighted when I read in her notes: "It could all be too rich an experience, too heady a wine, but humor and a kind of robust irreverence give it a very human feel. That's been important for me. I have a tendency to feel I have to be like God, over-responsible for my clients' well-being, able to make all things well, more aware of fragility and the danger of doing harm than of the resources of the person and their other supports . . . I am not the saviour of the world!"

I hope I have managed to convey the many pleasurable rewards of a decision late in life to cease to be an authority, abandon the demanding field of training, and hand-pick a few really interesting post-graduate psychotherapists whose gifts and personalities appeal to me and then set out with them on a new journey of discovery.

REFERENCES

Coltart, N. (1987). Diagnosis and assessment of suitability for psychoanalytical psychotherapy. *British Journal of Psychotherapy* 4(2): 127–134.

———(1988). The assessment of psychological-mindedness in

the diagnostic interview. *British Journal of Psychiatry*, 153: 819–820.

————(1992). *Slouching towards Bethlehem*. London: Free Association Books.

————(1993). *How to Survive as a Psychotherapist*. London: Sheldon Press.

Lee, R. R. and Martin, J. C. (1991). *Psychotherapy after Kohut*. Hillsdale, NJ: Analytic Press.

Meissner, W. (1992). *A Psychological Study of St. Ignatius of Loyola*. New Haven: Yale University Press.

Winnicott, D. W. (1971). *Playing and Reality*. London: Tavistock. (1982: Reprinted by Penguin Books.)

————(1982). *The Maturational Processes and the Facilitating Environment*. London: Hogarth.

VI

Approaches
to the
Supervisory
Process

6

Psychoanalytic Supervision as the Crossroads of a Relational Matrix

EMANUEL BERMAN*

* The ideas outlined here will be discussed more fully in the author's forthcoming book, *Clinical supervision: a relational psychoanalytic approach*, to be published by Guilford Press.

Clinical supervision is a task in which a psychoanalytic orientation can be expressed not only in content, but in the nature of the process as well. Psychoanalytic scrutiny can be effectively directed towards our own work as supervisors and allow us a critical self-analysis. When this is achieved, we could become—within supervision—less preoccupied with formulating what we *should do* and more receptive to an exploration of what we *actually do and undergo*—which may not be always dictated by our theoretical rationales and goals as we once believed. If we go that way, the programmatic and ideological dimension in our thinking could be modified and enriched by the good qualities of a social anthropological study.

The dynamic understanding of the patient is an important component in any supervision, but if it is not supplemented by a dynamic understanding of the other partners in the situation (the therapist, the supervisor, often the institution), and of their complex interrelationships, this implies that psychoanalysis is *underutilized*. Discussions of supervision which focus upon the didactic study of the patient–therapist dyad treat the supervisory process as if it were "transparent," just as authors who are naive about transferential and countertransferential currents might discuss therapy as a "transparent" process teaching us about the patient's childhood and inner world. The result may be texts about supervision which are actually about therapy and not about supervision *per se*.

Once we pass this barrier, we come to realize that supervision is the crossroads of a matrix of object relations of at least three persons, in which each person brings her or his psychic reality into the bargain. It is a crossroads of actual interpersonal encounters (involving also social issues such as authority, power, gender roles, economic stratification) and of less visible intersubjective relations.

In spite of the risks involved in introducing clinically derived terms, which Ekstein and Wallerstein (1972) advised us to avoid, it may be helpful to also speak of the interaction of several simultaneous transference/countertransference trends in each therapeutic-supervisory combination. In view of my belief that transference and countertransference are basically identical (as I will elaborate later on), I do not welcome the idea of adding yet another term, supertransference (Teitelbaum 1990), in describing the supervisor's experiences. While Teitelbaum emphasizes the negative impact of this phenomenon (loyal to the tradition of viewing countertransference as a hindrance), his suggested term paradoxically may acquire the connotation of viewing the supervisor as "superhuman," and above ordinary transference.

In considering supervision as the crossroads of several relational paths, I am painting a complicated picture. I am aware of the hopelessness of fully deciphering all its levels within the limited time span of one supervisory process. I am arguing, however, that all these levels should be at least acknowledged and allowed as legitimate contents in the supervisory discourse. If this is not achieved, some components (most typically both the supervisor's subjective contribution and institutional dynamics) may be defensively denied or rationalized away, and consequently supervision may become stilted or even oppressive (see Shevrin, in Wallerstein 1981).

In the next pages, I will go over the major relational components of the therapeutic-supervisory matrix.

THE PATIENT—THERAPIST RELATIONSHIP AS A TOPIC IN SUPERVISION

While a broad discussion of the therapeutic relationship cannot, naturally, be attempted here, I will briefly outline the way I view it, as well as its implications for supervision. This view is an outgrowth of a long tradition, including authors such as Ferenczi, Balint, Winnicott, Racker, Gill, Ogden, Bollas, Casement, Mitchell and others, although the specific formulations are, of course, my own. The issues I address are common to psychoanalysis and psychoanalytic psychotherapy, and I will therefore refer to both settings interchangeably.

Psychoanalysis is both a "one-person psychology" (studying intrapsychic processes) and a "two person psychology" (studying interactions); the concept of intersubjectivity attempts to integrate both aspects. The psychic realities of both analyst and analysand are involved in their encounter. Transference is both a reaction to the patient's life history and a reaction to the personality and actions of the therapist, who can never fully become a "blank screen" or an "empty container" (Aron 1991, p. 46). Transference, in its broader definition, unavoidably combines displaced and projected elements with realistic perceptions, and the therapist is never sufficiently "objective" to separate these out definitively. We can raise questions and offer ideas about the sources of different elements, but to attempt a definitive judgment as to what is true and what is distorted in the way we are viewed implies absolute knowledge of ourselves—that is, denying that there are unconscious aspects in our personalities.

Likewise, countertransference unavoidably combines issues stemming out of the basic psychic reality of the therapist and aspects that are responsive to the specific patient. Some authors have attempted to separate these out into different categories (Springmann 1986), but I suspect this attempt is futile. In my own experience, in self-analysis and in the supervision and analysis of therapists, every reaction that first appears as pure projective counteridentification (Grinberg 1979) or mere role responsiveness (Sandler 1976) turns out upon further scrutiny to have aspects that are related to the therapist's unique personality (in other words, there are reasons why a projective identification can "catch on"). And conversely, the therapist may be certain he or she reacts out of a purely personal vulnerability, but fuller exploration reveals that a particular patient powerfully activates that vulnerability while others do not.

Transference and countertransference constantly activate and mold each other, and are actually parts of one total cyclic process which has no starting point (Berman, 1986). Studying each separately makes as much sense as studying a game of chess by analyzing the moves of the white figures alone. In this respect the "counter" in the word countertransference may be misleading, as *transference is also counter-countertransference* (Racker 1968).

All of this has an enormous impact on what is expected from supervision. It becomes clear that didactic supervision, emphasizing the dynamics of the patient alone or demonstrating "correct" technique, is of limited value. If we assume that important elements in the transference are reactive to the therapist's actual personality and behavior, it follows that we cannot understand the patient if relevant aspects of the therapist's personality are not explored in supervision. I do not believe that the supervisor has the capacity to pass a final verdict as to the accuracy of the patient's attributions, but the supervisor can become an invaluable (and slightly less vulnerable) partner in thinking about their possible validity. It is potentially very helpful—though not easy—when a supervisor

says, "You know, I also heard that interpretation as aggressive."

If we assume that countertransference is both a clue to
understanding the psychic reality of the patient and an influence on its further development in therapy, it follows that
countertransference cannot be disregarded in supervision,
including its more personal sources which cannot be separated
out in advance. We need to know that the patient reminds the
therapist of her or his brother if we are to help in the process
of attempting to sort out what belongs to the actual patient and
what to that brother, and to uncover the ways in which this
association colors the therapist's actions and verbalizations
and therefore unknowingly influences the patient as well.

> Another example: A supervisee raises his difficulty with
> the patient's idealization of him. When listening to the
> material, the supervisor fails to hear the idealization,
> experiencing the patient as expressing realistic gratitude
> to this really competent and empathic therapist. Raising
> the issue leads to the therapist's low self-esteem, which
> made him blind to the progress these remarks signify for
> the patient, who is harshly critical of his parents and
> almost everybody else, in addition to being quite lonely.

In the framework I suggest, the idea of a standard technique
becomes obsolete. Haynal (1993) speaks of "the illusion that
there can be a technique that one needs only to learn and apply
'correctly'" (p.62). The actual challenge is to follow carefully
the therapeutic interaction, paying close attention to minute
details, and to pause and consider the intersubjective implications of each verbal or non-verbal exchange. In this context
interpretations, silences, or slips of tongue of the therapist are
examined in terms of their affective antecedants and consequences rather than on the basis of their conscious intention,

and they occupy the same ground as associations, requests, or jokes of the patient.

The analytic impact of interventions can be evaluated only in retrospect. What was formulated as an empathic interpretation may be experienced as an insult, what first appears as the therapist's blunder may eventually lead to an important insight, and so forth. Beyond some basic ideas about the setting and its boundaries, which are important to make this scrutiny possible (a loose and inconsistent setting makes the water too muddy), what needs to be learned is not any list of steadfast rules but an introspective and empathic sensitivity to the actual sources and actual impact of our actions and inactions. This is a most personal learning process, which requires considerable exposure. *One cannot learn to swim in a tuxedo.*

One more point: Within the framework I describe, there is room for selective countertransference disclosures (Bollas 1987, Tansey and Burke 1989, ch. 9). In my experience, such interventions—if they are judicious, well-timed, and not too frequent—can have a valuable therapeutic impact. Many younger therapists, however, are afraid to make such interventions, and their avoidance may be costly at times, especially when these younger therapists attempt to sidetrack an involuntary expression of countertransference already noticed by the patient—consequently, the therapists are perceived as defensive and anxious. The encouragement of a supervisor to be truthful, after thoughtful joint consideration of all risks and benefits, may be an important step towards breaking a stalemate in treatment. Naturally, countertransference disclosure cannot be considered if countertransference in general is not patiently explored first.

> A supervisee reports that his patient constantly blames him for identifying with his wife rather than with him, and attempts to reassure the patient are ineffective.

Fuller discussion in supervision makes it clear the patient is correct. The therapist experiences the patient as a bully and his wife as a victim. This reaction turns out to have some sources in the therapist's life, but to also be molded by the patient, who consciously disparages his wife but unconsciously invites empathy toward her much more than toward himself. It becomes clear that the therapist's apologetic denials make the patient confused and suspicious, while a judicious acknowledgment of the patient's perceptions could become a springboard to the understanding of his marriage not as the external battlefield he portrays but as a stage of an inner drama in which many of his own dissociated experiences as a battered child are projectively expressed through his wife.

THE SUPERVISOR–SUPERVISEE RELATIONSHIP

The supervisor–supervisee relationship arouses in itself a rich and always complex transference/countertransference combination, even if supervision appears to be utterly impersonal. After all, teachers are a major focus of transference feelings throughout our lives. Naturally, the more personal focus I advocate may add to this complexity; it may undermine some of the more defensive modes of avoiding anxiety in the situation and increase the fear of intrusion and humiliation. On the other hand, it may allow greater awareness and better resolution of supervisory conflicts and crises by encouraging the joint exploration of the supervisory relationship itself (Berman 1988).

While the wish of the supervisee to learn and develop and the wish of the supervisor to teach and be helpful are in most cases quite sincere, there are many factors which make their relationship potentially conflictual. Epstein (1986) thoroughly discusses its negative impact upon supervisees. The learning of new skills requires acknowledgment of their lack, which is a source of shame. The need for evaluation turns the supervisor into a threatening judge, a potential source of embarrassing exposure and rejection. Preoccupation with the need to remember the session, as well as with the supervisor's past or potential criticism of one's interventions, may easily immobilize a younger therapist, or at least inhibit one's spontaneity. Moreover, the therapeutic encounter is a very intimate dyadic situation, and a third partner in it may be a burdensome intrusion, a chaperon on a honeymoon. Therapists often experience rescue fantasies toward their patients (Berman 1993), projecting their own vulnerability onto them, while a supervisor reintroduces their vulnerability and neediness into the picture, and may be seen as a potentially superior rescuer. "I am sure you would have done it much better" is a common beginners' fantasy; it may be often untrue (with difficult cases a beginner's investment and optimism may be at times more helpful than a seasoned professional's sober apprehension), but would the supervisor help in dismantling it? When idealization is collusively maintained, oedipal and narcissistic dynamics may combine in producing in the younger therapist a painful sense of inferiority. An image of supervisor and supervisee as fundamentally differing in their therapeutic capacity may become part of "a myth of the supervisory situation" (Berman 1988), equivalent to "the myth of the analytic situation" as involving an interaction between a sick person and a healthy one (Racker 1968, p. 132).

From the supervisor's end, an inherent conflict of identifications with the supervisee and with the patient is a source of many difficulties. An equivalent issue appears in analysis itself. The analyst may be conflicted between "concordant identifications" with the analysand and "complementary identifications" with the analysand's inner objects as personalized through other individuals in the analysand's life (Racker 1968, p. 134). However, once we realize that these other individuals (e.g., spouse, children, etc.) also represent unacknowledged aspects of the analysand, an integration of the conflicting identifications becomes conceivable, and both kinds of identifications become the basis of potential empathy toward the analysand. This point is made by Tansey and Burke (1989) and is an important advance over Racker's original view that only concordant identifications can be sublimated into empathy.

Such understanding may be relevant at times in supervision as well (e.g., a resistant patient may represent a side of the therapist, just as a rebellious adolescent may represent a side of the parent), but not as consistently. After all, the therapist has not raised the patient and often has not chosen him or her (as we choose friends, lovers, or spouses on the basis of unconscious needs).

In other words, this conflict of identifications is harder to resolve. The supervisor is "a servant of two masters," often experiencing an ethical commitment towards the patient discussed, especially if that patient is treated within an agency to which the supervisor belongs. The dilemma surfaces when the supervisor is unhappy with the supervisee's work and becomes torn between loyalty to the latter's needs (to develop gradually at the individual pace required, without disruptions due to feeling too criticized and threatened) and a sense of responsibility for the patient's well-being. The supervisor may feel quite helpless in dangerous situations (e.g., risk of suicide or psychosis) and is tempted to assume a more directive position: putting words in the supervisee's mouth, and turning into a Cyrano de Bergerac). This leads to the risk of an authoritarian disruption of the younger therapist's growth.

A powerful example of a supervisor's negative counter-transference towards a supervisee is supplied by Teitelbaum (1990), involving: "(a) Dreading sessions—a wish to cancel them—a wish to get rid of the therapist . . . (b) Persistent feelings of irritation, annoyance, impatience, and disdain. (c) A desire to protect his patients from him, and empathy for the patients who were not being understood . . . (d) I felt deprived of seeing that my work with a therapist was having an impact . . . I did not want this therapist to be my product . . . (e) I often felt alone, angry, helpless and shut out . . . (f) . . . sadistic feelings . . . (g) Feelings of frustration because the therapist . . . appeared to simply screen out my reactions" (p. 252).

Narcissistic needs of supervisors; possible competitiveness with younger colleagues and fear of being displaced by them; an urge to impress by one's brilliance and to become indispensible; anxiety about the way supervisees describe them to their peers or to other faculty members—all may add burdensome components to the relationship. To follow once more in Racker's footsteps, just as in analysis the direct countertransference to the patient may be supplemented by indirect countertransferences involving the reactions of third parties ("What will my supervisor think"), in supervision the direct countertransference to the supervisee may be supplemented by indirect countertransferences as well ("What will her analyst think"). Disregarding this aspect is part of the denial of the reality of the institutional context to which I will return, just as Etchegoyen (1991) tends to deny it by interpreting indirect countertransferences in analysis as displacements of the direct countertransference to the patient (Berman 1994a).

While most existing literature focuses on the contribution of supervisees to difficulties in the process, I am convinced that the role of supervisors is not any lesser. The literature is written mostly by faculty members, but the other side of the coin is often thoroughly explored in informal discussions among trainees, which are never recorded. Similarly, papers by therapists about their patients massively outnumber papers by patients about their therapists, though the latter may be equally useful for our understanding of achievements and failures in treatment.

As in any relationship, many other aspects are determined not by its stated structure but by the personal idiosyncrasies of both partners. The possible variations are naturally innumerable and can be studied only through individual examples. The resulting difficulties can be conceptualized in terms of resistances and counterresistances (though with time I am less prone to use this potentially judgmental vocabulary), and at times even of negative supervisory reactions—creating crisis and regression after an apparent progress in supervision which may have been accompanied by unnoticed affective burdens for the supervisee (see Berman, 1988, where numerous examples are offered).

I believe that such issues should be a legitimate topic within the supervisory discourse. Their avoidance may pose a bad role model and undermine the supervisor's message as to the need to pay constant attention to the affective nuances of the therapeutic relationship, and to verbalize these nuances without being deterred by inhibitions and conventional norms. Empathy towards the patient which is unaccompanied by empathy towards the supervisee is a confusing mixed message (see Sloane 1986). Acknowledgment of the supervisor's possible role in difficulties is not only crucial in creating an unthreatening atmosphere but also crucial for a truthful understanding of the actual dyadic process.

The exploration of supervisory process issues has been initially introduced and legitimized through the idea of parallel process (Arlow 1963, Searles 1965, Doehrman 1976). This was a valuable historical move, but we should recognize the risks involved in this conceptual framework (compare Lesser in Caligor et al. 1984). Talking about parallel processes may offer an outlet for the expression of difficulties in supervision. However it may limit it (through a dogmatic expectation to find exact parallels), or may inhibit it (through the too easy attribution of supervisory conflicts to the patient) while avoiding more direct sources within the supervisory dyad itself. Parallel processes should be understood as one potential aspect of the complex network of cross-identifications within the supervisor-therapist-patient triad (Gediman and Wolkenfeld 1980, Wolkenfeld, in Lane, 1990). Some supervisory stalemates may develop irrespective of who is the patient supervised, and they require full attention despite being "unparallelled".

The valuable contribution of a joint exploration of the supervisory relationship is demonstrated by Sarnat (1992), whose views are close to mine. Here is her summary of her main example.

> A supervisee's character problems became a focus of supervisory attention. The supervisor's conflicts (i.e., her impatience to see her supervisee change, and her need to assert her own competence by too-active intervention) played into the student's problem (i.e., submissiveness), contributing to the development of a supervisory crisis . . . The supervisor's acknowledgment of her contribution to the crisis seemed to shift the interpersonal context to one in which the supervisee could safely and vividly experience and process her own conflict . . . Had the supervisor tried to "help" her with this problem, while pretending to be the uninvolved expert, the supervisee would very likely have felt humiliated and endangered (p. 399).

THE PATIENT—SUPERVISOR RELATIONSHIP

This is an aspect of the matrix which is often overlooked, though it may be quite important. Unlike the two relationships discussed before, this is one which usually involves no direct contact. Nevertheless, it may develop in fantasy and ultimately gain a powerful real impact, both of the two related parties on each other (even though in a mediated manner), as well as on the "mediator," the therapist.

Many analysands and patients are aware that their treatment may be supervised, especially those who are themselves mental-health professionals or are personally related to such professionals or acquainted with them. In some cases (e.g., being analyzed by a candidate in an analytic institute) this is a given. Some patients may find out who the supervisor is, or develop their wishful or anxious hypotheses about the supervisor's identity. Many more develop a mental image of the supervisor and a transference reaction to this imagined person. This reaction may be directly expressed or indirectly implied, and both therapist and supervisor play a role in the degree to which this experience is explored or kept as a secret.

I will mention briefly a few of the divergent themes which I have encountered. "You are too young and inexperienced to understand me, but your supervisor will help you out." "I feel that our relationship is very close, but it's hard for me to be open because you talk about me to a stranger." "You and your supervisor must have a field day, laughing about my stupidity." "Bring this dream to supervision, I feel we are stuck with it". "Were you in supervision today? This interpretation did not sound as your own." "You probably raise my fee because you were told in supervision you allow yourself to be exploited." "As a man you cannot understand menstruation, but hopefully you have a female supervisor."

Mayer (1972) relates the tendency to idealize the supervisor while denigrating the therapist to life histories involving traumatic disruptions of the tie to the parents and the presence of alternative caretakers within the family. Windholz (1970) describes a case in which a patient attempted to exclude her analyst (experienced as a competitive brother) from her relationship with the "maternal" supervisor. Another intriguing example is offered by Luber (1991):

An analyst spent 5 years of analysis under the auspices of an institute. When his patient correctly sensed he was close to graduation, she developed intense anxiety about the possible switch to a private-patient status. Analytic exploration revealed that she was fearful about losing the background presence of her analyst's supervisor (never alluded to before), and remaining alone with her analyst. Transferentially, the analyst came to represent her brother, with whom she experienced incestuous feelings, and the supervisor represented a protective father.

Luber suggests that these split transferences may belong to two main categories: attempts to split off one side of an ambivalent transference from the therapist to the supervisor, and cases in which the transference is primarily triadic, based on the patient's past involvement with two related figures. In my view, these categories are not mutually exclusive, as the initial split in the patient's history may have also been related to splitting off (see Fairbairn's (1954) analysis of the Oedipus complex as an externalization of an initial ambivalence regarding the mother).

Naturally, the patient's transference to the supervisor may influence both the therapist's countertransference (e.g., feeling put down or else seduced into an exclusive alliance), and the supervisor's countertransference to the therapist (e.g., seeing the therapist as weak because the patient yearns for reinforcement) or to the patient (feeling a guardian angel, or, at the other extreme, an unwelcome intruder). Consequently, it may influence the supervisory relationship.

In addition, the supervisor may develop an autonomous, unique countertransference to any patient being discussed: affection, curiosity, annoyance, etc. This in turn becomes interconnected with the supervisory relationship, and various (counter)transferential triadic patterns evolve (compare Winokur 1982). Let me give three examples, each of which creates a different supervisory climate.

1. Supervisor and therapist form a close alliance as the concerned and mutually supportive parents of a problematic child.
2. Therapist and patient form a close and secretive involvement; therapist withholds a lot in supervision (e.g., self disclosures, affective expressions, and other interventions that the supervisor may disapprove of), summarizing sessions in a brief guarded form, and as a result the excluded supervisor becomes bored and uninvested in both supervisee and patient.
3. Supervisor is deeply interested in the appealing patient, is critical of the therapist's unempathic work, and develops a fantasy of rescuing the patient from the therapist; the result may be a harsh, critical attitude leading to a crisis in supervision, at times "reporting" the supervisee to the relevant authority as unfit.

The most famous (but unacknowledged) example of the latter constellation is the case reported by Greenson (1967, pp. 220–221), where his supervisee failed to express interest in the health of his analysand's sick child. Greenson used this situation very persuasively to show the dangers of an analytic technique devoid of human sensitivity. It can be argued, however, that his identification with the patient made him insensitive to the supervisee's apparent emotional inhibition, and that scolding him and sending him for more analysis may not have been the most effective way of encouraging his growth into a more empathic analyst. A similar view is expressed by Teitelbaum (1990).

RELATING TO THE INSTITUTIONAL SETTING

Except for supervisions arranged privately, most supervisory dyads operate in a broader institutional context of a clinical training program or of a treatment agency. The institution typically has its own agenda: ideological commitment to a particular therapeutic or analytic approach, economic considerations (which may dictate preference to longer or to shorter treatments), encouraging hospitalization (if budgets depend on "filling beds") or avoiding it, safeguarding the institution's reputation, and so forth. In addition to such specific goals, most institutions are invested in maintaining control over staff and trainees, and this is served by having considerable information about them. These are all goals which are not relevant to the quality of learning in supervision, and yet may be the source of considerable pressure on both supervisor and supervisee, at times rationalized in order to appear motivated by more intrinsic values.

The influence of the institutional context can also be conceptualized as an additional set of transferences. If the patient is seen within an institutional setting, the patient is likely to develop a unique transferential attitude to the setting (clinic, hospital, etc.) which is often distinct from the transference to the therapist: "You understand me but they don't"; "I am mad at you for leaving but I trust them to assign me another therapist, hopefully more experienced." Reider (1953) describes traumatized patients who are unable to sustain an intimate relationship with one person and find it easier to fantasize being cared for by a motherly institution, the hospital. Meyerson and Epstein (1976) talk of analysands who split off their unreliable candidate-analysts from the psychoanalytic institute experienced as reliable and nurturant. I would argue that these are extreme versions of a widespread phenomenon, which may often remain unrecognized in its subtler versions, possibly because it threatens the therapists' self-image.

The therapist, as an employee or trainee, naturally has transferential feelings to the setting (whether it is experienced as a prestigious place one is proud to belong to, as a disappointing substitute, as generous or exploitative, etc.). So, too, does the supervisor as an employee or faculty member (gratified or frustrated, secure or struggling for recognition, etc.). In addition to transference to the setting as a whole, each of them may have transference/countertransference patterns with specific authority figures within it (e.g., being the director's favorite or rival).

My point is that all these transferential currents (I am using the term in its broader sense, which does not exclude realistic perceptions) may influence the supervisory process. The different agendas and feelings may coincide or clash. Let me give a few examples:

1. Patient, therapist, and supervisor create an alliance, wishing to prove to the director of a clinic that continuation of treatment for another year is crucial, contrary to clinic rules or economic interests.

2. The analysand and candidate-analyst both feel that at the present stage of the analysis it will be better to conduct it face to face, seeing the institute's insistence on using the couch as dogmatic and coercive; the supervisor, identified more with institute ideology, sees this as acting out or, in a different version, fears for her or his status if the change is legitimized.

3. The supervisor is secretly, maybe unconsciously, gratified that treatment is failing, because assignment of the case (or admission of the trainee into the program) was decided by another faculty member whom the supervisor despises and will be delighted to expose as incompetent.

A major influence of the institution is in the area of evaluation, which in turn has a powerful impact on learning. I see a basic difference between the inherent critical-evaluative element in any honest supervisory intervention (enthusiasm or concern about what happens in the treatment discussed, attention to blind spots, ideas about possible improvements), and the evaluative reporting to education committees and other authorities. The former, in my experience, may be painful but in the long run productive in promoting growth. Within the live relationship in the dyad—just as in the therapeutic dyad—narcissistic vulnerability to criticism can be contained and worked through. In most cases, the supervisor's caring puts possible insults in perspective, and these can be discussed and resolved, especially if the atmosphere is free enough to allow it and when the supervisor avoids assuming an omniscient position and is willing to admit blind spots or blunders when relevant. Basic trust in the trainee's capacity for future growth creates a *background of safety*, which makes it possible for the supervisor to honestly express criticism and point to shortcomings in the supervisee's present work.

The exploration of personal aspects of countertransference, some of which may be experienced as guilt-producing or humiliating, is naturally also easier in a more egalitarian and friendlier atmosphere. The facilitation of maximum openness and of effective learning is enhanced if supervisees and supervisors have a chance to choose each other, or at least (if assignment is necessary due to logistics) to veto those partners that they wish to avoid.

In contrast to my view of the value of straightforward face-to-face criticism, I find that reports to higher authorities and to anonymous committees, while generating anxiety and paranoia, rarely serve any productive purpose. Committees may spend long hours in discussing the personality of trainees. This discussion could border on a clinical case conference or degenerate into gossip. But committees can do very little to help the development of a troubled younger colleague. Extensive forms or reports are likely to accumulate in some drawer and to serve no purpose save the director's sense of mastery (and at times the gratification of a secretary's curiosity).

Another problem with training committees (especially in

psychoanalytic institutes, Berman 1994b) is that they are prone to adopt perfectionistic standards, at times influenced by a utopian vision of molding "a purified new person" in the tradition of many religious, political, and national movements. These utopian ambitions often lead to the humiliation and suppression of actual individuals who fall short of the yearned-for ideal and are seen as marred by materialism, bourgeois individualism, hubris, or (in our case) narcissism. This may be the root of the persecutory atmosphere which exists in some psychoanalytic training settings, as noted by Balint (1948) and others, and of their tendency to devote more time to compulsive evaluation of candidates than to efforts to improve their own teaching.

Moreover, the existence of an elaborate evaluation system may allow the supervisor to "pass the buck" and avoid the stressful moment of expressing criticism within supervision. The trainee lives in a "fool's paradise" until reaching the overwhelming moment of hearing from the (little-known and awe-inspiring) director of training about misgivings some unidentified faculty members have about his or her work. This is a formula for a defensive anxious confrontation, which is not likely at all to teach the trainee anything, while the chance for effective learning within the supervisory dyad has already been missed and the supervisor may now be suspected and feared as an informer.

On this background, I would guess that effective learning is most enhanced by a supervisor who is openly critical (though also self-critical), but conveys to the trainee that little reporting to external authorities will take place. If reporting is necessary, its content is ideally fully discussed within supervision (compare Caruth, in Lane 1990, and Sarnat 1992). Learning is least enhanced by an inhibited but submissive supervisor who reports about the trainee much more than is ever discussed in supervisory sessions.

Of course, there may be extreme cases, such as ethical

misconduct or dangerous incompetence, which raise the question whether a younger colleague's training or work should be discontinued. Then, deliberations by a committee may be necessary. These cases are luckily rare, and in such cases a special initiative may have to be taken to keep from penalizing all other trainees by continuous stressful discussions or endless evaluation forms. Even if the institution needs a formal evaluation of trainees towards the conclusion of training, in my experience such procedures can be easily minimized if learning itself—rather than control—is the purpose.

SUPERVISION AND PERSONAL ANALYSIS

My focus on exploring personal experiences in supervision (countertransference to patient, kernels of truth encountered in patient's view of therapist's personality, transference to supervisor and to institution) naturally raises the old issue of the boundaries between analysis (or therapy) and supervision. In a way, my approach could bring me closer to the view of the Budapest school (Balint 1948) that the ideal supervisor is the trainee's analyst. Nevertheless I reject this suggestion because of the risk that such a combination (either simultaneously, or even if supervision is planned to start after analysis) may undermine the quality of the analysis, discourage the expression of negative transference, sabotage real work on termination, and introduce an unanalyzable collusion (Berman 1992). I prefer the treatment of therapists and future analysts to be a very private affair, not directly mobilized for any training goals and unregulated and uninterfered with by training settings. The "reported training analysis," still practiced in London and elsewhere is in my mind a sad anachronism, defying all powerful arguments condemning it (Kairys 1964, and many others).

My image of good analytic and clinical training includes

therefore the division of labor, and, at times, the troublesome split between a personal analyst (maybe more than one along the way) and several supervisors. It also involves a certain *overlap* between the contents of analysis and supervision. Telling trainees, "bring it up in your analysis" is of no use, both because this is intrusive and unrealistic (a genuine analytic process cannot follow assignments) and because it deprives supervision of the understanding of crucial issues, without which we cannot figure out what goes on in treatment. Still, a personal analysis or analytic therapy is to me a basic assumption of any dynamic clinical training. I would find it enormously difficult, and ethically troublesome as well, to supervise therapists who have never been in treatment themselves, although as I said I would not want to interfere in the choice of analyst or in the content of the work done.

When I am totally unaware of my supervisee's personal life and major personal dilemmas, I may be grappling in the dark in my attempt to understand many issues in this supervisee's work with patients. I reject, however, the idea of communicating with the supervisee's analyst (mentioned by DeBell 1963), which would be a violation of confidentiality on both sides. Such paternalistic interventions (which happen at times, usually informally) are infantilizing and potentially humiliating. If a trainee accepts them knowingly, this is a worrisome sign of masochistic submission. Moreover, in my experience such discussions, while initially appearing to be useful, turn out eventually to be detrimental to both analysis and supervision (Berman 1995, Langs 1979). The only way out of this dilemma is to create in supervision a tolerant and interested atmosphere, which will make it easier for the trainee to share personal information and feelings whenever they appear potentially relevant to the task at hand.

In principle, no personal topic is out of place in supervision. A supervisee's impending divorce may be a major influence on countertransference to all patients, a childhood event may be the source of identification with a particular patient, a dream may be the key to the stalemate in a certain case, and so forth.

> Another example. A young trainee is assigned an older woman patient, and he immediately expresses concern that she may resemble his mother. After the first session the trainee reports with relief that he saw no similarity. A month later, however, he describes annoyance with the patient, hope that she will miss her sessions, and has difficulty in remembering their interactions. Upon exploration it turns out that these are his typical reactions vis-à-vis his clinging, dependent mother. Further discussions of both mother and patient enable him eventually to differentiate the 2 better in his mind, and to become more empathic to the patient.

Naturally, the extent, direction, and style of exploration are very different in treatment and in supervision. The analyst attempts to reach the deepest and broadest understanding, proceeding open-mindedly with no immediate goals; the supervisor is much more selective and goal oriented, focusing on these aspects of the personal theme which can be directly related to consequences and actual dilemmas in the trainee's work with patients.

Likewise, the supervisor wishes to identify the supervisee's transference towards her or him, but without searching for its deeper historical roots, at times simply relying on the trainee's word about such roots, as a summary of analytic work already done. The relevant focus is rather on possible reality elements, such as aspects related to the supervisor's personality (this helps in putting things in place and is also a valuable role model), as well as on the effective resolution of troublesome influences of this transference. While in analysis negative transference—or erotic transference—must often be allowed to develop fully, and premature attempts to dissolve it are usually counterproductive, the supervisor is more likely to strive towards a faster establishment (or reestablishment) of a calmer friendly atmosphere, which is more conducive for fulfilling the shared goals of this team.

CONCLUSION

My central points could be summarized in the following way. If we accept that psychoanalysis and psychotherapy, in addition to exploring the patient's intrapsychic reality ("one-person psychology") are also unavoidably interactive and intersubjective processes ("two-person psychology"), it follows that dealing in supervision with more personal experiences of the supervisee (countertransference both as a reaction to transference and as a factor in molding it) is crucial, and without it central aspects of the treatment process will remain in the dark. This necessity, however, increases the risk (which exists in any supervision to begin with) that supervisory work will become intrusive and threatening for the supervisee. To counteract this risk, open joint exploration of the interactive and intersubjective nature of supervision itself—including the supervisor's contribution—is necessary. This also implies understanding and discussing the influence of the institutional context of therapy and supervision on all those involved. The latter is often an additional source of stress in supervision, especially when evaluation is given central weight at the expense of learning itself, with which it may be at odds.

REFERENCES

Arlow, J. (1963). The supervisory situation. *Journal of the American Psychoanalytic Association* 11: 576–594.

Aron, L. (1991). The patient's experience of the analyst's subjectivity. *Psychoanalytic Dialogues* 1: 29–51.

Balint, M. (1948). On the psychoanalytic training system. *International Journal of Psycho-Analysis* 29: 163–173.

Berman, E. (1986). Transference/countertransference as a comprehensive interpersonal process. *Sihot (Dialogues: Israel Journal of Psychotherapy)* 1: 6–15.

———— (1988). The joint exploration of the supervisory relationship as an aspect of psychoanalytic supervision. In *New Concepts in Psychoanalytic Psychotherapy*, J. Ross & W. Myers, eds. Washington, D.C.: American Psychiatric Press.

———— (1993). Psychoanalysis, rescue and utopia. *Utopian Studies* 4: 44–56.

———— (1994a). Review essay on Etchegoyen's "The fundamentals of psycho-analytic technique." *Psychoanalytic Dialogues* 4: 129–138.

———— (1994b). Psychoanalytic training: Dynamics, social processes, pathology. *Sihot* 9: 28–37.

———— (1995). On analyzing colleagues. *Contemporary Psychoanalysis* 31: 521–539.

Bollas, C. (1987). Expressive uses of the countertransference. In *The Shadow of the Object*. New York: Columbia University Press.

Caligor, L., Bromberg, P. M. and J. D. Meltzer, eds. *Clinical Perspectives on the Supervision of Psychoanalysis and Psychotherapy*. New York: Plenum.

DeBell, D. E. (1963). A critical digest of the literature on psychoanalytic supervision. *Journal of the American Psychoanalytic Association* 11: 546–575.

Doehrman, M. J. G. (1976). Parallel processes in supervision and psychotherapy. *Bulletin of the Menninger Clinic* 40: 3–104.

Ekstein, R. and Wallerstein, R. S. (1972). *The Teaching and*

Learning of Psychotherapy. New York: International Universities Press.

Epstein, L. (1986). Collusive selective inattention to the negative impact of the supervisory interaction. *Contemporary Psychoanalysis* 22: 389–409.

Etchegoyen, H. (1991). *The Fundamentals of Psychoanalytic Technique*. London: Karnac.

Fairbairn, W. R. D. (1954). *An Object Relations Theory of the Personality*. New York: Basic Books.

Gediman, H. K. and Wolkenfeld, F. (1980). The parallelism phenomenon in psychoanalysis and supervision: Its reconsideration as a triadic system. *Psychoanalytic Quarterly* 49: 234–255.

Greenson, R. (1967). *The Technique and Practice of Psychoanalysis*. New York: International Universities Press.

Grinberg, L. (1979). Countertransference and projective counteridentification. *Contemporary Psychoanalysis* 15: 226–247.

Haynal, A. (1993). Ferenczi and the origins of psychoanalytic technique. In *The Legacy of Sandor Ferenczi*, L. Aron & A. Harris eds. Hillsdale, NJ: Analytic Press.

Kairys, D. (1964). The training analysis. *Psychoanalytic Quarterly* 33: 485–512.

Lane, R. C., ed. (1990). *Psychoanalytic Approaches to Supervision*. New York: Brunner/Mazel.

Langs, R. (1979). *The Supervisory Experience*. New York: Jason Aronson.

Luber, M. P. (1991). A patient's transference to the analyst's supervisor. *Journal of the American Psychoanalytic Association* 39: 705–725.

Mayer, D. (1972). Comments on a blind spot in clinical research. *Psychoanalytic Quarterly* 41: 384–401.

Meyerson, A. and Epstein, G. (1976). The psychoanalytic treatment center as a transference object. *Psychoanalytic Quarterly* 45: 274–287.

Racker, H. (1968). *Transference and Countertransference*. New York: International Universities Press.

Reider, N. (1953). A type of transference to institutions. *Journal of the Hillside Hospital* 2: 23–29.

Sandler, J. (1976). Countertransference and role responsiveness. *International Review of Psycho-Analysis* 3: 43–48.

Sarnat, J. (1992). Supervision in relationship. *Psychoanalytic Psychology* 9: 387–403.

Searles, H. (1955). The informational value of the supervisor's emotional experience. In *Collected Papers on Schizophrenia*. New York: International Universities Press, 1965.

——— (1962). Problems of psychoanalytic supervision. In *Collected Papers on Schizophrenia*. New York: International Universities Press, 1965.

Sloane, J. (1986). The empathic vantage point in supervision. *Progress in Self Psychology* 2: 188–211.

Springmann, R. R. (1986). Countertransference clarification in supervision. *Contemporary Psychoanalysis* 22: 252–277.

Tansey, M. and Burke, W. (1989). *Understanding Countertransference*. Hillsdale, NJ: Analytic Press.

Teitelbaum, S. H. (1990). Supertransference: The role of the supervisor's blind spots. *Psychoanalytic Psychology* 7: 243–258.

Wallerstein, R. S., ed. (1981) *Becoming a Psychoanalyst*. New York: International Universities Press.

Windholz, E. (1970). The theory of supervision in psychoanalytic education. *International Journal of Psycho-Analysis* 51: 393–406.

Winokur, M. (1982). A family systems model for supervision of psychotherapy. *Bulletin of the Menninger Clinic* 46: 125–138.

7

Toward a Model of Psychoanalytic Supervision from a Self-Psychological/ Intersubjective Perspective*

JAMES L. FOSSHAGE, PH.D.

* Portions of this paper were presented at the Spring meeting of the Division of Psychoanalysis, American Psychological Association, Philadelphia, April 14, 1994, and at the Postgraduate Center for Mental Health Conference on Supervision, New York City, March 10, 1995.

Viewing the supervisory situation as comprised of three inter-acting perspectives requires substantive changes in understand-ing and facilitating the supervisory process. The paradigmatic transition from positivistic to relativistic science has provided the required underpinnings for the ongoing shift in the psy-choanalyst's stance from an "objectively based" authoritarian-ism to a perspectivalist-based co-participation. In the analytic arena there are 2 perspectives; in the supervisory situation there are 3; and no one perspective can be elevated as "objec-tive." Borrowing from contemporary theoretical developments within self psychology, the purpose of this paper is to utilize the concepts of listening perspectives, intersubjectivity, self- and motivational-systems, and the organization model of transfer-ence to explore further a model for psychoanalytic supervision. Clinical vignettes will be presented for illustrative purposes.

LISTENING PERSPECTIVES

It was in keeping with the emergent perspectivalism that Kohut (1959, 1982) more systematically formulated the em-pathic mode of observation. Essentially this mode of observation is a listening stance aimed at understanding from "within" the perspective of the analysand. Of the 2 perspectives involved in the analytic endeavor, the analysand's perspective needs to be in the foreground for purposes of illuminating the analysand's subjective world. While all analysts variably listen from within the analysand's perspective, Kohut and, subsequently, self psychologists have emphasized listening *consistently* from within the analysand's perspective. Listening from within the analysand's frame of reference is relative, however, for we can never truly extricate ourselves from our own subjectivities.

All analysts aim to understand the analysand's inner world; yet, analysts differ as to the use of various listening stances. Recently, in 1995, I proposed two principal listening/experiencing stances: the analyst experientially can resonate with the analysand's affect and experience from *within* the patient's vantage point, the empathetic mode of perception, or what I also call the *subject-centered listening perspective* —self psychology's emphasis; and the analyst can experience the patient from the vantage point of the *other person in a relationship with the patient*, what I call the *other-centered listening perspective*—an emphasis in object relations and interpersonal approaches. Countertransference discussions traditionally have involved listening from the other-centered perspective (for example, "he's manipulative," "she's seductive," "he's provocative," "she's sensitive"). I believe that in relationships we naturally oscillate between these two listening perspectives and both provide us with important data about the analysand. Listening from the other-centered perspective tells us about how another person might feel in a relationship with the patient, tempered by the fact that the analyst's particular subjectivity variably shapes the experience as the other.

We, as analysts, differ, often without awareness, as to our relative use of these two listening perspectives. We also vary as to which listening perspective we base our inquiry, as well as the degree to which we introduce our subjectivity in interventions. Whereas one analyst begins exploration by using directly his other-centered experience with the patient, for example, "I'm experiencing you as hostile!" or "I wonder why you're being hostile!" (an approach variably used by interpersonalists); another tends to deemphasize this experience in order to focus on an inquiry into the analysand's subjective experience, for example, "What are you experiencing?" (self psychology's emphasis). To start from within the analysand's experience facilitates the analysand's self-articulation and protects against possible derailments due to the imposition of the analyst's viewpoint and agenda onto the analysand. To attempt to remain totally within the analysand's perspective, however, can deprive the analysand of the input from the analyst as the other that can further illuminate relational scenarios as well as provide the relational experiences necessary for facilitating development. Thus, I have proposed that while inquiry needs to emanate *primarily* from an empathic perspective, the analyst's listening from "within" and "without," oscillating in a background-foreground configuration, can illuminate more fully the patient's experience of self and of self-in-relation-to-others. As the interpretive sequence clarifies the patient's feeling via the empathic perspective, the focus on interpersonal consequences of the patient's state and corresponding behavior via the other-centered perspective becomes useful in illuminating the patient's experience of self and self-with-other experience.

How do these two listening perspectives affect the supervisory situation? Within a psychoanalytic supervisory setting the intersubjective field (Atwood and Stolorow 1984) consists of three interacting subjectivities, namely, the analysand's, the analyst's and the supervisor's. Supervision can focus on six possible overlapping areas, namely, the subjective experience of each of the three individuals and the intersubjective experience between any two individuals within this field. For example, the supervisor might focus on the *content* of the analysand's description of a relational experience outside of the analytic relationship, or on the ongoing *process* (Fosshage 1994) between the analysand and analyst *as experienced by* the analysand, analyst, or supervisor. As the analyst presents the analysis, the supervisor can listen from *within* the analysand's experience, wondering what the analysand was experiencing; or the supervisor can listen from *within* the analyst's frame of reference, inquiring as to the analyst's experience of the analysand. In addition, the supervisor can listen to the analysand from the other-centered perspective, which might help to illuminate the analyst's experience of the analysand and the analysand's relational patterns; or the supervisor can listen to the analyst from the other-centered stance, which might help to illuminate the analyst's contribution (via the analyst's relational patterns) to the analysand's experience. Finally, focusing on the supervisory process, the supervisor can listen to the analyst's experience of the supervision from an empathic perspective or gain information about the relational scenario through the other-centered stance.

This intersubjective system between analysand, analyst, and supervisor is exceedingly complex and is probably rarely captured through addressing a single linear process. A number of analysts (Caligor 1984, Gediman and Wolkenfeld 1980, and Searles 1955), for example, have delineated what has been called "parallel process," namely, the transferential pattern emergent in the analysand-analyst relationship is re-created in the analyst-supervisor relationship through the presentation of the clinical material. In other words, the supervisor's experience of the analyst "reflects" (Searles 1955) the relationship that is occurring between analysand and analyst. This formulation is based on a number of presumed processes:

1. the analysand is the principal, if not sole, contributor to the transferential experience;
2. the analyst is a minimal contributor to the transference;
3. the analyst in relating the case material momentarily identifies with the analysand's experience (Arlow 1963)

and relates to the supervisor as the analysand relates to the analyst;

4. during this re-creation the analysand's transferential configuration is sufficiently powerful to shape substantially the analyst's and supervisor's interactive experience; and, finally,

5. during this re-creation, although the analyst and supervisor bring to each interaction unique subjectivities, they are viewed as contributing minimally to their experience.

The concept moves us toward a one-person psychology, that is, the interactive experience in both the analytic and supervisory situations at a given moment emanates from the analysand. Clinical evidence indicates that the analysand's transferential configuration, through triggering affect states in the analyst and supervisor, is, on occasion, sufficiently powerful to affect these 2 interactive processes; yet, because of the uniqueness of each analyst and supervisor, each responding to the analysand's transferential configuration in his or her particular way, parallel process, it would seem, is too readily assumed.[1] For example, the patient blames the analyst for a stalemate and the analyst feels at fault and immobilized; the analyst blames the supervisor for the stalemate and the supervisor begins to be rendered impotent. One could invoke the concept of parallel process and note that the scenario began with the patient's criticism of the analyst. This framing,

---

1. Searles (1955), who first wrote about this phenomenon, cautioned us as to its frequency of occurrence: "This reflection process is by no means to be thought of as holding the center of the stage, in the supervisory situation, at all times. Probably it comprises, in actual practice, only a small proportion of the events which transpire in supervisory hours" (p. 136). Yet, in discussions of supervision, the concept is frequently invoked.

however, conceals the analyst's and supervisor's unique, although in this instance similar, contributions to their reactions to being blamed. The analyst and the supervisor might have reacted quite differently to the patient's accusation. Rather than concluding prematurely that parallel process is operative, we need to illuminate carefully the contributions of each participant to understand the triadic intersubjective encounter.

The primary task of the supervisor is to understand as well as possible the patient and the patient-analyst interactive experience occurring in the analysis in order to facilitate the analytic process and development of the supervisee. To listen as-the-other contributes important data, yet it is too-often assumed that this data is directly revelatory of the patient's experience, thus creating the danger of imposing the supervisor's perceptions and agenda onto the analysis. To enter into the patient's and the analyst's respective experiences is best facilitated with the use of the empathic mode of listening. However, using the empathic mode does not preclude premature and (therefore) distancing, impositional organizations onto the material. To listen closely to the analysand's and, subsequently, the analyst's experiences requires us to live in suspense for a sufficient period of time in order to enable the material, not our schemas, to be primary in the shaping of our experience. The typical once-a-week supervisory experience makes this especially difficult. To inquire consistently into the analysand's experience and, then, the analyst's experience both illuminates the respective experiences and provides an important model for the analyst.

As supervisors listening closely to the unfolding of the analytic process, what criteria do we use to assess an analyst's intervention or sequence of interventions? We know well that the various psychoanalytic models inform and shape both analytic interventions and their assessment. Any given intervention will be applauded by some and repudiated by others. In this sea of contradictory opinions is there any criterion we might rely upon to steady ourselves? When reviewing the process, the most sensible criterion for assessing interventions is, in my judgment, the analysand's response or sequence of responses. (While our models and subjectivities affect the evaluation of any given response, more agreement may be arrived at if we examine a sequence of responses.) We have all heard interventions that at first seemed either mystifying or ill-suited, if not destructive, and were surprised to discover that the analysand's sequence of responses evidenced these interventions to be facilitative. Clearly our models affect what we assess as facilitative; yet, placing the analysand's sequence of responses as central for assessing the analyst's interventions provides the best hope for understanding and evaluating the process at hand.

While an experience-near approach *mitigates* (not elimi- nates) the imposition of a theory-dominated assessment of an analytic process, a phenomenological emphasis is often criti- cized for not dealing with the "unconscious." Theory-dominated assessments that, to my mind, steal away from the process at hand frequently involve, even require, the invocation of the "unconscious" and assertions that the analyst is not dealing with the unconscious or some specified unconscious material. The content of one analyst's view of the unconscious, however, can look vastly different from another's view (e.g. the vastly different understandings of the same dreams by representa- tives of various psychoanalytic persuasions, Fosshage and Loew 1987). Experience is always more or less affected by unconscious mentation. Illumination of experience expands awareness, which includes the gradual emergence of uncon- scious factors. An experience-near approach in supervision tends to bias the supervisory process to a lesser degree and keeps the process for the analyst and supervisor more open, facilitating the emergence of the unique affects and meanings of the analysand and of the analyst.

While an experience-near approach to supervision, in my view, has much to offer, we, as all analysts, still must posit goals for an analysis in order to assess the analysand's responses. These goals vary from one analyst to another—for example, to make the unconscious conscious, to manage conflict with more mature defenses, to transform the internalized bad objects, or to develop and consolidate a positive sense of self. Lichtenberg, Lachmann and I (1992) recently delineated 3 fundamental goals for an analysis, namely, self-righting, expansion of awareness and symbolic reorganization. While an experience-near approach to supervision, in remaining close to the analyst and analysand's respective experiences, facilitates the analytic and supervisory process, each supervisor approaches the supervised analysis with formulated or unformulated goals which uniquely affects the analyst and the analysis.

SELF EXPERIENCE

While there were many important contributors (for example, Hartmann, A. Reich, Lichtenstein, Sullivan, Winnicott, Guntrip) in the evolution of psychoanalytic thought to the conceptualization of the self and recognition of the need to maintain a sense of identity and self-regard, perhaps Kohut most legitimized self concerns and the need to develop and maintain a positive cohesive sense of self. While within self psychology the vicissitudes of the self and self experience are central, the importance of the analysand's self-regard has become highlighted throughout psychoanalysis. Whereas previously the goal was to make the unconscious conscious, from today's perspective no intervention aimed to make the unconscious conscious will be optimal unless it is framed in such a way that the analysand can digest the interpretation without serious threat to his sense of self. If the interpretation is experienced as threatening or as shame-provoking (Nathanson 1987, Morrison 1989), the analysand will either accommodate and feel deflated or become aversive to the interpretation and the analyst.

Similarly, the supervisor needs to pay close attention to the analyst's sense of self, particularly to the analyst's sense of competence and ability.[2] Regardless of the professional level, revealing an analytic process—a highly intimate process—increases each presenter's feeling of vulnerability. The supervisor's use of the subject-centered or empathic mode of listening in investigating the analyst's experience supports self-cohesion. To be listened to, to have one's experience acknowledged and to be taken seriously bolsters a sense of self, what Kohut (1982) noted as the therapeutic impact of using the empathic mode of perception. Entering into the experience of the analyst and analysand helps to create an ambience of respect for, and understanding of, the unique dyadic process that the analyst is discussing. It is from this within perspective, based on the recognition of multiple perspectives, in contrast to an authoritarian teaching stance, that understanding of the process can proceed and alternative suggestions can be provided more easily without threatening the analyst's sense of competence and ability.

Mismatches occur that make it difficult for the supervisor to understand the analyst's approach, creating mutually frustrating and undermining scenarios. A few years ago, for example, a psychoanalytic candidate came to me feeling seriously doubtful of herself as an analyst and of her work with a particular analysand. While the candidate was emotionally connected, she tended to lead with cognitive understanding. In contrast, the style of the supervisor, whom I also knew, was to aim for affective expression. The supervisor reportedly would become disgruntled with the candidate for not being more emotive herself and for not pursuing fuller affective expression from

---

2. Just before completion of this paper I had the opportunity to read Martin Rock's paper on "Effective Supervision." His thesis (chapter 4, this volume) with which I concur, that "what is learned will be a function of the relational context in which it is learned" emphasizes the importance of the supervisee maintaining self-esteem and a sense of autonomy.

the analysand. The supervisor and candidate were caught up in a frustrating and deteriorating impasse. Meanwhile, the analysand, a graduate student in this field, wanted more cognitive understanding and denigrated the analyst for its lack. The analytic candidate was barraged from both sides, which seriously undermined her confidence.

Our first task, as I saw it, was to understand what had gone wrong in the previous supervision through a close subject-centered listening to the candidate. This approach, in contrast to the previous more authoritarian "teaching," helped to create a respectful, facilitative ambiance within which the analyst could regain her self equilibrium (a self-righting process). The second task was to investigate from a within perspective, as best as we could, as to what was occurring in the analysis, not what ought to be occurring. We recognized underneath the disappointments and criticisms the analysand's striving for an idealizing self-object connection with the analyst that centered on the analyst's demonstration of comprehending the analysand. This recognition aided the analyst to feel less deficient and to understand and ally with the positive strivings in the patient. As the analyst regained her self-equilibrium and began to offer more self-assured interpretations of the disappointments and search for an idealizable figure currently and historically, the analyst became more idealizable to the analysand, an experience sorely needed. Both the analyst and analysand began to feel more positive about themselves as they formed an effective relationship.

ORGANIZATION MODEL OF TRANSFERENCE

As the analyst spells out the case material, the supervisor listens for the emergent transferential configurations from the analysand to the analyst and from the analyst to the supervisor. Each person—analysand, analyst and supervisor—enters the arena with shifting motivations (Lichtenberg 1989) and

characteristic ways of organizing experience. The conceptualization of transference, itself, centrally shapes the organization
of data and tends to create a specific supervisory ambience.
Anchored within the positivistic scientific tradition, the classical or "displacement" model of transference refers to those
feelings, thoughts, and attitudes inappropriately displaced and
projected onto the analyst, distorting the "reality" of the
analyst. The analyst's task is to remain anonymous, neutral,
and a blank screen in order to "reflect back" these distortions
and their intrapsychic origins. The analyst takes on an "objective" tone that tends to create a hierarchical arrangement
between analyst and analysand. Within the supervisory situation, as the supervisor picks up on the distorting and pathological
countertransference of the analyst, the same authoritarian
relational arrangement is created. (This is an example where
the theory, not the patient, tends to create the parallel process
"from the top down.") [see Martin Rock's Chapter in this book.]
A supervisor's recommendation that a supervisee take back to
his analysis his countertransference problems—as if one could
choose at the behest of an authority-figure to work produc-
tively on what are often largely unconscious issues—can easily
be experienced as exhortation and criticism, thus further
destabilizing the supervisee's sense of self.

In contrast, over the past decade a number of authors,
including Wachtel (1980), Gill (1982, 1983), Hoffman (1983,
1991), Stolorow and Lachmann (1984, 1985), Lichtenberg
(1990), Lachmann and Beebe (1992), and myself (1994) have
contributed with many variations to an emergent, what I call,
organization model of transference. This model corresponds in
many respects with what Berger and Luckmann (1967), Hoffman (1983), and others call the social-constructivist model.
This model, in part based on theory by Piaget (1970), refers to
the characteristic ways of organizing experience that have
gradually crystalized out of thematic lived-experience. "These
organizing principles or schemas (the 'mental sets,' if you will)

do not distort a supposed 'objective reality,' but are always contributing to the construction of a subjectively experienced 'reality'" (Fosshage 1994, p. 7). Thus, transference refers to the analysand's experiences of the analytic relationship that are constructed, perpetually and interactionally, with the analysand's primary organizing patterns. The analysand's organizing patterns vary in frequency of use, openness to reflection, and modifiability. The analytic task is to illuminate the patient's particular thematic organizations and their origins in his or her lived experience. The goal of the exploration is to increase the analysand's perspective and subsequent flexibility of use, aided by the gradual formation of alternative views of oneself and the world, thus increasing the complexity and enrichment of experience.

Our capacity to form organizing patterns is a product of our cognitive sophistication. The patterns become pathological on the basis of thematic lived-experience, for example, a negative self schema formed on the basis of repeated parental criticism. Recognizing the cognitive sophistication inherent in a schema, understanding that the schema forms on the basis of lived-experience, and acknowledging its role in constructing relational and non-relational occurrences through such processes as "expectancies" and selective attention, all serve to create a more accepting ambience. The analysand's transference and, similarly, the analyst's countertransference are not distortions but constructions. The analysand selects particular cues, ascribes meaning, and interactively constructs. The analyst variably contributes to the transferential experience. Through recognizing the analyst's and analysand's variable co-determination of the transference, an atmosphere of co-participation is created. When the focus is on the analytic relationship, the analyst continually inquires about the meaning of the interaction for the analysand and consistently asks "Who's contributing what to the analysand's experience?" to make sense of the intersubjective encounter. No participant has a hold on the "truth." Similarly, the supervisor illuminates the analyst's ways of organizing (including the use of particular models), deciphering as well as possible the analysand's contribution and the analyst's to the analyst's particular organization. The supervisor may offer alternative ways of organizing which may fit or not, be facilitative or not. As issues emerge concerning the supervisory relationship, the door is open to explore the contribution of each. Anchored in relativistic science, this view of transference lends itself to a more accepting, co-participating ambience, an ambience which increases space for reflection and dialogue.

Based on Kohut's work (1971, 1977, 1984), the model of transference in self psychology has been expanded to include two fundamental interacting dimensions, the selfobject experience-seeking dimension and, what I call, the repetitive relational dimension (Stolorow and Lachmann (1984, 1985), Lachmann and Beebe 1992, Fosshage 1994). Within this model, developmental and restorative needs are viewed as embedded in conflict. Conflict, in part, emanates from traumatic failures of responsiveness in the past, leading to fears of their potentially self-fragmenting reoccurrence (Ornstein 1974) and expectations that failure will reoccur, all of which require various self-protective measures. These are the repetitive problematic relational themes that variably impede a person developmentally and in conflict resolution. Other transferential organizations are forward-looking crystallizations of developmentally or self-restorative-needed experiences. A patient hopes for the "new," expects the "old," and tends to construct the analytic experience in keeping with both the "new" and the "old." While traditionally psychoanalysts have emphasized the pathological themes, a number of contributors (for example, Jung, Fairbairn, Winnicott, Balint, Guntrip, Kohut) have stressed the strivings for the new. While both dimensions of the transference must be illuminated, picking up on what the analysand is striving for, what Kohut (Miller 1985) called the "leading edge" of the material, provides implicit self-consolidating affirmation and strengthens a vitalizing (selfobject) tie. The supervisor, in turn, needs to attend to both dimensions of the analyst's organization of the supervisory relationship. When the analyst's self needs come to the foreground, the supervisor must find a way directly or indirectly to attend to the analyst's momentary disequilibrium in order to facilitate the supervisory process.

Recognizing the co-participation of analysand and analyst in the analytic relationship has expanded the concept of countertransference "to include, not just the pathological, but the entire range of the analyst's experience and its actual usefulness in ongoing analytic work, what has become known as the 'totalist' perspective (see Kernberg 1965, for a review, also Gorkin 1987, Tansey and Burke 1989)" (Fosshage 1995, p. 376). *Defining countertransference as the analyst's organized experience of the patient* (Fosshage 1995) positions the supervisor to invite *all* of the analyst's experience into the supervisory situation. Recognizing that the analyst, as the patient and the supervisor, is always organizing his/her experience alleviates dichotomizing and categorizing the analyst's experience into pathological and non-pathological, which aids a more open investigation. In addition, to define countertransference as the analyst's experience of the patient nullifies the question as to whether or not to work on countertransference within the supervisory situation, for the analyst's experience of the patient is central in understanding and guiding the analytic process. Within this context, the "teach or treat" dichotomy is no longer a meaningful distinction, for "treating" corresponds with illuminating the analyst's experience, a necessary process for "teaching." Thus, supervision becomes another arena in which the analyst can reflect on the analytic process and oneself.

CLINICAL ILLUSTRATION

A brief clinical vignette will illustrate identification and use of the 2 dimensions of the transference, creation of reflective space and maintenance of the supervisee's self equilibrium.

A seasoned female psychoanalytic candidate presented in a small group supervisory workshop a 37 year-old male actor who had been in psychoanalytic treatment for 14 months. His reasons for seeking treatment were the recent breakup of a long-term relationship, anxiety, and intense feelings of inadequacy and guilt. The candidate described her patient as very bright and having a wonderful sense of humor. The patient's father was described as a gruff, pugnacious owner of a small business who either yelled or was depressed, often leaving the patient feeling scared, in the wrong, and not a part of the world of men. Mother was described as possessive, controlling and humiliating. She would dress the patient and call him "her little man." In relationship to women the patient described how the woman takes over and he loses himself. The candidate was presenting the analysis because it felt chaotic, keeping her "off-balance."

In the session on which we will focus, the patient first spoke of his sadness and guilt with regard to the woman from whom he had separated—"She's a good person and look what I've done. What's wrong with me?" He then related a recent get-together where he hung out with a group of male friends smoking cigars, and remembered a "terrible" dream. "I was in a fraternity and had been elected President. We heard a commotion upstairs. I went up to investigate. Upstairs I saw an older man trying to insert a rat in a woman's anus. I was repulsed and tried to stop him." The patient then lamented his "sadistic impulses" and dejectedly commented that perhaps the woman with whom he had lived was right about anal intercourse, that it is abnormal. In an attempt to capture the patient's experience, the candidate reflected at the end, "You're feeling like a rat." The patient assented. In the following session the patient appeared to be more agitated, disorganized, down, and apologetic to the analyst for not coping better. The analytic candidate had a disheartening sense that something had gone awry and, for this reason, was presenting the material.

In the group supervisory situation, we began to explore the candidate's experience—a potentially self-stabilizing process. She explained that using the structural model she had understood the dream to be the patient's struggle over his id impulses, specifically his sadism. While she was not experiencing him at that moment (from the other-centered perspective) as sadistic, her particular framing appeared to position her inadvertently to confirm the patient's self-condemning interpretation of the dream about his sadistic impulses with her statement, "You're feeling like a rat." Her feeling for the patient and her tone was empathic, not sadistic, which ruled out a sado-masochistic transference-countertransference enactment. This exploration suggested to the supervisor that the candidate's model at this juncture was primary in impeding understanding of the patient.

To create some space for reflection and for the consideration of alternative understandings, I attempted to guide a reentry to the patient's world by inquiring as to the patient's experience in the dream, initially his experience in the fraternity and being elected President. While the candidate had not pursued this line of inquiry with the patient, her general feeling, and that of the other supervisory group members, was that he was feeling the same pleasurable camaraderie with the men as he had been describing just prior to associating to the dream. This positive experience with men was a new experience, for, based on the relationship with his father, he had felt typically estranged and fearful. To be elected President of the fraternity in the dream was additionally affirming of him as a leader of men, an emergent vitalizing self organization.

We were immersing ourselves in the dreamer's experience with anticipation of juxtaposing it with the dreamer's waking experience. To enter into the patient's dreaming experience helped to dislodge the candidate from her organization which had implicity confirmed the patient's waking configuration that he was the rat. We continued to explore the dream—most strikingly, the older man's sadism and the dreamer's repulsion and assertion to stop the older man. In the dream he was not the sadist but the hero who was intervening. This corresponded with recent confrontations and assertions vis-a-vis his father. The patient in the dream appears to be envisioning and further integrating new feelings and attitudes about himself in the world of men—the developmental movement that needs to be picked up and facilitated. Not surprisingly, the patient's waking organization of the dream moved in his typical self-deprecatory fashion, which was in keeping with his negative self schemas. (The question is not whether or not the patient has sadistic impulses— presumably he does by simply being human and, more specifically, of being raised within his particular family matrix. The dream's scenario, in my view, is not *directly* addressing that issue. The dream's thematic structure directly reveals the dreamer's struggle with the older man's sadism which the dreamer is assertively attempting to curtail. To translate the image of the sadistic man to be a self-representation and thus to reflect the patient's sadism misses the relational scenario of self with other so evident in the structure of the dream and so thematic in the relationship with his father.) In keeping with the negative self schema, the patient apparently "heard" the candidate's statement, "You're feeling like a rat," as implicitly confirming—that he, indeed, is a rat. Hearing her statement as confirming the negative image of himself momentarily undermined his self-esteem and equilibrium, evident in the following session. The candidate, I believe primarily due to her model, had for the patient inadvertently become the denigrating, humiliating parent, momentarily replicating the repetitive traumatic experience (keeping in mind that transference is variably co-determined, it appeared, in this instance, that the patient's proclivity to feel negative about himself predisposed him to hear the candidate's reflective comment as confirmatory of his negative self image). In the state of disequilibrium, the patient in the following session apologized to the analyst for not coping better, thereby hoping to elicit a forgiving, if not affirming, response—that is, the search for the needed vitalizing (selfobject), self-restorative experience with the analyst comes to the fore.

To see the developmental thrust of the dream relieved the candidate's stressful quandary as to what had gone wrong and what to do about it. Her discomfort about having gone awry was relatively easily overcome with a renewed sense of confidence that she understood the dream and could easily use the dream in affirming the patient's emergent contrasting image of himself. The group similarly participated in the discovery of a new understanding, and felt relieved and supportive of the candidate.

Every analytic intervention variably affects the patient's sense of self. Analytic illumination of the repetitive transference must be closely monitored for the subtle and not so subtle impact on the patient's self experience. Similarly, every supervisory intervention variably affects the supervisee's sense of self. In this instance, the supervisor, with the candidate and the group, had to find a way to facilitate the candidate's openness to reflection and to the consideration and integration of an alternative understanding, quite discrepant with hers, without triggering her feeling aversive, crushed or depleted—not a small task. Exploring the candidate's experience, respectfully addressing the candidate's model of dream interpretation, and attempting to enter into the patient's dreaming experience and then his waking experience, were the ways in which I attempted to facilitate a supervisory process in which the candidate and group could discover new ways of viewing the material and to further consolidate the candidate's sense of competence.

While each supervisory experience is unique and varied, one guideline of sequential steps for the supervisory process, especially applicable to process material, is as follows:

1. listen carefully to the interval and interactive experience of analysand and analyst, attempting to understand the experiences of each and what is occurring within the interactive system;
2. inquire of the analyst's experience of the session;
3. track closely the entire session if time permits, or at least sequences that involve poignant internal and interactional moments;
4. inquire and assess together the patient's meaning, offering alternative formulations if needed;
5. inquire and assess together the analyst's aims and interventions and their impact as revealed by the patient's response; understand and affirm facilitating interventions; understand why other interventions are problematic and offer alternatives.

This close tracking provides a useful model for following the analytic process and facilitating change.

In conclusion, the awareness of different listening perspectives and the different data generated, the primary use of the empathic mode of listening for inquiry, the awareness of the repetitive transference and the search for the vitalizing (self-object) experience in the analytic relationship, all have far-reaching value for the supervisory process as we continue to make the shift from an "objectively based" authoritarian stance to a co-participatory, perspectival stance.

REFERENCES

Arlow, J. (1963). The supervisory situation. *Journal of the American Psychoanalytic Association*, XI, 576–594.

Atwood, G. and Stolorow, R. (1984). *Structures of Subjectivity*. Hillsdale, NJ: The Analytic Press.

Berger, P. and Luckmann, T. (1967). *The Social Construction of Reality*. Garden City, NY: Anchor Books.

Caligor, L. (1984). Parallel and reciprocal processes in psychoanalytic supervision. In *Clinical Perspectives on the Supervision of Psychoanalysis and Psychotherapy*, L. Caligor, P. Bromberg, and J. Meltzer, eds. New York: Plenum.

Fosshage, J. (1994). Toward reconceptualizing transference: theoretical and clinical considerations. *International Journal of Psychoanalysis 75*, 2:265–280.

———(1995). Countertransference as the analyst's experience of the analysand: the influence of listening perspectives. *Psychoanalytic Psychology*, 12(3), 375–391.

Fosshage, J. and Loew, C., eds. (1987). *Dream Interpretation: A Comparative Study, Revised Edition*. Costa Mesa, CA: PMA Press.

Gediman, H. and Wolkenfeld, F. (1980). The parallellism phenomenon in psychoanalysis: its reconsideration as a triadic system. *Psychoanalytic Quarterly*, 49: 234–255.

Gill, M. (1982). *Analysis of Transference I: Theory and Technique*. New York: International Universities Press.

———(1983). The interpersonal paradigm and the degree of the therapist's involvement. *Contemporary Psychoanalysis*, 19: 200–237.

Gorkin, M. (1987). *The Uses of Countertransference*. Northvale, NJ: Jason Aronson.

Hoffmann, I. Z. (1983). The patient as interpreter of the analyst's experience. *Contemporary Psychoanalysis*, 19:389–422.

———(1991). Discussion: toward a social-constructivist view

of the psychoanalytic situation. *Psychoanalytic Dialogues*, 1:74–105.

Hoffmann I. Z. and Gill, M. (1988). Critical reflections on a coding scheme. *International Journal of Psycho-Analysis, 69*. 55–64.

Kernberg, O. (1965). Notes on countertransference. *Journal of the American Psychoanalytic Association*, 13:38–56.

Kohut, H. (1959). Introspection, empathy, and psychoanalysis. In *The Search for the Self*, vol. 1, ed. P. Ornstein, pp. 205–232. Madison, CT: International Universities Press.

———(1971). *The Analysis of the Self*. New York: International Universities Press.

———(1977). *The Restoration of the Self*. New York: International Universities Press.

———(1982). Introspection, empathy, and the semicircle of mental health. *International Journal of Psycho-Analysis*, 63:395–407.

———(1984). *How Does Analysis Cure?* Hillsdale, NJ: Analytic Press.

Lachmann, F. and Beebe, B. (1992). Representational and self-object transferences: a developmental perspective. In *New Therapeutic Visions, Progress in Self Psychology*, vol. 8, ed. A. Goldberg, pp. 3–15. Hillsdale, NJ: Analytic Press.

Lachmann, F., and Fosshage, J. (1992). *Self and Motivational Systems: Toward a Theory of Technique*. Hillsdale, NJ: Analytic Press.

Lichtenberg, J. (1984). The empathic mode of perception and alternative vantage points for psychoanalytic work. In *Empathy II*, ed. J. Lichtenberg, M. Bornstein, and D. Silver, pp. 113–136. Hillsdale, NJ: Analytic Press.

———(1989). *Psychoanalysis and Motivation*. Hillsdale, NJ: Analytic Press.

———(1990). Rethinking the scope of the patient's transference and the therapist's counterresponsiveness. In *The*

Realities of Transference, Progress in Self Psychology, ed. A. Goldberg, pp. 23–33. Hillsdale, NJ: Analytic Press.

Miller, J. (1985). How Kohut actually worked. In *Progress in Self Psychology*, vol. I, ed. A. Goldberg, pp. 13–30. New York: Guilford Press.

Morrison, A. (1989). *Shame: the Underside of Narcissism.* Hillsdale, NJ: Analytic Press.

Nathanson, D. (1987). *The Many Faces of Shame.* New York: Guilford.

Ornstein, A. (1974). The dread to repeat and the new beginning. *The Annual of Psychoanalysis* 2: 231–248. Madison, CT: International Universities Press.

Piaget, J. (1970). *The Place Of the Sciences of Man in the System of Sciences.* New York: Harper and Row, 1974.

Sachs, D. and Shapiro, S. (1976). On parallel processes in therapy and teaching. *Psychoanalytic Quarterly*, 45:394–415.

Schwaber, E. (1984). Empathy, a mode of analytic listening. In *Empathy II*, ed. J. Lichtenberg, M. Bornstein, and D. Silver, pp. 143–172. Hillsdale, NJ: Analytic Press.

Searles, H. (1955). The informational value of the supervisor's emotional experiences. *Psychiatry* 18, 2:135–146.

Stolorow, R., Brandchaft, B., and Atwood, G. (1989). *Psychoanalytic Treatment: An Intersubjective Approach.* Hillsdale, NJ: Analytic Press.

Stolorow, R., and Lachmann, F. (1984/85). Transference: the future of an illusion. *The Annual of Psychoanalysis* 12/13:19–37.

Tansey, M., and Burke, W. (1989). *Understanding Countertransference.* Hillsdale, NJ: Analytic Press.

Wachtel, P. F. (1980). Transference, schema and assimilation: the relevance of Piaget to the psychoanalytic theory of transference. *The Annual of Psychoanalysis* 8:59–76.

8

From Parallel Process to Developmental Process: A Developmental/Plan Formulation Approach to Supervision

THOMAS ROSBROW, PH.D.

INTRODUCTION

In this chapter, a developmental approach to supervision will be elaborated. The developmental approach applies to 2 complementary levels: 1) as a model for the actual process of supervision, the interaction between supervisor and supervisee, and 2) as a specific theory, the *plan formulation model* that is used within supervision to understand the dynamics of the patient and of treatment.

Understanding psychoanalytic supervision as a developmental process is an obvious idea, just as supervision is an intense mentoring experience with significant effects on the analyst's identifications and actual functioning. There have also been many excellent writings applying a developmental model to treatment and contrasting this approach to a more traditional defense-resistance approach (see Emde 1990, Schlessinger and Robbins 1983, Settlage 1992, Shane 1977, Thoma and Kaechele 1986). However, this model has not been applied in any thorough way to the supervisory relationship. Like any significant formative relationship, both parties learn and change together. Along with the effects of the relationship on the supervisee, this is also a process with marked effects on the professional identity and clinical work of the supervisor. The meaning and effects of supervision on the supervisor is then another previously undiscussed area worth more attention. Looking at the developmental meanings of the relationship for both supervisee and supervisor will be one aim of this essay.

The initial impetus for this essay was to look at supervision from the perspective of the theory and research of the San Francisco Psychotherapy Research Group (formerly the Mt. Zion Psychotherapy Research Group) (Weiss and Sampson 1986). This is the theory that will be used to look at a case within supervision. Using the Research Group's plan formulation model provides an open, evolving framework for looking at both the patient's core psychodynamics and the patient's movement in treatment. It provides a developmental model of psychopathology and treatment, which delineates the patient's progressive, adaptive capacities. Formulating a plan entails thinking within the patient's own frame of reference, the same stance used in self psychology (Rosbrow 1993).

If supervision is truly a significant developmental process, what are the effects on the supervisor as well as on the supervisee? This question will be examined by looking at the effect of doing supervision on the supervisor's self-analytic process. Finally, the crucial importance of "being real" in supervision will be discussed.

FROM PARALLEL PROCESS TO DEVELOPMENTAL PROCESS

Recent developmental theories converge in seeing the infant/ person/patient as a constructive, intentional agent. Seeing the person as intentionally, if unconsciously, struggling to overcome crippling beliefs derived from traumatic experiences and interactions contrasts with the view of the patient as ruled by unconscious resistances, clinging to infantile or archaic fixations or gratifications. The concept of resistance has been criticized as an atavisitic relic of an earlier time when patients relied on the analyst's authority to elicit confession of secrets. By terming the patient's difficulties in relaxing and communicating resistances, the analyst suggests that the patient willfully chooses (even if unconsciously) to withhold and obstruct the process of treatment. For example, resistance-defense interpretation was criticized by Wolf as being part of a nondemocratic atmosphere where the analyst instructs the patient on how and when to disclose (Wolf 1991). Others have similarly advocated the replacement of the "basic rule"—to say everything that comes to mind—with an easier encouragement to talk as freely as possible (Bowlby 1988).

Ideas about resistance are particularly relevant to a discussion of supervision. The concept of the parallel process has been a dominant, probably *the* dominant, idea in the literature on supervision since its introduction by Ekstein and Wallerstein (Ekstein and Wallerstein 1958). It is prominently featured in current writing in supervision (see Caligor et al 1984). Before critiquing the parallel process concept, I need to say that Ekstein and Wallerstein's book remains surprisingly fresh and readable and has ideas that are, to my mind, very germane to current problems. The authors repeatedly advocate that the analyst's autonomy must be cultivated and respected. They warn against the supervisor looking for adherents rather than nurturing the originality of their supervisees. The supervisee's need to identify too readily can dovetail with supervisor's vanity, hampering genuine learning. The result is "to produce dependent admirers rather than independent co-workers" (pp. 58–9).

However, the main thrust of the book is quite different. Their thesis is that the supervisee unconsciously identifies with aspects of a patient's resistance, which thereby resonates with his or her own neurotic difficulties, and then enacts these problems via "parallel process" with the supervisor. The supervisee's "problems about learning" with supervisor stem from unresolved characterological difficulties. Though the authors go to great lengths to distinguish these learning problems from therapy issues, the distinction appears to be one only of different labels—calling it a learning problem rather than a character problem.

For example, speaking of a supervisee's initial skepticism, they state, "Overt skepticism can be dealt with as a resistance just as any other . . . the acknowledgment of this difficulty in the student is a foreshadowing of the particular way in which he will resist being taught" (p. 154). In the following passage where they describe "learning problems," their emphasis on the supervisee's character is clear:

> The major obstacle to the smooth growth of psychotherapeutic sensitivity and competence (and hence, of improved clinical service as well), is the mobilization during the process of learning of idiosyncratic patterns that determine the way in which a given individual learns— the ways in which mastery is sought and the specific difficulties that limit its effectiveness. These "learning problems" encompass the whole complex of ways of acting and responding within the psychotherapy situation that are determined not by the objectively ascertained needs of the patient but by the characteristic, automatic—and therefore, at times inappropriate—patterns of response of the would-be helper (p. 137).

The task of supervision is then to unknot the supervisee's neurotic interaction with patients and within supervision. Ekstein and Wallerstein declare that this is the great bulk of work with beginning therapists, and that technical skill cannot be taught *at all* until these problems are clarified:

only through unraveling the learning problems that he experiences with his patient, that therapist can come to see the other side of the therapeutic interaction, the technical-skill problems posed by the disturbed mental processes of the patient. This will be a rather late achievement in the training process of the young therapist. It may even seem that this achievement is not a part of the process of learning, but rather is the end-product of successful learning (p. 173).

The identificatory phenomena highlighted in parallel process thinking certainly occur, and I am not loathe to interpret them when needed. But putting the therapist's identification with unconscious resistance and characterological "learning problems" at the conceptual center of the supervisory experience, as many writers have, infantilizes and patronizes the therapist. Loewald has talked about the "differential" between analyst and patient, the experienced difference in psychological knowledge and mastery between them (Loewald 1980). He emphasizes that some gradient is necessary between the two, as the analyst must have a higher level of understanding and organization in relationship to the patient's problems. But he underlines that the gradient does not pertain to their relationship as two human beings, that the gradient is specific to the task at hand. A parallel process orientation can stretch the gradient between supervisor and supervisee to a dangerous degree. The supervisor is then in the postion of the omniscient interpreter/therapist, while the supervisee is in the position of the unknowing patient.

TEACH OR TREAT—A FALSE DICHOTOMY

The literature on supervision also discusses in a similar authoritarian-tinged vein the "teach or treat" question—what balance to take between being purely "educational" in supervision, that is, focussed on the patient, and analyzing the therapist's countertransference problems (e.g. Fleming 1971; for a contemporary discussion, see Sarnat 1992). The teach or treat question suggests that teaching technique and psychodynamics to the supervisee is suspect and constantly runs the risk of avoiding the "real stuff," the supervisee's problematic countertransference.

Using a developmental approach, one looks at this matter from a different angle which does not split up teaching and treating—for therapy or for supervision. In therapy, the analyst naturally provides information and knowledge in any number of ways depending on the person's needs, blindspots, conflicts, or deficits. He or she does so both in making interpretations, but also at times serving as a "developmental object"—taking on parental or caretaking functions, sometimes literally, sometimes symbolically (Modell 1990). The therapist does this for a multitude of reason—for example, to protect the patient from danger or to serve as a model of identification.

The teach-treat dilemma is a false dichotomy, which imagines there should be a pure, interpretive technique rigorously applied to the dynamics of the analytic situation untainted by contaminating advice, support, or encouragement. In supervision, the dilemma concept suggests at one point the supervisee is a student who receives instruction, and then shifts to becoming a patient who receives interpretation (or, is "treated" like a "patient" most of the time, offering up countertransference for analysis by a supervisor/analyst). The educational process and the therapeutic process are split and polarized. The split is well-illustrated in the last quote by Ekstein and Wallerstein, where technical learning can only follow work on the supervisee's characterologically based problems.

In a developmental approach, the process of learning in supervision is itself mutative and, in a broader sense therapeutic. The supervisee learns from the supervisor through instruction, affective experience, and identification. By listening to and formulating about patients, the supervisee also unconsciously as well as consciously self-reflects, associates, and deepens self-awareness. A great deal of the supervisee's anxiety can be resolved when he or she feels a better understanding of the case. Good education diminishes countertransference.

The therapist's intense emotional reactions often can be understood within a formulation of the patient's life and identifications. Often the therapist (unconsciously) either identifies with aspects of the patient's self or with qualities of the patient's primary objects. These are often termed projective identifications or, in Weiss' terms, passive into active tests. The supervisee does not usually have to "go on the couch" to look at these processes.

The supervisor works to make the supervisee feel safe to bring up countertransference feelings at a level of depth which is comfortable to that person. Those reactions to patients which stem primarily from the supervisee's own life—the supervisee's transferences to a patient—can more readily and genuinely be discussed at the supervisee's initiative. As in treatment, this type of self-disclosure, if it happens, takes place over a long period of time.

The particular orientation of the supervision will lead the supervisee to think about his or her life and reactions to patients in a distinct way. The supervisee is encouraged at times to stretch and try unfamiliar ways of relating and intervening. The supervisor needs to be empathic to the supervisee's hesitancy to do things differently but also respect the supervisee's inevitable real differences of opinion and different ways of working. This acceptance of difference is also mutative for the supervisor, who gets help in mastering his or her own needs to be in control and omnipotent by respecting the supervisee's individuality and initiative.

USING A PLAN FORMULATION

The basic assumptions of the plan formulation model about pathogenesis and therapeutic change, derived from detailed empirical observations and research, are common to other psychoanalytic developmental theories derived primarily from clinical and research observations of infants, children, and caretakers (Rosbrow 1993). These assumptions involve the person's (or infant's) basic healthy strivings for activity, self-regulation, and mastery (Emde 1990, Leichtman 1990, Lichtenberg 1989). In treatment, the patient works to accomplish specific forsaken developmental goals and to gain insight into how these goals were abandoned. In the crucial sequence of the plan formulation, the *patient works unconsciously to disconfirm pathogenic beliefs by testing them with the analyst.*

The following vignette illustrates, albeit sketchily, how to make a plan formulation about a case. Put briefly, a plan formulation constructs a picture of the patient's unconscious plan for treatment, what the patient is inferred to be seeking from treatment. This construct includes the patient's *unconscious goals*, the *pathogenic beliefs* which stop her from accomplishing the goals, the *tests* the patient will unconsciously enact with the analyst, and insights which would help the patient.

Pathogenic beliefs refers to how a child comes to understand and interpret painful events and interactions. Weiss emphasizes the significance of *the sense of personal responsibility* in the formation of pathogenic beliefs. Because of childish egocentrism and paucity of life-experience, a child is prone to interpret himself or herself to blame for environmental failure and mistreatment. If a parent is chronically angry and threatening, the child can infer that he or she is irritating and deserving of punishment. Or if a parent is listless and unhappy, the child can infer he or she is draining and demanding. Feeling responsible for the caretaker's failings, the child may unconsciously decide to compromise normal developmental goals, assuming his or her desires and strivings provoked the caretaker's wrath, withdrawal, or any other traumatic parental attitude. A pathogenic belief is the specific hypothesis the child constructs. For example, "If I was less demanding and weak, then my mother would not be so exhausted and overwhelmed." These beliefs are formed unconsciously, and subsequently the person uses them to avert psychic danger. If the child believes his or her "demandingness" drained a parent, the child might decide, unconsciously, to ask for as little as possible from others and present a front of pseudo-strength, while warding off feelings of need and disappointment.

While these beliefs are compelling and neurotogenic, the individual also unconsciously seeks experience with others which might contradict a belief, and give an opportunity for resumed development—Weiss defines this as *testing* of the environment, a universal phenomena. I have argued that in another part of the person's experience, he or she knows, or remembers, "evidence" that he or she is not at fault—a view shared by Bowlby (Rosbrow 1993). However, given the strength of the beliefs, the individual's view of the outside world usually confirms his or her beliefs. Sometimes in development, an experience with another person is so strikingly different from what is expected that a person's view of the world can be dramatically changed. This can happen with a friend, a mentor, or a lover, especially when the other person's different qualities are experienced in extremely stressful or significant circumstances.

The patient's strivings to work through, and discard specific pathogenic beliefs are constructed as the patient's goals for treatment and typically can be inferred during early sessions. In treatment, the patient continuously tests the therapist in two important ways. One is by simply scanning assiduously, mostly unconsciously, the character and behavior of the therapist and comparing him or her with significant others. The

second way is by reenacting key relationships with the therapist, again unconsciously, and finding out whether the therapist represents a new object with all that implies for resumed
development and working through of repressed, traumatic
experiences.

VIGNETTE

This vignette also illustrates how supervisor and supervisee
may differ over dynamics of a case, but still use the framework
of the plan formulation to look at the effects of the supervisee's
interventions. The supervision is a reciprocal, mutually enriching process, where both parties work and learn together.

The supervisee, an experienced clinician with a different,
well-formed theoretical orientation, usually refrained from
interventions which, to her, suggested advice-giving or intrusions into the patient's life. The patient quickly posed a
dramatic test which called for the analyst to inevitably either
directly respond to the crisis in the patient's life, or else let the
patient self-destruct. This vignette illustrates how differing
styles of responding to a patient can be accepted and understood.

> In this case, the patient, Ms. A, was a professional woman
> in her twenties employed in a blue-chip financial institu-
> tion. She was contemplating a serious breach of profes-
> sional ethics with the potential for scandal and public
> disgrace. Ms. A's mother was a bitter, cutthroat business-
> woman, a female version of the real estate sharks in
> David Mamet's *Glengarry Glen Ross*, who sneered at
> people who played by the rules as losers and wimps.
> During childhood, the mother frequently ridiculed and
> humiliated Ms. A verbally, and at the least threatened her
> physically. She had been, and still was, detached, disin-

terested, and unsupportive of the patient's professional strivings. The patient was aware at rare moments of feelings of hurt and anger towards her mother but was typically obsessed with her current preoccupations with little insight. Ms. A presented herself as greedy and impulsive, but was shocked at her frequent rejection by others. She described her female therapist as an establishment type from a more privileged, educated background. Her description, given with a mixture of respect, envy, and class animosity, was one of the superstraight, seemingly moral authorities she scorned and feared.

From a plan formulation perspective, the patient was currently posing a major test on multiple levels. She was testing to see if the therapist would permit her to destroy her newfound success, and agree with her view of herself as debased and despicable. From her mother's contemptuous attacks, she had developed the pathogenic belief that she was loathsome and weak, and that she did not deserve to be happy either professionally or personally. She also felt that if she shined, her mother would be hurt and enraged. At the same time, she also identified with her mother out of loyalty and guilt (Modell 1984a, 1984b, Weiss 1986). Imitating her mother's psychopathic tendencies in an exaggerated way was an act of fealty. Her toying with scandal and disgrace could involve a need—out of survivor guilt—to keep herself bitter and failed like her mother just at the time that respectability and security were potentially hers. Ms. A's professional aspirations and actual vocational choice, a field involving very strenuous ethics, suggested that she desperately wanted to individuate from her mother and feel respectable and socially responsible. These aspirations are inferred to be the patient's unconscious goals.

The current crisis pushed the therapist to explicitly demonstrate if she wished the patient to fail, akin to the mother, or whether she was a new object who believed in the patient's talents and wished-for self and would not let Ms. A destroy her hard-won professional success. Demonstrating this did not feel easy to the therapist, since Ms. A presented her imagined professional indiscretions in a provocative, defiant, ego-syntonic manner. The therapist had grounds to fear if she confronted the patient about the risks involved—Ms. A would perceive her as judgmental and intrusive and thereby confirm Ms. A's transference perceptions of her as obsessively moralistic and hostile towards her. If the negative transference intensified, Ms. A could become paranoid and untreatable. The therapist also had reservations, out of her own well-founded ideas, about intervening in ways that could be construed as telling the patient what to do.

The supervisor's advice was to spell out to Ms. A the dangers of her behavior in a full, lengthy fashion. This would include the present danger of professional disgrace, the therapist's concern about this, the hypothesis of unconscious guilt and identification with her mother, and the possible implications of this interpretation making the patient regard the therapist as excessively moralistic versus the therapist's interest in circumventing disaster for Ms. A. This type of intervention would give the patient the "big picture."[1] Even if the dynamics were rebuffed by Ms. A, which was likely, the seeds could be planted for future use.

The therapist chose to intervene in a quite different manner, sympatico with her own style and convictions. At a certain point when Ms. A was characteristically plotting

---

1. I am grateful to Harold Sampson, who introduced me to using a "big picture" approach in two ways: 1) to construct a broad overview of what the patient is striving to accomplish in treatment, and 2) to at crucial moments in treatment impart this total picture to the patient.

and scheming, the therapist calmly queried her about her proposed actions and their potential consequences. She wondered how Ms. A assured herself that her actions would work out beneficially, rather than backfire. At the time, Ms. A responded to these comments by pausing thoughtfully and then going on with her usual obsessive ruminations.

The therapist saw herself at this particular point in treatment as addressing a defect in the patient's reality-testing. The therapist's intervention reflected this frame of reference. At the same time, the therapist's intervention was also a response to—and a translation of—the supervisor's recommendations and exhortations. Although the therapist was not very interested in, or in agreement with, the formulation of the patient's pathogenic beliefs and goals, she came to agree with the idea that the patient's actions constituted a test which had to be addressed for the patient's sake and for the treatment to proceed.

This therapist had a strong need to work in her own way. She found a way to speak to the patient which incorporated supervisory input but expressed her own nuanced position. A parallel process view might see the therapist displaying her problems in learning through her need to assert her autonomy and do things differently, while wondering about the parallel nature of her identification with the patient. One could apply a testing model and wonder how the supervisee might be testing the supervisor by disagreeing and asserting herself, and what would be a passed test for the supervisor. However, I do not advocate using a testing model for the supervisory process, though this idea has been fruitfully discussed by members of the research group. To do so would bring back the problems I discussed as inherent in the parallel process literature—a patronizing emphasis on the therapist's patientlike inadequacies and character problems.

Rather than looking at the supervisee's actions as tests, they can be seen as constituting the supervisee's own plan for supervision—a way of understanding the supervisee's goals and needs at a crucial point in professional development. Often the supervisee's plan will involve complex needs to both identify with the supervisor, learn from the supervisor, and at the same time be his or her own person. The supervisor felt that the therapist had to have her needs for autonomy respected in order to take in the supervisor's help. At the same time, the therapist could not overidentify with the patient's need for autonomy or then she would let the patient self-destruct out of an overzealous interest in being non-intrusive. The supervisor dealt with this situation by repeating his understanding of the patient's testing over numerous sessions while also observing and listening to the therapist's different ways of handling the patient with interest—that is, by respecting the therapist's autonomy while asserting his own, different point of view. For each supervisee, the supervisor has to find a way to be "optimally responsive" (Bacal 1985).

In following sessions, it became clear that Ms. A had dropped her scheme as unwise without explicitly crediting this decision to the therapist. Over the next few months, she continued to feel aggrieved and entitled but no longer contemplated endangering herself. Most marked was a shift in affect, noticeable to both Ms. A and her therapist—she began to consciously experience depression and emptiness, along with feelings of shame and inadequacy. This shift suggested a marked lessening of defense and the beginning capacity to bear unpleasant emotions. Her psychological mindedness increased subtly as, with difficulty, she started to acknowledge her sense of frustration and limitation. Ms. A understood her experienced depression as a gain in awareness, and she began to look at relevant childhood memories. Ms. A's caustic perception of the therapist's moralism became tempered by grudging respect for the therapist's integrity.

This vignette illustrates the 2 issues of how to apply a theory, and how to work together with different theories. Ms. A's potentially ruinous scheme is inferred to constitute a major test with implications for her real life, her capacity to self-reflect in treatment, and with significant transference meanings. After this situation was addressed, the patient rapidly, albeit subtly, grew in her capacity to protect her self from acting self-destructively and grew in her ability to externalize less and self-reflect. This positive shift following the therapist's response to an inferred test constitutes a "passed test," in Weiss' terms. The patient unconsciously processes the therapist's reaction, feels reassured and perceives the therapist in a new, more protective light; then the patient can work in treatment with more confidence and openness.

Regarding working with different theories, the therapist made a different type of intervention than the supervisor suggested, a reflection of both stylistic and theoretical differences. We cannot predict how the patient might have responded to the proposed intervention. But the way the therapist spoke to the patient "passed the test" regardless: The therapist called the patient's attention to the therapist's concern and perception of the self-destructive dangers of the patient's actions. The plan model, if used flexibly, can explain the effects of the various modes of intervention by formulating what the patient is asking (or "testing") and then by seeing how the patient responds to the therapist's actions.

This method looks at process—the patient's psychological mindedness, capacity to experience affects, and so forth—rather than at content as a way of retrospectively appraising therapeutic action. It is not important whether the patient "agrees" with an intervention but how the patient's psychological work is affected. Others writing on supervision have similarly emphasized the need to look at the clinical evidence to see the effects of an interpretation or intervention rather that relying on theory (Ekstein and Wallerstein 1958, Haesler 1993). The plan model does the same thing but more systematically, as the research has used process measures to look at the effect of interventions both immediately and more long-term (Weiss 1993). The plan model can respect and give clarity to inevitable differences in approach. From the point of view of theoretical pluralism (Bernardi & Bernardi 1993), people of different orientations can work together and learn from one another using this framework.

Regarding differences stemming from personal manner, the supervisee can learn more about what is curative or enhancing about his or her own "personal equation." Perceiving what works in therapy stemming from the person's natural way of being is an important function for supervision. This self-awareness is a key element in knowing how to use oneself fully in doing treatment. This heightened positive self-awareness can make the analyst appreciate more easily, with less narcissistic vulnerability, when these same traits do not work in other situations or with other patients.

For the supervisor, learning repeatedly that "there is more than one way to skin a cat" is a valuable lesson against theoretical rigidity or personal omnipotence. Seeing how other styles or ways of thinking work helps me to stretch or improvise more freely when my habitual way of working does not connect with a certain patient. My potential repertoire can include images of how others make contact and facilitate a patient's growth.

At the same time, I am not just espousing modesty and eclecticism. When a supervised treatment is going well and has become more open or has changed course in response to supervisory input, the supervisor can powerfully experience a sense of conviction of the "rightness" of what he or she espouses. This strengthened self-feeling of confidence and effectiveness is valuable and sustaining, and can paradoxically allow one to tolerate the equally important feelings of doubt and uncertainty inherent in our work.

During supervision, the supervisor constructs a complex representation of the patient and has the opportunity to add depth and detail to the representation over time. The same capacity to make representations of other unseen people, the important people in a patient's life, is an important part of the analyst's empathic capacities. Doing supervision greatly stimulates the analyst's ability to represent and visualize another's reality.

SUPERVISION AND SELF-ANALYSIS

For some time, the attainment of the self-analytic function has been a sine qua non of a successful analytic treatment, particularly for an analyst (e.g. Fleming 1971). Today, analysts are describing in ever-finer detail actual experiences of self-analysis (Barron 1993), or self-inquiry (Gardner 1983). This movement toward more open scrutiny and elaboration of the analyst's personal associations and lived experience inside and outside of sessions is stimulating and salutary. Reading this literature heightens the analyst's awareness of barely conscious thoughts and feelings which persist as a stream parallel to the patient's associations.

Typically, the self-analytic activity is explained as a final internalization of the analyst's own analysis—the internal structure formed through a successful analysis, in large part through identification with one's own analyst. I can talk to myself and ask myself questions, as my analyst did with me. While this is undoubtedly true, the effect of supervision on the development of the self-analytic function is both obvious and subtle. As analysts, our self-analysis is constantly activated—indeed demanded—in our work with our patients. Doing treatment, I have time and space to systematically observe my associations and self-reflect. What is sometimes referred to as self-supervision is inseparable from self-analysis. In this process, thoughts about a patient flow seamlessly into thoughts about one's own life and psychology. How we hear and categorize our patient's material is centrally involved with what we have learned and experienced in supervision, perhaps as much as in our own treatment. This is especially so when long-term relationships with important mentors have taken place. My organization of my patient's material then becomes the first step, the impetus for my ongoing self-analytic work.

Doing supervision then allows the supervisor the opportunity for deeper self-analytic work through his contact with the supervisee and the supervisee's patients. While listening to patients, the analyst is usually aware of a concurrent track of associations related to the analyst's own life and concerns. When doing supervision, the analyst more often has associations with patients related to his work-life rather than related to his personal life. When I associate to a patient during supervision, it prods me to think about what affinities and differences there are between my patient and the supervisee's patient. Later, I'm prodded to think more about my own patient, which then leads into self-analysis as well. While writing this article, I've become more aware of how listening to a supervisee describe a patient reminds me of a present patient of my own. Suggesting with the benefit of the supervisor's distance an intervention that is helpful with the supervisee's patient then encourages me to try something new with my own patient. Usually, the situations have a common thread, but the actual patients and interventions are quite different. Listening to the supervision material triggered a network of associations and actions with unintended beneficial effects on my own clinical work and self-reflection. I imagine this is a background phenomena for supervisors which has been little explored or acknowledged.

I was supervising a case of a very depressed woman with a history of physical abuse, which was mentioned only at the beginning of a long-term treatment. At a certain point, the patient was becoming increasingly numb, withdrawn and unproductive in work and in therapy, and the therapist was feeling helpless and alarmed. I suggested introducing to the patient the idea that her chronic feelings of numbness and hopelessness might relate to her rarely discussed childhood trauma, and I would encourage her discussion of these experiences. Over some time, introducing the topic stirred up the patient in many ways and opened up current secrets and symptoms she had been unable to touch in treatment, specifically severe bulimia. While supervising this case, I found myself consistently thinking of a seemingly quite-different patient I was treating, a man with some depression but who was bothered primarily from sexual and professional inhibitions which he was steadily overcoming. His treatment was at times plodding, but overall he was moving along and in no state of crisis. I wondered for a while why I was thinking about him and what was happening now in his treatment.

I realized that the common thread(s) between the two cases related to the latter's tendency to be flat and undescriptive, and that I felt—without usually realizing it—a certain ennui about his treatment. Though there was not a parallel trauma in his history, he shared with the other patient longstanding difficulties in self-regulation—with her it was bulimia, with him it was restlessness and difficulties sleeping and organizing himself. My ennui stopped me from pursuing various leads in his material which could foster his self-reflection and his taking more responsibility for getting his life on track. Thinking about these parallels helped me to make a renewed, refreshed effort with him. This effort has enlivened our work. This is an undramatic, everyday example of how supervision effects, often preconsciously, the supervisor. My guess is this goes on all the time with supervisors.

Thinking about supervision has highlighted for me the intrinsic, deeply reciprocal value of the supervisory relationship. When supervision works, both parties can grow and benefit enormously, more than is commonly understood. After being supervised, the analyst is fortunate if supervision becomes part of a person's professional functioning. The supervisor owes a debt of gratitude towards his or her supervisees for extending his capacity to listen to himself and to his patients. All analysts must undergo, enjoy, and struggle with the need for continuous self-analytic scrutiny. Doing supervision constantly rejuvenates and assists the analyst's capacity for self-inquiry.

For the supervisee, the potential gains are much greater. When supervision works, the supervisee first gains the conceptual tools needed to harness that person's intuitions and unique therapeutic style. Then, through careful observation of the treatment process by supervisor and supervisee, the supervisee gains a different, sharper, picture of his or her own idiographic character and how it effects patients. By underscoring key moments in treatment, when the patient poses unavoidable tests and the analyst successfully "passes the test"—resulting in discernible shifts in the patient's therapeutic capacities—the supervisor constructs for the supervisee a picture of his or her actual strengths and style of working. Having his or her creativity understood and described—made conscious—by the supervisor helps the supervisee establish a clearer sense of personal agency and identity as an analyst. After supervision, the analyst retains a supervisory introject which consists of a distillation—or fusion—of the teachings and relationships with important supervisors.

BEING REAL

For the supervisee to "complete supervision," to feel finished, to be able to internalize the supervisor, the quality of the relationship is paramount. Impossible to "teach," but possible and important for the supervisor to model, is a manner of openness, honesty, and "realness." By that I mean the supervisor should relate to the supervisee without pretension, airs of superiority, or artifice. Winnicott stressed the crucial importance of the analyst's aliveness and realness (Winnicott 1965a). He saw it as an antidote to the patient's false-self compliance with the analyst, repeating the person's environmental trauma with parents who demanded or appeared to psychologically need overcompliance (Winnicott 1965b).

Until a certain point down the road in the supervisee's training, it is inevitable for the (relatively) new analyst to be at times stiff and lacking in spontaneity. While mastering new skills and anxieties as an analyst, the supervisee will often be pulled to act like he or she imagines one should, rather than as oneself. While this is inevitable, this constrained way of being, often based on imagined rules, runs counter to what both patient and analyst need, which is for the analyst to relate in a natural, genuine manner (see Heimann 1989). A supervisor can help the supervisee understand and utilize his or her own "personal idiom" (Bollas 1992) in two ways. One is by the supervisor relating to the supervisee in a frank, real manner while respecting differences of opinion and character. The other is helping the supervisee recognizing when his or her own spontaneous, true-self relatedness has a mutative effect with patients and knowing how to use this part of themselves more freely.

REFERENCES

Bacal, H. (1985). Optimal responsiveness and the therapeutic process. In *Progress in Self Psychology, vol. 1*, A. Goldberg, ed., pp. 202–227. New York: Guilford.

Barron, J., ed. (1993). *Self-Analysis; Critical Inquiries, Personal Visions*. Hillsdale, NJ: Analytic Press.

Bernardi, R., and Bernardi, B. (1993). Does our self-analysis take into consideration our assumptions?. In *Self-Analysis; Critical Inquiries, Personal Visions*, J. Barron, ed. Hillsdale, NJ: Analytic Press.

Bollas, C. (1992). *Being a Character*. New York: Hill and Wang.

Bowlby, J. (1988). Attachment, communication, and the therapeutic process. In *A Secure Base: Parent–Child Attachment and Healthy Human Development*, pp. 137–157. New York: Basic Books.

Caligor, L., Bromberg, P., and Meltzer, J., eds. (1984). *Clinical Perspectives on the Supervision of Psychoanalysis and Psychotherapy*. New York: Plenum.

Ekstein, R., and Wallerstein, R. (1958). *The Teaching and Learning of Supervision*. New York: Basic Books.

Emde, R. (1990). Mobilizing fundamental modes of development: Empathic availability and therapeutic action. *Journal of the American Psychoanalytic Association* 38: 881–914.

Fleming, J. (1971). Freud's concept of self-analysis: Its relevance for psychoanalytic training. In *Currents in Psychoanalysis*, I. Marcus, ed. New York: International Universities Press.

Gardner, M. R. (1983). *Self Inquiry*. Hillsdale, NJ: Analytic Press.

Heimann, P. (1989). On the necessity for the analyst to be natural with his patient. In *About Children and Children-no-longer: Collected Papers 1942–80 Paula Heimann*. M. Tonnesman, ed. New York: Tavistock/Routledge.

Leichtman, M. (1990). Developmental psychology and psychoanalysis; I. The context for a revolution in psychoanalysis.

Journal of the American Psychoanalytic Association 38(4): 915–950.

Lichtenberg, J. (1989). *Psychoanalysis and Motivation.* Hillsdale, NJ: Analytic Press.

Loewald, H. (1980). On the therapeutic action of psychoanalysis. In *Papers on Psychoanalysis*, pp. 221–256. New Haven: Yale University Press.

Modell, A. (1984a). On having more. In *Psychoanalysis in a New Context*, pp. 71–82. New York: International Universities Press.

——— (1984b). On having the right to a life. In *Psychoanalysis in a New Context*, pp. 55–69. New York: International Universities Press.

——— (1990). Play, illusion, and the setting of psychoanalysis. In *Other Times, Other Realites; Towards a Theory of Psychoanalytic Treatment*, pp. 23–43. Cambridge: Harvard University Press.

Rosbrow, T. (1993). Significance of the unconscious plan for psychoanalytic theory. *Psychoanalytic Psychology* 10(4): 515–532.

Sarnat, J. E. (1992). Supervision in relationship: Resolving the teach-treat controversy in psychoanalytic supervision. *Psychoanalytic Psychology* 9(3): 387–403.

Schlessinger, N., and Robbins, F. (1983). *A Developmental View of the Psychoanalytic Process.* New York: International Universities Press.

Settlage, C. F. (1992). Psychoanalytic observations on adult development in life and in the therapeutic relationship. *Psychoanalysis and Contemporary Thought* 15(3): 349–374.

Shane, M. (1977). A rationale for teaching analytic technique based on a developmental orientation and approach. *International Journal of Psychoanalysis* 58(1): 95–108.

Thoma, H., and Kaechele, H. (1986). *Psychoanalytic Practice 1; Principles.* New York: Springer Verlag.

Weiss, J. (1986). Part I. Theory and clinical observations. In *The Psychoanalytic Process; Theory, Clinical Observations & Empirical Research*, pp. 3–138, J. Weiss, H. Sampson, and T. M. Z. P. R. Group, eds. New York: Guilford.

——— (1993). *How Therapy Works*. New York: Guilford.

Weiss, J., and Sampson, H. (1986). *The psychoanalytic process; theory, clinical observations & empirical research*. New York: Guilford Press.

Winnicott, D. W. (1965a). The aims of psychoanalytical treatment (1962). In *The Maturational Processes and the Facilitating Environment*, pp. 166–170. New York: International Universities Press.

——— (1965b). Ego distortion in terms of true and false self (1960). In *The Maturational Processes and the Facilitating Environment*, pp. 141–151. New York: International Universities Press.

Wolf, E. S. (1991). Advances in self psychology: The evolution of psychoanalytic treatment. *Psychoanalytic Inquiry* 11(1–2): 123–146.

9

A Proposal to Enlarge
The Individual Model of
Psychoanalytic Supervision*

BENJAMIN WOLSTEIN, PH.D.

* Presented, with minor changes, to the Council of Fellows, W. A. White Institute, April 1983.

In this essay, I shall describe a proposal to reconsider and enlarge the individual model of psychoanalytic supervision into the small case seminar model. My aim is not simply to replace the model of current practice, but to modify it so as to reflect the changes already made in psychoanalytic therapy since the 1940s, when the one-to-one model of supervision was first instituted. The psychoanalytic supervision of transference and countertransference, which was not thought feasible then but is sought as a routine matter now, gives rise to a direct extension of the candidate's personal psychoanalysis, and also, of course, to the supervisor's as well. But since one-to-one supervision is not, in fact, a personal psychoanalytic experience for either participant, I believe it yields a form of psychoanalytic teaching and learning that tends to constrict, to interfere with, even to distort the transmission of psychoanalytic knowledge.

A number of problematic aspects of individual psychoanalytic supervision makes it rather difficult, occasionally impossible, for a supervisor and candidate to carry out their responsibilities toward one another. First is the important historical fact that psychoanalytic institutes organized the current patterning of individual supervision from the late 1930s into the

1940s, when the structure of psychoanalytic inquiry differed from what it is today in some major respects, such as the relativity of transference and countertransference, as the experiential dimensions of the ego or the interpersonal self, as the clear distinction of psychology from metapsychology, or, in alternate terms, of psychic truth from narrative truth.

Supervision approximately 40 years ago, like the psychoanalytic inquiry to be supervised, was not a context for articulating forms and processes of experience directly between the two individuals involved. Nor, indeed, were countertransference, counterresistance, and counteranxiety directly essential to the supervisory experience. By the 1950s, however, when we began to observe candidates re-creating patients' communications with their supervisors, we described those re-created communications as parallel with the original. I then thought of it as retransference, as though candidates were not, there and then, articulating their own immediate experience of transference, resistance, or anxiety undergone directly with their particular supervisors (Wolstein 1959). However, conceptions of the psychoanalytic experience have continued to develop since the 1940s and the 1950s, especially toward a larger view of the psychology of the self. The critical issue becomes therefore, the transference, resistance, or anxiety that candidates actually experience directly with supervisors through the medium of their presented clinical material. So candidates, I now believe, who tend to re-create and retransfer their patients' communications in supervision are, instead, making their own direct response to the collaborative inquiry with their supervisors.

In the 1950s, we drew a hard and clear line between individual supervision and personal psychoanalysis. "Take it up with your psychoanalyst" is the counsel that supervisors gave candidates who showed evidences of countertransference, counterresistance, or counteranxiety toward patients. A coherent and workable approach in the perspectives of the time, we were, nonetheless, teaching candidates to treat psychic experience indirectly, reflectively, at a distance from its dynamic field of origin and function. In retrospect, that approach proved fundamentally ambiguous because we, then, also believed that the countertransference, counterresistance, and counteranxiety of the psychoanalytic inquiry to be studied were not part of the psychoanalytic supervision in which we were to study it.

Consider, further, some ambiguities involved for both the candidates and for their supervisors. Candidates were doublebound. They were to be evaluated on the basis of their presented work, but they could not, at the same time, present their private experience of it. That did not belong in supervision: "Take it up with your psychoanalyst," they were told. Some, of course, anticipated this state of affairs and took the path of educational deception. They did not, while still matriculated, tell it to their supervisors or, in some instances, even to their personal psychoanalysts. They managed to cover up successfully all around and did their real learning, as far as that was still possible, with other training and other supervising psychoanalysts after graduation.

But candidates were not alone. Supervisors were also doublebound. "Take it up with your psychoanalyst" meant that supervisors both did and did not become directly involved with the private experience of their candidates as it intertwined with patients; nor, we may note, were they (or their candidates) to explore their own private experience that intertwined with candidates. However, in referring candidates back to their personal psychoanalysts, of course, supervisors did become directly involved; in order to evaluate their candidates' work for training committees, however, they did not.

One way to cut through both double-binds at once would be, obviously, to construct the one-to-one field of supervision itself as a sort of mini-psychoanalytic experience, and as adjunctive to personal psychoanalysis, for both the candidates and for the supervisors (Wolstein 1972). Then the supervisory experience becomes congruous with the common commitment to study the psychoanalytic process between therapist and patient and also follows the lead of their one-to-one inquiry wherever it goes between therapist and supervisor. As a result, it makes supervision directly relevant to the candidate's entire practice with patients. That, we may observe, usually happens when the candidates themselves are the ones for whom we set the focus of the supervisory experience.

But consider, in greater detail, a structural problem already built against this view. It derives from treating candidates, on the one hand, as students whose reporting must not trespass into personal psychoanalytic issues, and from treating supervisors, on the other, as teachers whose commentary also must not trespass into personal psychoanalytic issues, neither candidates' nor their own. They are both expected to work together as though that standard were possible, as though, from either side, they could do their work without touching on such issues. For all personal psychoanalytic issues are, of course, governed by the principle of confidentiality. So the problem is set: How can supervisors best teach, and candidates best learn, psychoanalysis in the absence of a genuinely psychoanalytic field of inquiry?

Ultimately, I think, candidates learn the most about the range and the depth of psychoanalytic inquiry from direct personal experience, first with their own psychoanalysts, then with their patients. In both these instances, the work is done under the defined conditions of psychoanalytic inquiry without reservation. I do not include individual psychoanalytic supervision because of its limitations from the standpoint of realized psychoanalytic experience. For when we attempt to follow psychoanalytic inquiry during the actual experience of supervision, we encounter a series of ineradicable difficulties, if, that is, a candidate's personal psychoanalyst works within the principle of confidentiality, and if, in addition, the candidate's personal psychoanalyst also accepts its confines. Or, as at the

W. A. White Institute, unlike some others, training analysts are present at meetings of the Training Committee, listen to its deliberations about their candidates based on the reports of various supervisors and on the comments of seminar leaders, but do not speak. So training analysts must treat what they hear about their candidate from supervisors and colleagues as they treat information received about any other patient from all other collateral sources—the referring agency, previous psychoanalysts, parents and children, spouses and lovers, friends and coworkers, and so on.

Consider, further, the following two sorts of difficulties. First, candidates, no less than other patients, have deeply private life histories to tell, idiosyncratic issues to explore, and personal anomolies to make conscious, which they are free to do only in the context of unimpeachable confidentiality. Candidates cannot do these things in supervision, which is not, of course, covered by confidentiality; nor, indeed, do they even introduce deeply private psychoanalytic issues into supervision, even though countertransference, counterresistance, or counteranxiety becomes, at times, eminently relevant to the particular patient being presented—not to mention, also, the probable countertransference, counterresistance, and counteranxiety which supervisors themselves may undergo with a particular candidate. Supervisors are, of course, neither bound nor expected to discuss these issues directly with the particular candidate they are supervising.

A second sort of difficulty arises when supervisors, instead, undertake a direct psychoanalytic approach with candidates. Here, candidates appeal to the confidentiality of the required material, often enough with, or occasionally without, the support of their training analysts. Candidates, now, turn the instruction "Take it up with your analyst" into its counterpoint, "This belongs in my analysis." By so doing, they effectively sidestep the intensification of the supervision of the psychoanalytic therapy. In such circumstances, supervisors have to back off from studying with their candidates the relevance of transference and countertransference, resistance and counter-resistance, anxiety and counteranxiety, and, I believe, correctly so.

I have already suggested the reason for both sorts of difficulty. Candidates, not unlike their patients, expect confidentiality from their personal psychoanalysts, but not from their supervisors and teachers. Supervision is, finally, not therapy, nor, therefore, covered by confidentiality. So it cannot be, or be considered, genuinely psychoanalytic. But questions remain. Do supervisors, as a rule, have to divert their candidates with "Take it up with your analyst"? Why not let them decide how to take care of it themselves? Or, do candidates, by the same token, have to divert both their supervisors and their patients with "This belongs in my analysis"? Why not let them, here too, decide for themselves? The point is not that candidates during supervision are, in this way, resisting transformation. For most training analysts are, I believe, able to observe that sort of resistance. The point is, rather, that the experience of individual psychoanalytic supervision is fundamentally flawed by built-in structural difficulties around the principle of confidentiality.

As a result, the resistance of indirection, evasiveness, and obduracy during individual psychoanalytic supervision is unavoidable. While both the inner experience and outer procedure of candidates are, inevitably, part and parcel of all their psychoanalytic inquiries, they are not, both, equally open to supervisory discussion. It is not possible to study the most private, confidential material of psychoanalysis within a patently public, unconfidential field of inquiry, unless supervisors and candidates are prepared to waive confidentiality in their work—which, paradoxically enough, would turn the supervision of psychoanalysis into psychoanalysis itself. The relation of supervisors to candidates thus resembles that of candidates to the patients being supervised in a most extraordinary

respect. Both the supervisors and the patients may say anything they wish about candidates doing the therapy, and the
candidates have no recourse—since, obviously, their personal
psychology is not covered by confidentiality with either one. In
this circumstance, the options reduce, at best, to a paranoid
mode of study.

Certain things follow from the fact that both patients and
supervisors bear this same relation to candidates doing the
therapy. And they are worth considering. We might, for example, infer that candidates appear in their work with supervisors as they do with their patients. Not so, of course, because
candidates are supposed to accomplish something with supervisors quite different from that with patients—in short, learn
about psychoanalysis. Or, rather, are patients and supervisors
both struggling with the same problem—that is, bring out the
genuine psychoanalytic capacities latent in the psyche of
candidates? It is interesting to speculate about. For such might
be the case at the ideal psychoanalytic institute at which the
ideal candidate would not interpose parallels with the patient's
personality in resistance to the supervisor, at which the ideal
patient would not split the transference, and so on, between
the candidate and the supervisor, and the ideal supervisor
would not infringe on the candidate's confidentiality, at which
the ideal training analyst would not be threatened by the
supervisor's inquiry. But that's not the way it is in the real
world.

To state my proposal in brief: The training analyst should be
called the personal psychoanalyst, whose primary function is
therapy; and the supervising analyst becomes the teaching
psychoanalyst, whose primary function is training in small
case seminars of 3 to 5 candidates, each of whom may present
clinical material on a rotating basis following the model of the
continuous case seminar. Instead of the one-to-one model of
individual psychoanalytic therapy, I am proposing that we
adopt the one-to-several model of the continuous case seminar.

My suggestion is to teach psychoanalytic inquiry in small case seminars, somewhat more intimately and more intensively than we do in the large case seminar.

In this model, once the candidate presents the material, whether he or she then wishes to take part or not, that material is out in the open for public discussion by the other participants, including the teaching psychoanalyst. Any candidate may, in some respect, always resist transformation, but no candidate can, in any case, actually prevent the other members who wish to study how that particular therapist and patient are constituting their particular psychoanalytic experience. It is precisely because the relation of candidates and supervisors is not one-to-one on the individual psychoanalytic model that candidates and supervisors can no longer obstruct one another—candidates saying "That belongs in my analysis," supervisors, "Take that to your analyst." They may both together, or each in turn, obstruct the small case seminar, but the seminar can, however, continue to explore that particular psychoanalytic experience, whether or not the particular candidate or teaching psychoanalyst takes part in it.

To the presenting candidates who bring discussion to halt with "This belongs in my analysis," for example, we may say:

Let us not confuse the privilege of silence with the state of immutable privacy—which, as such, does not exist in the human domain; for the private is a term of distinction that holds only in dynamic relation to the public. As in the distinctions between psychic and social, between individual and group, between unique and shared, there is a dynamic connection between private and public such that neither is ever definable in the absence of the other. So you may choose to speak or remain silent. But since this seminar, including yourself, meets to study aspects of psychoanalytic inquiry, the group continues to observe, makes inferences, interprets and speculates about the interactive process between you and your patient. Indeed, it even does this about your choice of speaking or remaining silent. That way, in its discussions of your therapeutic work, it learns about the varieties of countertransference, at least as many as the several individuals who are participating in this seminar.

True, candidates may, because of unconscious pressures, stop exploring their work as easily in a small case seminar as they now do in individual supervision. But the two situations differ, however. Candidates can block inquiry by supervisors on a one-to-one basis, simply because supervisors have no one else in the room to talk to; they cannot block inquiry by the other members of the small case seminar, including the teaching psychoanalyst, even though they, themselves, no longer choose to take part. Here, for example, resisting transformation itself becomes the focal point of discussion. And that is, in my opinion, the constructive difference between the two models from the standpoint of teaching psychoanalytic inquiry, especially, I might add, for candidates who balk at continuing to explore their work. For they too, now, are involved in the study of, among other things, varieties of counterresistance.

Most important, finally, the principle of confidentiality no longer applies to this small case seminar studying psychoanalytic inquiry, and its members may follow the lead of their discussion wherever it takes them. That is so, I think, because candidates are presenting clinical material in the public domain *ab initio*. They are cautioned to remain silent about things they cannot speak of. But their reporting to a small case seminar is a public event, in principle no longer confidential, so it no longer generates the sense, or supports the standard, of privacy that obtains in one-to-one psychoanalytic therapy, or in one-to-one supervision.

CLINICAL ILLUSTRATIONS

In further support of this proposal to enlarge the model of psychoanalytic supervision, I propose, now, to sketch out some illustrations of the difficulties indicated above. These illustrations come from private practice and from training and supervisory psychoanalyses. Personal psychoanalysis and supervision differ in one essential respect, absolutely for all. Though the therapeutic field of psychoanalysis is, of necessity, governed by the principle of confidentiality, the supervisory field is not. The fortunate coincidence of doing both supervisory and training psychoanalyses enables me, nevertheless, to see the issue from both sides of the principle of confidentiality, and to observe the sort of difficulties that I list below. In some instances during supervision, clinical intuition has sufficed to grasp the cues for these observations; in others, only direct clinical psychoanalytic inquiry in explicit detail would yield the desired information. Not all these instances are, in fact, derived from direct personal experience with those who suffer the difficulties being discussed; a few are derived, as well, from the reports of others at case seminars and clinical conferences.

I mention my association with a number of different institutes during the last 35 years, reassuring those who may need it that nothing I say here discloses the identity of anyone with whom I have been involved clinically, in personal psychoanalysis or supervision. Nor do I even try to differentiate observations made during supervisory from those made during psychoanalytic inquiries, again, for the purpose of protecting the identity of the individuals involved. I state these things at the very outset, moreover, to let them know that, from what I say in this paper, they will not identify who they are. I am, certainly, keeping their personal identities confidential, and, given the way it really is in the present historical state of social and cultural development, it is only common good sense that they keep private the issues that I am about to discuss.

The selected instances fall into two groups: (1) those candidates who engage in private lives that, for reasons of social prejudice and cultural distortion, they choose to keep private; and (2) those who passively bear a burden of psychic pain and suffering that, for reasons of personality structure, they cannot bring into their own awareness, or the awareness of significant others—that is, make them conscious.

Candidates in the first group have deeply private agenda which, if exposed to broad public view, would, in at least their own opinion, expose them to harsh social judgment, prejudice, and, they are convinced, ostracism from the psychoanalytic community. They are afraid of becoming opprobrious outcasts. What is worse from a practical point of view, they are afraid of being dropped from the rolls of the institute at which they have matriculated and losing the friendship and fellowship that they have come to enjoy with other candidates, graduates, and faculty. In this first grouping, then, are the candidates who live secret lives with complete awareness of their required secrecy, individuals who have, for example, made varieties of sexual adjustment that are not viewed in the popular mind as being consistent with genital primacy. Note the following: varieties of heterosexual arrangements, premarital, marital, extramarital; sado-masochistic perversions with spanking and beating for sexual arousal; masturbatory practices involving anything from kinky photographs to group orgies; bestiality with animals of both sexes; and, of course, homosexuality and bisexuality— none of which practices is considered entirely acceptable even to those who pursue them. Then, there are some candidates who are deeply involved with drugs and/or alcohol. In addition, I find with increasing frequency, are those with strong defenses against openly speaking about money, not only in relation to their own fees for personal psychoanalysis, which some persistently shy away from discussing, but they also refrain from fully inquiring about their patients' attitudes toward money, its symbolic meaning, and actual use, as both individual and familiar experience. For the topic of money is, these days, gradually moving higher on the list of social taboos, even, curiously enough, to the point of becoming a matter of incestuous distortion, no less unspeakable than sex was about 100 years ago.

In the second grouping are candidates who suffer deeply rooted psychic complexes which, valiantly but vainly, they try to cover up. In so doing, however, they not only undergo psychic suffering, they also introduce a secondary or derivative elaboration to defend against acknowledging the suffering as well. They, in other words, put forth a facade of security operations shot through with anxieties and tensions, to cover over the sources of their basic insecurities beyond conscious awareness, their own and their other's. They have psychic complexes such as: sadistic dependency, irrational anger and competitiveness, irrational rage and authority, unresolved guilt and guilt-induction, uncontrollable defensiveness and depression, and fears of direct therapeutic inquiry expressed as disturbed nurturance, aggressive dependency, a model of adjustment and health, hypercriticality, and distancing to the schizoid borders for narcissistic purposes.

Those in the first group live out their secrets with awareness, appearing cold, calculating, or furtive in how they present—in fact, misrepresent—themselves and their experience of their clinical work as a caricature of their original capabilities; those of the second group live out their secrets without awareness, appearing anxious and disturbed in how they present—again, in fact, misrepresent—themselves and their clinical work as being far worse than they are capable of.

There are, in addition to these two groups, still other candidates who, for reasons of social status or personal vanity, desire to graduate from a psychoanalytic institute without actually learning how to do psychoanalytic therapy. They wish to practice some other kind of psychotherapy, usually some variant of behavior modification or client-centered therapy. Why then choose to attend a psychoanalytic institute, instead of finding the institute that would teach them the psychotherapy they are bent on practicing, is their unexplored question. From a psychoanalytic point of view, I suspect that these candidates see themselves as special, if oppositional characters who would most probably insist on learning psychoanalytic therapy at an institute for behavior modification or client-centered therapy. They are, in any case, far easier to deal with than are those in the first group who, despite their being severely burdened with secret lives within their own awareness, still pursue the wish to learn psychoanalysis.

Not unlike most other psychoanalysts, I believe in the freedom of inquiry into truth, and know, with certainty, that the last word in psychoanalysis has not yet been spoken. I am, therefore, not prepared to prohibit any of these candidates from studying psychoanalysis, so long as qualified psychoanalysts are ready to train them. Nor, indeed, would I support or sympathize with any who would deny them the opportunity of training on those grounds. However, the actual practice of psychoanalytic therapy requires a clear sense of psychic resolution. If they seriously attempt to meet this requirement, the work itself will, in my view, force them to shape up, or, in the end, stop them from continuing with it. Their patients' unresolved pain and misery and suffering, alone, will take care of that. So much for charlatanism in this field.

On the other hand, the fact that these candidates are so burdened with secret lives, both conscious and unconscious, of itself, does not mean that they lack the original intuition and creative intelligence to practice psychoanalytic therapy. Anyone who reads the new Sullivan biography[1] and closely attends

---

1. Perry, H. (1982) *Psychiatrist in America*, Boston: Harvard University Press.

to the intimate details of his personal development will quickly learn to avoid the embarrassment of this sort of psychogenetic fallacy. It is impossible to consider the stark realities of Sullivan's life without allowing them to penetrate through the stereotyped romantic images which may have clustered about him. The reduction of this man's ideas and procedures to the warp and woof of his personality is, happily, still untenable. My only point here, of course, is that such personal issues are deeply rooted in psychic structure, and that a thorough personal psychoanalysis alone illumines them. Scientific probity requires a line of distinction clearly drawn between ideas and procedures that someone contributes to psychoanalytic knowledge on one side, and the anxieties and secrecies embedded in the defense and dynamics of a contributor's psyche on the other.

But, given the current and, what promises to remain, lasting interest in countertransference, counterresistance, and counteranxiety, the practice of psychoanalytic supervision may continue under individual one-to-one conditions only with great difficulty. A particular candidate may, with trust, decide to open up to a particular supervisor, and choose to waive the principle of confidentiality. However, such a waiver on the part of the candidate is, in itself, a rather extraordinary gesture. It suggests an unexplored psychodynamic complex of issues about his or her relation to authority, even about psychic and social reality. What, in other words, does it mean that a candidate offers to confer such authority on the supervisor, who is not his or her personal psychoanalyst? And is that authority, then, also his or hers to withdraw at will? Even so, when a candidate waives confidentiality under present arrangements, the supervisor must, regardless, still submit an evaluation. From the other side, the supervisor may choose not to evaluate, so as to facilitate the discussion of personal issues, but the candidate, this time, may remain closed to further inquiry into the relevance of transference and countertransference, and so on, because that inquiry leads, inevitably, into issues that belong in his or her own personal psychoanalysis. Actually, of course, the principle of confidentiality is not a candidate's to affirm or ignore in supervision, since it does not belong to the supervisory experience in the first place.

So there are problems arising from both sides during the study of countertransference in the current model of psychoanalytic supervision, whether a particular supervisor attempts to evaluate the candidate, or whether a particular candidate attempts to waive confidentiality with the supervisor. These problems cannot be overlooked, and they cannot be talked out of existence. They tend to persist for a number of reasons. I consider two: first, that from Breuer and Freud to the present day, all psychoanalysts locate the source of the therapeutic action of psychoanalysis in their direct experience with patients and their inquiry into it, no matter their preferred perspective on metapsychology for interpreting and speculating about the source of therapeutic action. Second, the model of psychoanalytic supervision in use today was originally constructed during the late 1920s and through the 1930s, the period in which character analysis, ego psychology, and interpersonal and object relations first came into being. The psychoanalyst increasingly was seen as the professional, the expert, and the patient as the lay person, the sufferer—that is to say, before critical attention to the relevance of transference and countertransference in the actual field of their occurrence changed the psychoanalytic landscape, from the middle 1950s and into the present. But if the direct experience of psychoanalyst and patient is, in fact, the real locus of their therapeutic inquiry, what better place for a psychoanalyst to study countertransference, for example, than in the actual field of its relevance to transference *in vivo*—that is, as the candidate's countertransference emerging with the patient, or, what is the same thing in psychic experience, as the candidate's transference emerging with the personal psychoanalyst, both appear in their respective fields of therapeutic inquiry?

Hence, the model of psychoanalytic supervision, as now constructed, is at least once removed from the complex of experience that it is supposed to study. For even when a supervisor and candidate claim, with the best intentions, to study countertransference, and so on, they are, in fact, incapable of studying it *in vivo*, because of the derived, secondary, and unconfidential nature of their inquiry. They cannot study it directly, but can, instead, study it only indirectly—which is to say, study the study of it.

I turn, now, to still another aspect of this theme. One clear sign that a candidate is under some special stress and anxiety about countertransference emerging in his or her clinical practice is the request made of the personal psychoanalyst to provide supervision after their work together is over. Not, I should add, to study the candidate's countertransference appearing as his or her transference there and then, but to agree to a course of supervision at some future date, after the proposed psychoanalysis will have been completed. That means, in my view, that the candidate is suffering the distortions of countertransference but, at the same time, is not free to discuss them openly with a current supervisor who is, also, required to evaluate his or her work, let alone with the patient who directly experiences those distortions of countertransference.

Consider the complexity of this curious situation: The personal psychoanalyst, because of having that special function in the candidate's training, cannot freely discuss or evaluate the candidate's work with the training committee. The candidate cannot seek this sort of supervision with anyone else connected with the public dimensions of his or her training. For whatever real or imaginary reasons, the candidate still does not believe that the psychoanalytic world, any more than the world at large, is ready to accept his or her self-diagnosed pathologies. Such a candidate carries a heavy burden of psychic stress and cannot, therefore, genuinely accept the full and free study of countertransference with anyone, including the personal psychoanalyst. His or her secret life prevents the emergence of a clear picture of the therapeutic work—not with the supervisor, the patient, or, even, curiously enough, the personal psychoanalyst. The candidate has secrets, conscious as well as unconscious, and, with respect to them, remains defensive, stubborn, bull-headed, or, as one put it—neatly, if unpsychoanalytically— avoidant. He or she, instead, presents everyone with a fictional facade, which may appear in the guise of a need to be loved but, in fact, represents a coverup of secrets still unacceptable even to his or her own self.

To summarize the major difficulties with the current model of psychoanalytic supervision: Some candidates, in defense of their secrets, actually leave supervision before completing the required number of hours already agreed upon for receiving credit. Others lay it down, as a firm condition for completing their hours, that their countertransference be left alone during supervision, even through it is transparently involved in counterdistorting the patient. "That belongs in my personal psychoanalysis," they insist, usually with the support of their ego-interpersonal psychoanalysts. Still others, no longer in personal psychoanalysis, cannot make that a condition for completing the supervision, and discontinue in *medias res* because they feel the anxieties about possibly revealing their secrets becoming too strong. They often do so with the promise of returning to supervision after they resume their personal psychoanalysis at some future date. But they do not mean to return, essentially, I believe, because the supervisor broke the agreement not to discuss their experience with the patient from a psychoanalytic point of view, as it tends to appear in their experience with the supervisor.

I want to close this discussion with a word of acknowledgment to candidates, colleagues, and teachers who, like myself, were puzzled by the artificial limits imposed on their freedom of inquiry by the ego-interpersonal model of psychoanalytic supervision, and on the possibilities inherent in the study of psychoanalytic inquiry when done unencumbered by those limits. And the possibilities are, of course, being realized. How, for example, can a supervisor and candidate study the relatedness of transference and countertransference, and so on, if they are not supposed to acknowledge that it exists between them, and that, if not psychoanalytically explored, also has therapeutic consequences for the patient? How, that is, can they refuse to acknowledge its presence in the supervisory field of experience even in the context of clinical data from the therapy, the supervision, or both, that unerringly depict its existence between the supervisor and the candidate? Especially under conditions of supervision, where the supervisor, as a matter of principle, always referred the candidate's ego-interpersonal experience back to his or her personal psychoanalyst? But what happens, here, to the supervisor's own ego-interpersonal experience with his or her candidate? Under these circumstances, do they make psychoanalysis into a purist, antiseptic, and idealized version of the ego-interpersonal therapy and supervision that, they believe, should be done? I am, of course, grateful to those who have taken part in my struggles with these issues, and have attempted to struggle through them with or without me, for they will inevitably, in some unique ways, all arrive at results other than my own. For this is, after all, what the new psychoanalytic awareness of the uniquely individual varieties of countertransference means.

Finally, I present this proposal to enlarge the model of psychoanalytic supervision, in order, most especially, to accommodate the study of countertransference, and so on, in the form of a working hypothesis. This, of course, is open to experiment, inquiry, modification and further enlargement.

REFERENCES

Wolstein, B. (1959). *Countertransference*. New York: Grune & Stratton.
—— (1972). Supervision as experience. *Contemporary Psychoanalysis* 8:165–172.

VII

ISSUES,
PROBLEMS,
AND
RESOLUTIONS

10

Towards Autonomy: Some Thoughts on Psychoanalytic Supervision

PATRICK J. CASEMENT, M.A.

Paula Heimann used to point out to student psychoanalysts that it is useful to bear in mind, from the very beginning, that one of the aims of an analysis is for the patient to reach the point of not needing the analyst. In many ways the same is true of psychoanalytic supervision.[1] I have therefore chosen a title for this paper which reflects that aim, which is the ultimate autonomy of the supervisee.

My examples are from the supervision of student psychotherapists, but I believe that the principles I shall describe are also relevant to the supervision of analysts and analytical psychotherapists, qualified or not, and so are many of the issues illustrated.

I shall not attempt any overall view of supervision or the different phases of this. But, within the ambit of my title, I plan to focus on a few concepts that I have found useful.

---

1. The main exception to this statement is that it is always prudent for analysts, after qualification, to return for periods of supervision as a way of extending their skills—or at least for occasional consultation.

THE SUPERVISORY TRIAD

I wish to begin with some thoughts on the supportive function of formal supervision, as there are crucial dynamics which can operate in the supervisory triad: that of the supervisor, the student, and the patient (see also Crick [1991], for a consumer's view of this triangle in supervision). These dynamics can be overlooked with consequences that are sometimes serious and unjust.

The role of supervisor needs to be that of supporting the student as *therapist to the patient*. This means believing in, and fostering, the potential in the student to become a competent therapist to the patient. And if the supervisor is not able to believe in that potential then there is already something wrong, either in the selection of this student's training patient or of the student for training, or in the selection of the *supervisor*!

There are a number of ways in which the supervisory triad can break down. Too strong a model of how the analysis "should" be done can be profoundly undermining of the student's own thinking. This can foster an exaggerated dependence on the supervisor so that a student can sometimes feel reduced to being a messenger between the patient and the supervisor, as if the supervisor were the patient's real analyst/ therapist. There is also a problem when students feel that supervisory insights should not be allowed to go to waste, as this can lead to a tendency to use, inappropriately, too much of the supervision in an ensuing session. It is then likely that patients will sense that there is a different hand at the helm in sessions immediately following a student's supervision.[2]

When I hear too much of my own thinking turning up in a

---

2. It is likely that some patients in treatment with student therapists/ analysts could say, if asked, which session in the week follows most immediately after the weekly supervision.

student's work with a patient, I know that I should not just question the student's lack of independence. I must also examine my own way of supervising. Am I being too active in the supervision, too directive, or too dogmatic? Am I being too quickly critical of the student's way of interpreting? Am I leaving enough room for the student to develop his or her own thinking, in supervision and in the clinical work with the patient? In other words, I need to bear in mind what my own contribution might be to the difficulties being experienced by the student.

We can see a similar dynamic operating in a training analysis, as both the training analyst and supervisor have a part to play in the triad that supports, or fails to support, the student in clinical work with training cases. Therefore, when as training analyst I hear of things going wrong in a trainee's work with patients, I regard this as a prompt for me to review my own analytic work with that trainee. It is possible that some difficulties a trainee is having with a patient may reflect difficulties not being dealt with sufficiently in the trainee's analysis with me.

It is always tempting to question someone else as supervisor, or someone else as analyst, when there is something amiss in a trainee's clinical work. I therefore think that we should always first examine our own possible contribution to a student's difficulty before settling into criticism of the student, or of someone else who "ought" to be helping the student better.

It is also salutary to remember that a mother, when feeling insufficiently supported as mother to her baby, can experience her baby's crying as an attack upon her own capacity as a mother. At times of stress some mothers retaliate. Students can likewise feel threatened by a patient's failure to thrive, being dependent upon the patient for qualification. If at the same time the student is feeling blamed by a supervisor for these difficulties, further inappropriate dynamics can ensue.

A student can have quite problematic feelings about a

patient who is raising doubts in the training organization about the student's eventual qualification. Even though students are careful not to retaliate—at least for the duration of the training—that reaction may surface later, however unconsciously. And I have wondered about this when some patients are dropped from treatment so soon after a student's training has been completed. Another possible consequence of feeling that qualification is being threatened by a difficult patient is that a student may resort to pacifying the patient in ways that are aimed to prevent this training case from leaving at a time that would be inappropriate for the student. This can result in some patients being kept in treatment by means that are manipulative, even seductive, this being nonanalytical and inappropriate to both treatment and psychoanalytic training. I feel that these issues are too rarely discussed.

I believe that it is essential that a supervisor, as far as possible, should convey a sense of shared responsibility for difficulties in the analysis of a training case. These difficulties often signal the need for more effective supervisory support, or more work in the training analysis, as much as they may indicate some deficiency in the student. When this dimension of the supervisory triad is overlooked a student can be left feeling burdened with a problem that can effectively jeopardize qualification. I would therefore like to see more evidence of supervisors and training analysts examining their own parts in relation to any training case that fails.

INTERNAL SUPERVISION

As I have already indicated, there is always a risk that an inexperienced supervisee may invest too much in the authority and assumed wisdom of the supervisor. This can inhibit the autonomous working of a student at the time when it most matters—when the student is with a patient. I have described elsewhere (Casement 1985, chapter 2, 1991, chapter 2) the course of development from external supervisor to internalized supervisor, and the development of a student's own internal supervision as separate from that. It is with this last that I am primarily concerned in this paper.

It is not unusual to hear a student in supervision saying; "At this point in the session I began asking myself what *you* might have said here." I therefore regard the concept of an internal supervisor as representing the student's own thinking as distinct from that of the internalized supervisor: both are important, what the actual supervisor *might* have said and what the student *is* thinking in the session. I therefore try to foster a supervisee's sense of this inner dialogue, so that the thinking represented by the internalized supervisor can be processed, taking into account the immediacy of the present session. I consider formal supervision to be a dialogue between the internal and external supervisors.

The functions of internal supervision evolve from a student's experience of his or her own analysis, from formal supervision and clinical seminars, and from following the clinical sequence of many sessions. It is therefore fundamental that students become able to process for themselves what is taking place with a patient, particularly when under pressure in a session, in order to become aware of different options and the implications of each. Interpretation, and sensing when to remain silent, can then more readily become the skill it needs to be, rather than being too much a matter of intuition or (sometimes) paralysis.

For the more immediate processing of internal supervision to become possible, students need to establish a mental "island" within which to reflect upon a session at the time rather than later. Along with this, it is also valuable to develop a benign split between the participating ego and the observing ego in the therapist, similar to that recommended for the patient (Sterba 1934). This allows greater freedom for a therapist to be drawn into the dynamics of a session whilst still preserving, in the observing ego, sufficient detachment for monitoring the vicissitudes of a session. This double use of the ego, and the capacity to reflect upon what is happening, can also help toward making sense of a therapist's affective responses to the patient, and sometimes of being flooded by feelings in a session, without being incapacitated by what is experienced.

TRIAL IDENTIFICATION WITH THE PATIENT

Another technique that I often focus upon in supervision is that of encouraging a student to trial-identify with the patient in a session, most specifically to consider *from the patient's point of view* how the patient might experience what is being said, looking for ways in which the patient's experience might be different from what is intended. This self-monitoring is essential because it is always more difficult to interpret transference meaningfully if the analyst is also affecting the patient through the way in which interpretations are given, their style and manner, and/or the timing of them.

A very simple example of a supervisor trial-identifying with the patient can be illustrated in relation to a student's attempts at finding a focus in the transference.

EXAMPLE 1

A patient has just been saying: "I feel that no-one understands . . ." The student replied: "Do you feel that *I* don't understand?"

As supervisor, I took a few minutes to go through this sequence with the student, saying something like the following:

Let me be the patient for a moment. If I (as patient) have just said that I feel no-one understands, "no-one" here includes *you*. I could therefore hear your question as if you have either not heard me properly, or as not believing me. So this question "Do you feel that *I* don't understand?" sounds as if you are expecting the answer "No." I could therefore hear this as indicating that you don't like to consider the possibility that I might think of you as not understanding. If I feel able to be directly angry with you I might then say something like: "Don't think you are so clever that you understand everything." Or, I might feel a need to placate you by agreeing with you.

The student then reported the patient's response:

Of course I am not meaning to include *you*. I know that you do understand really. But my father often made me feel so distant from him that it was as if I would never be able to get across to him what I was feeling, even if I shouted. He was always so sure that he was in the right.

Comment

From a sequence like this it is possible to demonstrate to a supervisee that the patient's response to this question may well have been to hear it as defensive. The patient attempts to reassure the student, and follows this with a displacement onto some other figure (here the father) of the sense that the student had not been hearing. It therefore does look as if the patient had been anxious that the student may have to be treated with caution, as the student seemed unwilling to be seen in a negative light—as not understanding. The echo of this problem, now spoken of in relation to the father, can be seen as an example of unconscious supervision (Langs 1978), as if the patient were saying: "I don't know how to reach you. Will I have to shout before you will hear?"

What I am particularly wanting the student to learn from this is how easily a patient can be deflected from being allowed to develop a negative transference, thus keeping negative feelings split off from the analysis.

EXAMPLE 2

A patient has been talking about a recent TV program in which someone had been telling a psychiatrist that he possessed a dangerous knife and he was afraid that he might kill someone. The psychiatrist seemed not to have taken this seriously enough and this person, in the program, had then gone out and *actually* killed someone.

Following this, the patient subjected the student to a persistent enquiry as to what he would say in court if he (the patient) had really killed someone. The student proceeded to focus on the question of confidentiality, saying: "I think you are anxious about whether it is really safe for you to be confiding in me or might I disclose to others some of what you tell me?"

As supervisor, I felt that this was a misleading focus. I therefore made the following comments:

I feel that you are staying with the question of confidentiality, in this hypothetical future, which may be easier to think about than the issue of potential violence referred to in the opening statements of this session.

We have been hearing of someone whose thoughts of violence have not been taken seriously enough,

fantasy leading to action. If you listen to yourself
from the position of the patient here, you might
notice that he could be wondering if *his* thoughts of
violence have been taken seriously. They need to be,
as the patient is pointing out. If they are not, the
sequence might move into this hypothetical future
with some actual act of violence. The matter of
confidentiality is clearly secondary to that of the
patient's violent feelings and fantasies.

Comment

Again, we can see a therapist deflecting from the more difficult
matter that is current in the session. Here it is that of the
potential violence. The choice of focus demonstrated could
leave the patient feeling that his therapist may be afraid of this
violence too. No patient will feel securely contained when the
therapist can be seen as backing off from what most needs to be
addressed in the current session.

EXAMPLE 3

A male patient has been expressing anxiety about showing his feelings to his female student therapist, particularly in crying. He added: "It is sissy for a man to cry, isn't
it?" He goes on to say how he has always been very careful
not to cry in front of anyone. The student replied: "You are
afraid that I might reject you if you cry in front of me."

I notice that the specific idea of rejection had not been
introduced here by the patient but by the therapist. I
therefore commented:

There are two things to draw attention to here: the
rhetorical question, that is asked as if it needs no

answer, and your actual response. How might you feel, as the patient here, in relation to these two points?

When I listen to you, from the patient's point of view, I could hear your nonresponse to the rhetorical question as your agreeing that it *is* "sissy" for a man to cry. I am sure that there is more work to be done in finding out how the patient has come to regard crying in this light, and he will need to discover that it does not have to be that *everyone* regards a man's crying as "sissy."

Also, where does the notion of your rejecting the patient come from? I do not hear this in the patient's communication. He could therefore misunderstand you to be suggesting that, if he were to cry, you might then *actually* reject him. I think it is always important to listen for those ways in which a patient could mishear what you are meaning to say. We can better avoid that if we monitor what we are saying from the patient's point of view, not jumping ahead of the patient's actual communication.

Comment

I am using this example to remind the student to be careful to notice who introduces what into a session, and that a patient can regard something that is brought in by the therapist as perhaps revealing some unconscious truth about the therapist. This "reading" of the therapist by the patient can sometimes lead to a patient beginning to negotiate with the therapist *now seen in this way*, a sequence that is not uncommon. It can become confusing if too much of the patient's reactions to the therapist are then treated as if they were only a matter of transference, unconnected to some recent reality in the therapy.

EXAMPLE 4

A patient had been at a school where teachers used to speak of masturbation as "self-abuse," and he now uses this term as his own way of speaking of it. The therapist reports a session in which she too had been using the patient's own words for masturbation.

I commented:

When I listen to you speaking here of "self-abuse" I am hearing two things that you may not be considering from the patient's point of view. First, I hear you being euphemistic, which suggests that you too may be feeling embarrassed by this. The patient is using a euphemism here as his way of speaking of masturbation, but it will not help him to feel any more able to talk about it if he feels that you too find this difficult.

I am also hearing you as if you too regard masturbation as a bad thing, literally as "self-abuse." The point I want to stress is that it is fundamental for the patient to find that there can be another view of this. It might therefore help to open up the analytic space, in which other views can be considered, if you were to be more direct in your own language—or if you are careful to indicate that you are not regarding masturbation in the same way as the patient. You could then refer to what he has been saying by referring to masturbation as: "what you have come to think of as self-abuse." That could open up some analysis of how the patient has been affected by the attitudes of others in relation to this.

Comment

I am trying to illustrate here that there always needs to be a
sufficient difference between how things are viewed by a
therapist/analyst and how they have been viewed before in a
patient's life. It is this difference that establishes the analytic
space within which to think about things differently from before.
If a therapist appears to share a patient's pathological view on
some matter, it is likely to seem confusing if the therapist then
questions the patient's view on this.

EXAMPLE 5

The day before the session being reported, a female
patient had been kept waiting by her male student
therapist. The student had not been immediately available when the patient had rung the doorbell, even though
she had arrived on time for the session.

The following day, the patient was speaking about
someone at work who had been insisting on her keeping
an appointment by being there "sharp on time." The
student naturally linked this to the previous day by
saying: "I think you are referring to yesterday when I did
not open the door to you at 2 o'clock sharp." Once again,
I felt there was something worth noticing in the student
using the patient's own words back to her. I therefore
commented:

I would like you to be the patient here, to reflect
upon how it could feel when I speak to you in terms
of being sharp on time. If I say, as you did there, "I
know that I did not open the door to you at 2 o'clock
sharp" I think that you might feel rebuked for
making a fuss about just a few minutes. In the

session this language is coming now from you, even though it is quoting from the patient's own words, and it feels like pointing the finger of blame at the patient.

Compare that with the quite different implications if I were to say to you: "You are raising the question of punctuality, which reminds me of yesterday when I failed to be punctual for your session." I am unequivocally accepting that it is my responsibility to be punctual and I had failed in that, never mind the matter of how many minutes it may have been that I was late. I think that the patient could then feel more clearly entitled to her feelings about my lack of punctuality, rather than being made to feel that she should not be getting upset over just a few minutes.

It may then not be surprising to hear that the patient responded with the comment: "Well, it *was* only a few minutes . . . It isn't that important really." It sounds as if the patient felt that her own view of this failure by the therapist had been treated as not important. She then dismisses this herself, perhaps identifying with the aggressor—the dismissive therapist.

Comment

I am wanting the student to learn here the value of abstracting the more essential theme from the detail. The question of punctuality does not so readily lead to a sense of quibbling over how long or short the delay had been.

I also want the student to recognize that there is a matter of importance being presented in the transference, but which gets deflected here. The patient is entitled to make a fuss over a failure of this sort, particularly when it is recalled that she had experienced her previous therapist as unreliable. Is this new therapist about to let her down too? In this session at least, it looks as if that anxiety is being brushed to one side as not important. The patient is thus denied the freedom to explore that negative transference here which is so crucial to her security in this second therapy.

EXAMPLE 6

Another patient, also a woman, had been in a previous attempt at therapy which had failed. One specific factor in that failure was said to have been the counselor's frequent cancellation of sessions.

Now, in this second therapy, the student therapist had canceled a session at short notice. The patient had reacted badly to this and, in the session following that cancellation, she has made multiple references to feeling insecure. She has been saying that she feels her boss wants her to leave; her husband has been rejecting her; she was late for the session because the bus driver, at the bus station where she has to change buses, had just driven off without giving her time to get on the bus. The student had then said: "I think that you are, perhaps, telling me you are not feeling very secure in your therapy with me."

I commented:

I think that your patient has been telling you very clearly that she is not feeling secure with you. We have heard of someone who may be wanting the patient to leave; someone who is felt to be rejecting of her; and someone who did not want her to be on the bus, so that she was not allowed to continue her

journey. This patient has already had to change
therapists once. The idea that this second therapy
could also be in trouble might well make her extremely anxious. She might well feel in crisis about
her therapy with you. She therefore needs to know
that you are really in touch with what it could be
meaning to her. It might even mean having to
change again to another therapist.

When I trial-identify with the patient here, your
use of "perhaps" suggests to me that you are not
really registering what a crisis this could be for the
patient. Also, "not feeling very secure" sounds as if
you are again minimizing the insecurity the patient
could be feeling. If you had listened to what you had
in mind to say here, from the patient's point of view,
you could have picked up these points for yourself.

Comment

I make a lot of this small detail as a teaching point. There will
certainly be other occasions when this therapist will need to be
more firm than tentative, so it is worth learning about this
now. A patient who is in crisis needs to have a clear sense of the
analyst/therapist being genuinely in touch with this fact,
feeling some of the impact of that crisis as well. It is not then
enough to be commenting, as it were, from afar. But, the
opposite problem exists too—that of the therapist appearing
too sure.

EXAMPLE 7

A patient has been describing a row with his wife after
which she had walked out. The male student therapist

said: "You must have felt very rejected." The patient replied: "I suppose so," and continued to talk about feeling that his wife had just not understood what the row had been about.

I commented:

I am concerned about two things here. First, you say that the patient *must* have felt rejected. Why must he have felt that? I think that you may be putting yourself too literally into the patient's shoes here.

When we try to trial-identify with the patient we need always to bear in mind that we are not literally putting *ourselves* into the patient's shoes. That is almost bound to be misleading as we are then likely to note what *we* might have felt in that situation rather than what the patient may have felt. So, in trial-identifying, we need to use all that we know about the patient in trying to explore what the patient might feel in that situation.

If we bear in mind what else we know about this patient we may remember that he has been playing with the idea of provoking his wife to leave, with a view to staying in the marital home and bringing his girlfriend in to live there with him. He also likes to put his wife in the wrong. So, he may well have felt all sorts of other things here than just feeling rejected. For instance, he might have felt triumph.

As we actually do not know what this patient felt we might be able to help him to reflect upon his own feelings here. It would have been enough to say: "It is not clear to me what you felt about her leaving." The patient could then begin to clarify this, if he wishes. And, in this particular session, I hear the patient replying that he felt not understood—by someone. That could be some unconscious supervision by the patient. He may have felt not understood by you.

Comment

I would like to note several points about my response here. I am, as so often, teaching about technique. But, as in an earlier example, I also find myself using the plural here—"we." I have sometimes thought of this as the plural of supervision. I try not to stay too much with "I" and "You," as if I am telling the supervisee what he or she might do. I think that can all too easily be experienced as undermining, even persecutory. I am therefore putting myself alongside the supervisee, trying to consider different options, speaking of what "we" might notice and what "we" might say.

I am also illustrating here the value of using a stance of not-knowing, as a way of encouraging the patient to reflect, rather than too often seeing interpretation as making *statements* about the patient's unconscious. We are frequently in a position where we cannot be that certain, so it is necessary to develop ways of enabling the process of joint exploration with the patient. This also creates a less confrontational style of working, which for many patients is more appropriate. And it does not have to be just a matter of asking questions which can be experienced as intrusive and controlling.

EXAMPLE 8

A patient has been in therapy for 2 years as a student training case. The patient is now talking of ending. At one point in a session the student reports having said: "I think that you are taking flight into health because you are afraid of what else we need to face in your therapy. And,

if you take flight from this, you will find that you can't get
away from yourself and you will eventually regret ending
prematurely."

I commented:

I am unhappy about this for a number of reasons.
First, "flight into health" is jargon. Could we not find
some other way of addressing this so that we do not
invite an intellectualization of the problem? Second,
we do not *know* why this patient is wanting to leave.
It could be that she is anxious about whether she
will be less welcome as a low-fee patient when she
has served her time as a training case. (She had
discovered early in her treatment that her therapist
was a student.) Third, you build upon your untested
hypothesis (that this is flight into health) before you
have determined whether that is even a relevant
point here. And then you can be heard as threatening the patient with internal consequences if she
leaves.

Comment

I think that there are critical object lessons to notice here.
Some students do slip into intellectualizing the process, with
the use of jargon as part of that. Also, I want the student to
notice when there is an untested hypothesis already being
built on, which can easily happen in a two-tier interpretation.
And I want the student to recognize the need to explore what
the various strands might be in this idea of leaving just now, as
there are likely to be several elements in this—not just one. In
addition, we must notice when an interpretation can be experienced as a threat, and not just as a cautionary warning.
Patients can be very seriously disturbed by this kind of inter-

pretation and the therapist's contribution to that disturbance is, I think, sometimes overlooked.

CONCLUDING REMARKS

As well as illustrating some specific technical issues, I have been trying to give a more general sense of encouraging students to learn about technique for themselves within the ongoing process of a session. Another step in this, which I have not illustrated here, is when I encourage students to share their own thoughts of internal supervision as an integral part of their presentation of a session.

For all analysts and therapists, as well as students, there will always be more to learn about technique. In most sessions there are technical points to notice and different ways of dealing with them. Learning to trial-identify with the patient is therefore a necessary step in learning to recognize what the issues are, the different options, and the implications of each for the patient. This can then become a natural part of the process of internal supervision, which in turn becomes the heir to formal supervision.

There will of course be much else that is necessary in any supervision of a student therapist/analyst, beyond what I have discussed here. But I hope to have shown some ways in which we can in particular foster the autonomy that students need to have begun to acquire before being qualified to work without supervision.

REFERENCES

Casement, P. J. (1985). *On Learning from the Patient*. London: Tavistock Publications.

———(1991). *Learning from the Patient*. New York: Guilford

(which includes Casement [1985] together with *Further Learning from the Patient* [1990]). London: Routledge.

Crick, P. (1991). Good supervision: On the experience of being supervised. *Psychoanalytic Psychotherapy* 5:235–245.

Langs, R. J. (1978). *The Listening Process.* New York: Jason Aronson.

Sterba, R. (1934). The fate of the ego in analytic therapy. *International Journal of Psycho-Analysis* 15:117–126.

11

Collusive Selective Inattention To the Negative Impact Of the Supervisory Interaction*

LAWRENCE EPSTEIN, PH.D.

---

* I want to thank Dr. Irwin Hirsch for his critical commentary on this paper which included several useful suggestions.

It has become increasingly clear to me that the traditional tutorial psychoanalytic supervisory relationship, because of its authoritarian tilt, may easily lead both participants to collude in a process of selective inattention. This collusion is to indications of the negative impact of supervision on the supervisee and on his functioning with the patient under supervision. It is my aim in this paper to identify and discuss those features of supervisory practice which are likely to disadvantage the supervisee and the treatment relationship; and to suggest how the supervisory relationship might be conducted so as to minimize its potential for negative influence and to limit the development within the relationship of tacit agreements to take no notice of signs of this influence.

Fiscalini (1985) has discussed the issue of parataxic interferences in the supervisory relationship. He derives his understanding of such interferences mainly from a retrospective review of the varying impact of two successive supervisory relationships on himself and on his treatment of the same patient during the period that Fiscalini was a candidate in psychoanalytic training. The first supervisor focused mainly on Fiscalini's failures to confront "the patient's hostile security operations and his self-centered disregard for others." Fiscalini writes, "My initial sympathy with the patient's plight and empathic feel for his anxiety were gradually submerged in a one-sided emphasis on his hostile and alienating defensive operations" (p. 594). Fiscalini's second supervisor:

> . . . soon diagnosed the parataxic difficulty between the patient and myself, helping me to see the impact of my anxiety and anger on the analytic relationship. . . . In the supervisory situation, the supervisor focused on my anxiety in the supervision as well as on my anxiety in the analysis. . . . As I became more secure in the analytic relationship and in supervision and grasped my parataxic participation in both, the analytic inquiry became broader and deeper . . . and in time, the patient began to show genuine concern and sympathy for others in his life and he became better able to see them and himself realistically (p. 596).

It is striking that the actual emotional impact of the supervisor's conduct of the supervision on the supervisee and on its carryover to the supervisee's conduct of the treatment has received scant attention in the psychoanalytic literature. It has been mentioned but not elaborated, in papers by Searles (1962) and Gediman and Wolkenfeld (1980).

The subject has, however, been studied in depth by Doehrman (1976) in a setting for the training of clinical psychologists.

Among Doehrman's conclusions, the following are noteworthy:

> . . . if [the] transference-countertransference binds which developed in the supervisory relationship had not been recognized and worked through, the supervisory and therapeutic process would have suffered. Supervision had

to become something more than a didactic or consultative experience. . . . It seems reasonable . . . to generalize that all supervisors should be extremely sensitive to unknown and intense effects that they will have upon their supervisees, as well as the effects their supervisees may have upon them, and not assume that their relationship with a trainee is a simple didactic one. . . . Almost exactly at the points where the resolutions of the transference binds in the supervisor-therapist relationships occurred, resolutions of the transference binds in the therapist-patient relationships also occurred and the emotional climate of both relationships changed (p. 76).

A candidate-in-training recently provided me with a clear example of such "unknown and intense effects" of supervisor upon supervisee.

During a session with his patient, the supervisee found himself unable to concentrate on what the patient was talking about. His attention kept drifting away and he found himself preoccupied with personal concerns. Unable to bring this process of involuntary distraction to a halt, he decided to associate to the problem. He recalled his experience of the last supervisory session in which this patient was discussed. At a certain point in the session, his supervisor began to talk about his own work with a similar kind of patient. The candidate remembered feeling slightly unsettled by this but resolved the matter by thinking to himself as follows: "Oh, that's good. He's treating me like a peer." It came to him, while associating, that he had actually suppressed feelings of being emotionally abandoned by his supervisor, and he then understood that he had been unwittingly and uncontrollably subjecting his patient to similar mistreatment.

In this example, the impact of the supervisor's empathic failure was apparently so subtle as to lead the supervisee to suppress his negative thoughts and feelings so that they remained at the level of unformulated experience.[1]

I think it is reasonable to infer from this example, as well as from Fiscalini's experience and Doehrman's research, that the treatment relationship is likely to be especially vulnerable to a carryover of negative impact from the supervisory relationship when the supervisee's experience of such negative impact is unformulated. In order to limit the development of this problem, or to correct for it, it would be important for the supervisor to develop a relationship with the supervisee in which the supervisee is enabled, with a minimal sense of risk, to contact and put into words whatever negative thoughts and feelings he may be experiencing vis-à-vis the supervisor or the supervision.

In the traditional tutorial supervisory relationship, the supervisor is generally not interested in the problem of his potential negative impact. Such information may actually be unwelcome. Should the supervisor have an actual aversion to discovering any negative impact he might be having, the supervisee is likely to join him in a tacit collusion to be selectively inattentive to such matters.[2]

My own awareness of the problem of collusive selective inattention as a pitfall of the traditional tutorial supervisory relationship has emerged mainly from experiences of supervisory failure and near-failure and from my participation in the process of group supervision both as a group member and as a group supervisor. Before discussing those features of group supervision which both limit the operation of selective inattention and facilitate awareness of subtle signs of negative super-

---

1. See Stern (1983).

2. Lesser (1983) stresses the importance of the supervisor's conducting "an indepth inquiry into and analysis of each member's transferences and countertransferences which are directly experienced by and observable to one another. . . ." (p. 127).

visory impact, I want to define what I mean by the traditional tutorial supervisory relationship and to discuss its built-in pitfalls.

THE TRADITIONAL TUTORIAL MODEL

In this model, following the example of my own supervisors, I would monitor my supervisee's treatment of his patient, teaching him to listen for derivatives of unconscious processes and to understand the genetic and dynamic meaning and function of variations in the transference. I would call attention to subjective countertransference interferences and help the supervisee identify the objective component of the countertransference experience and to learn how to address this component as data in order to better understand the patient's ongoing unconscious processes. I would routinely call attention to lapses in maintaining the treatment frame, to failures to set appropriate limits, to errors of intervention, to lapses of observation and understanding, and to lost opportunities for making facilitating interventions. I would confront the supervisee with such resistances to the supervisory process as came to my attention: lateness, absences, sloppy preparation, desultory presentation of material, etc.

The implicit definition of tasks in this tutorial approach would seem to be the following: the supervisor's task is to guide, advise, and teach, by informing, correcting, challenging and confronting; the supervisee's task is to learn, and it is hoped the supervisee's analyst will deal with those characterological or neurotic problems that constitute interferences to the supervisee's capability for assimilating and integrating his supervision experience.

The main focus of this approach is the patient-therapist relationship. As the patient becomes more difficult to treat and/or as the supervisee shows himself to be more at a loss as to how to treat his patient, the supervisor, should he follow his natural inclinations to get the therapy situation under control, will be found, increasingly, to attempt to influence the supervisee to treat the patient as he, himself, would. Thus supervision can easily become a process in which the supervisor attempts to treat the patient through the supervisee.[3] Should such be the case, the needs and feelings of the patient become more important to the supervisor than the needs and feelings of the supervisee, with ensuing negative effects.

In the traditional supervisory context neither the concept nor the practice of participant-observation seems to apply to the supervisor's conduct of the supervision. Both participants, therefore, are likely to be selectively inattentive to any negative impact that the supervisory process might be having.

AN EXPERIENCE OF SUPERVISORY FAILURE

I was consulted by an analyst who, a year earlier, was graduated from an institute in which he said he had been exposed to varying and somewhat diverging points of view regarding both theory and practice. He said that since graduating he had been in a state of confusion. He wanted help in gaining a clearer grasp of the analytic process. He no longer wanted to operate "by the seat of his pants." He felt especially ineffective in treating a number of difficult borderline patients. He said that he was consulting me because he had heard from others who had taken classes and supervision with me that I had an effective approach to treating such patients and that in my approach I had integrated different points of view. He also hoped to get some help in dealing with his countertransference.

When the supervisee began to present cases, it became clear

---

3. Fiscalini (1985) has aptly termed this, "analysis by ventriloquism."

immediately that things were much as he had said they were. Because he had little understanding of the resistances presented by his difficult patients, he was very frustrated and intervened ineffectively under the sway of intense negative countertransference feelings.

I found him very easy to supervise. He was very cooperative with my suggestions for getting the cases he was presenting under control.

> One case in particular was upsetting to him and was, in fact, going very badly. A married female patient complained incessantly and repetitiously about the way people in her life were treating her. She frustrated all of his efforts to get her interested in understanding anything, and when she wasn't complaining, she talked trivia. In his efforts to get her to make some sort of meaningful connections, the supervisee invariably found himself in a sadomasochistic interaction. He found himself criticizing her and attempting to control her, sometimes verging on being punitive. He felt guilty and terrible about himself as a therapist. I explained that the patient was using the same passive-aggressive tactics with the supervisee that she had used all of her life with her mother, and that she was currently using with her husband, and that these tactics came into play whenever she was found wanting or was criticized. I suggested that the patient probably needed, at this time, to use the therapy sessions as an emotional toilet into which she could evacuate her accumulated emotional debris and, should that be the case, she needed the therapist to do nothing more, for the time being, than to tolerate the situation. I suggested that the face-to-face situation was probably overstimulating to this patient and that she would probably feel more relaxed and be less troublesome on the couch. I suggested that, for the time being, the supervisee make no interpre-

tations, nor ask probing questions, nor attempt to get the patient to understand anything that she wasn't interested in understanding. I suggested too that he restrict his interventions either to occasional comments reflecting some empathic understanding of the patient's feelings or to questions that had only the purpose of clarifying some information given by the patient.

The supervisee followed my suggestions. He no longer felt provoked to treat his patient sadistically, and her functioning in her outside life showed progressive improvement. The supervisee, however, felt very uncomfortable with this way of practicing. He complained that he did not feel like an analyst with his patient, that he felt useless and that it made no sense to him that the patient should progress in such a context. He felt like a fraud and, out of his need to feel legitimate, he felt strong urges to explain to the patient what I had explained to him about this toilet situation. I told him that the patient would be unlikely to welcome such information, that she would probably feel criticized and that he might soon find himself treating her sadistically. I told him that he had two ungratifying choices: to feel like a useless fraud or to feel like a sadist and that it would be better for his patient if he chose the former. I explained that at this stage of the treatment his patient, in order to feel secure and comfortable, apparently needed to feel in control of the treatment relationship. She needed the therapist, for the time being, to function as a self-object rather than as a separate person with a mind of his own. His countertransference reactions of feeling underemployed or useless were, therefore, nothing more than the normal counterpart of his patient's self-object transference. Sooner or later, I said, when his patient was more ready to bring her aggression out into the open, she would probably begin to find fault with his lack of input. He would then be in a good position to investigate what other interventions might be of use.

In a similar way, I helped the supervisee with his other difficult treatment situations. For the most part, he got them under control, and his patients were doing well.

At the end of the eighth session, the supervisee, giving me some reason that I did not believe, informed me that he was unable to continue supervision at this time. He thanked me for the help I had given him and said that he would like to return at a later date. This was many years ago and he never again contacted me for supervision.

My first reaction was to feel both terrible about myself and intense anger and contempt for the supervisee. When I asked myself what it was that I had done wrong, the answer that came to me was embarrassingly simple. While I was focused on helping this supervisee to function effectively with his patients, I neglected his more basic problem, namely, his complex of terrible feelings about himself as a therapist. In being so successful in helping him with his patients, I failed to consider the possibility that I was making him feel so stupid and inadequate about his own analytic understanding and therapeutic skill that he probably came to find the supervision unbearably painful. It might have made the situation more emotionally tolerable for my supervisee had I—before displaying my quick and confident understanding of his induced countertransference—taken his complaints about feeling fraudulent and useless seriously enough to investigate them thoroughly and empathically.[4]

---

4. My conclusion concerning the main reason for my supervisee's abrupt termination has been criticized as taking insufficient account of other possible motives. In the absence of any confirmatory data, this criticism is, of course, warranted. The issue of the rightness or wrongness of my conclusion, however, is of less importance to me than

My own bad feelings about this fiasco are eased somewhat by a feeling of camaraderie with Freud (1905). I am reminded of his being cut off by Dora at the peak of his analytic potency after less than three months of treatment. The problem was that whatever Dora might have felt she wanted or needed was irrelevant to Freud. According to Erikson (1964) Dora needed Freud to affirm the actuality of her experience of having been, as an adolescent, so ill-used by the significant adults in her life. As Freud saw it, what Dora needed was the analysis of her unconscious conflicts.

My supervisee's need to have his low self-esteem as an analyst taken into account was for me irrelevant to the project of teaching him how to do more effective therapeutic work.

GROUP SUPERVISION

Now let me describe group supervision as I have experienced it as a group member and as I now conduct it as a group supervisor. The work is done on two levels. The supervisees present current cases with which they are experiencing difficulty. The supervisor, using the group, works with the presenting supervisee in such a way as to enable him to resolve the ongoing impasse with his patient. The more experienced the supervisee, the more likely are his problems rooted in a countertransference resistance than in technical ignorance. The second level is the process level. The group supervisor is alert to ongoing tensions that might be building up within the group and interfering with the work of supervision. He works with the group members' resistance to verbalizing whatever latent or withheld thoughts and feelings they might be having

---

its value in alerting me to the ever-present possibility of my negative impact.

in response to each other, the leader, or the supervisory situation. Following the resolution of such resistances, the group is enabled to bring their intellectual and emotional resources more fully to bear on the task of supervision. The group supervisor's method of dealing with group resistances constitutes a paradigm that seems to become internalized and carried over to the supervisees' work with their patients.

In the process of conducting group supervision the supervisor gets feedback that is rarely forthcoming in the one-to-one tutorial situation. From such feedback I have learned the following:

Most standard supervisory interventions that are spontaneously offered to the presenting supervisees, either by myself or by others, are likely to be experienced as unhelpful or critical, making the supervisee feel anxious, wrong and inadequate, thereby increasing his reluctance to present cases in the group. In effect this means that the "supervisory impulse," if acted upon without being internally processed for its possible impact on the other, is, more likely than not, to be unresponsive to the supervisee's need.

I also learned that the more I follow the practice of explaining and formulating whatever it is that I might feel like formulating and explaining, the more I will be admired by the group members yet the worse they will feel about themselves. The connection between my behavior and the supervisees' reactions is not usually immediately apparent either to myself or to them. They might report during the group session that they are feeling depressed, or they might later report that they left the session feeling depressed, or during a given session members might report that they feel some resistance to being in the group that day. It is through investigating such symptomatic negative reactions that the latent connection becomes clear.

A MODIFIED SUPERVISORY APPROACH

Such is the power of the reverse parallel process that it applies as well to the unconscious transmission of the supervisor's positive impact to the treatment situation. More than this, the supervisory process can profoundly influence such processes of internalization as the assimilation of enduring therapeutic values and enduring identifications with the supervisor. For this reason I have become increasingly interested in understanding how the supervisory relationship might be conducted so that the supervisor's treatment of the supervisee can be internalized with good effect.

In considering how my supervisory approach has changed in response to the above considerations, I would conclude that there are two main revisions. One is that I make a conscious effort to focus no less of my interest and attention on the supervisee than on his work with his patient. This means that I attempt to take full account of his feelings and reactions vis-à-vis both the supervisory and treatment situations. The other revision is the application to the supervisory relationship of the practice that I have termed, following Sullivan (1940), active-participant-observation (Epstein 1982).

This practice requires the supervisor to be consistently alert to the impact of his personality style, his interventions, and of the entire supervisory process on the supervisee. It requires him to be ready at all times to investigate this impact and to enable the supervisee to put his feelings and reactions into words with a minimal accompanying sense of risk. The management of the supervisee's gradient of anxiety—in working with his resistances, both to the supervisory process and to the therapeutic interaction—becomes as important in the supervisor's conduct of the supervisory interaction as is the management of the patient's gradient of anxiety in the therapist's conduct of the therapeutic interaction. The practice of participant-observation models is an interactional process that becomes internalized by the supervisee and is carried over to his work with his patients.

Now I would like to move from the general to the specific.

In applying participant-observation to a new supervisory relationship, I am, to begin with, less focused on how I treat the supervisee than I am on studying his reactions to my interventions. As I learn how he is affected, I adjust my communications accordingly. I take notice, for instance, of his facial expressions and body language. I notice behaviors that signify anxiety such as nail biting or fidgeting. One supervisee would signal a heightening of anxiety by frantic note-taking. Should I comment that I seem to be making the supervisee uncomfortable, I am alert to whether my comment enables him to elaborate his thoughts and feelings vis-à-vis his experience of the supervision or whether he becomes more defensive or self-conscious. I ask myself such questions as: Should I back off? Should I ask the minimum number of questions—and only out of a need for clarification? Should I wait until the supervisee contacts me or should I respond to signs he may be giving of needing something from me?

I operate on the assumption that persisting negative behaviors, such as lateness or missing sessions, are resistances signifying negative reactions to the supervision. I might ask, "What is there about the way I am conducting this supervision that might be making you less than eager to get here?" Should the supervisee fail to carry out agreed upon interventions, I would ask him what he felt was wrong with the intervention and/or the supervision. It may turn out that his failure to intervene effectively is due to intense negative countertransference reactions toward the patient which he needs help in contacting and putting into words. He may, for instance, discover that unwittingly he has been withholding potentially helpful interventions because of unformulated hateful thoughts and feelings toward a patient who has been tormenting him.

More often than not when a patient is going into a decline,

it is due to the therapist's failure to enable the patient to put ongoing, selectively inattended negative feelings about the therapist and the therapy into words. This usually requires the supervisor to resolve the supervisee's resistance to receiving and accepting such feelings from his patient. This is most effectively done by resolving the supervisee's resistance to contacting and expressing any feelings of disappointment and dissatisfaction he might be having vis-à-vis the supervision and the supervisor. An effective approach to resolving this resistance is to suggest to the supervisee that since the patient is continuing to get worse, there must be something wrong with the supervision and that the supervisee's help is needed in discovering what it is that is wrong. If the supervisor can overcome his own resistance to accepting, as a simple matter of fact, that the supervision is failing the supervisee, he will be in a good position to initiate a process that results in the therapist helping the patient contact and communicate feelings of being failed by the therapist—as the patient was by his parents—thereby transforming a passive-aggressive, treatment-destructive, negative therapeutic reaction into an open and direct expression of dissatisfaction and disappointment.

I favor, whenever possible the use of what Spotnitz (1969) has termed "object-oriented questions" as contrasted with "ego-oriented questions." These questions direct the supervisee's attention to the faults of the other, to myself, or to the patient, rather than to his own faults. This technique might appear to further the supervisee's tendency to externalize responsibility for his own contribution to the failure of the supervision or of the treatment situation. Actually it has the opposite effect. Object-oriented questions establish an atmosphere in which the supervisee becomes increasingly free, with a minimal sense of risk, to contact and directly communicate all of his feelings vis-à-vis both the supervision and his patient. The supervisee's experience of having his negative thoughts and feelings matter-of-factly received and accepted by the supervisor becomes transmuted into a greater capability for identifying, articulating, and tolerating his own faults and errors.

When the supervisee reports interventions that strike me as incorrect or ill-timed, I work hard to stifle my impulse to offer correction immediately. I try to wait until there is some evidence either that the intervention didn't take or that it has resulted in a negative therapeutic reaction. At that point I might ask the supervisee what he was attempting to accomplish with the intervention. Did he think his purpose was accomplished? If not, why not? In responding to this sequence of questions, the supervisee may contact selectively inattended anxiety aroused by something in the therapeutic interaction.

As an example of this, recently a supervisee reported that she reminded her patient that the patient had been treated badly by her brothers in the past. Because this intervention not only seemed to be irrelevant but also turned out to be disruptive to the flow of the session, I asked the supervisee what she had in mind in making this intervention. In response to my inquiry the supervisee recalled that she was beginning to feel anxious at that moment in the session. This was in response to her sense that the patient was running out of material. She realized that she wanted to keep the patient talking in order to prevent her from reaching the point where she would begin to complain about the therapy and question its usefulness. The intervention, in other words, was unwittingly designed to keep things going in order to enable the therapist to avoid experiencing the feeling of being a bad-, or no-good-therapist.

As a way of furthering the aim of enabling the supervisee to internalize the practice of participant observation, I am in favor of his making whatever interventions he may be inclined to make followed by a non-critical study of their positive or negative effects.

I place a great emphasis on working with the supervisee's countertransference reactions. This is especially important in supervising situations involving borderline and psychotic patients. I am referring to feelings of inadequacy, impotence, helplessness, stupidity, confusion, frustration, anger, hate, sadism, contempt, disgust, punitive feelings, wishing the patient dead, sexual feelings, and so forth. Supervisees will feel themselves to be gravely at fault for having such feelings and desires and are likely to be ashamed of themselves if they have been indoctrinated with the concept that analytic neutrality means emotional neutrality (Reich 1951, 1960). Emotional neutrality is a myth, and I believe that it may be dangerous for a patient if his therapist actually assumes that he can operate from a position of emotional neutrality.

When strong countertransference feelings are aroused in response to the powerful primitive projective processes of borderline and psychotic patients, it will be difficult and, at times, impossible to prevent such feelings from seeping either into the therapist's communications or into his way of being with his patient. The best way the analyst can protect his patient from the noxious effects of negative countertransference feelings is to begin by fully owning and confronting such feelings.

Supervisees, more often than not, conclude from the very fact of having intense emotional reactions to their patients that this signifies they are doing bad therapy. Frequently, in such a context, when asked if a patient is doing badly, the supervisee may say, matter of factly, that the patient is doing well—as if the patient's progress were something apart from, and having no connection with, this "bad therapy" of which the therapist presumes himself guilty. Usually the supervisee will resist any effort to address the issue of how or why it might be possible for the patient to be doing well in such a negative emotional context. He may be incapable of thinking seriously about such questions until he is enabled to accept all of his feelings and adopt a relaxed and tolerant attitude toward them.

I attempt to accomplish this by asking such questions, as "What is wrong with hating the patient?", "Wishing him dead?", "Wanting to have sex with the patient?" and so forth. If the supervisee complains that he feels helpless or impotent I would ask, "How does the patient prefer him to feel?", "Does the patient prefer him to feel like a good-competent-analyst or like a bad-incompetent one?"

I generally compare feelings to the weather. There is nothing you can do about a bad weather system except to wait for it to pass through the area.

I work to enable the supervisee ultimately to value his feelings, whatever they may be, and to understand that in owning and containing them, rather than acting on them, he will be performing an essential, maturationally corrective function for his more disturbed patients. He will be, in effect, breaching a lifelong, compulsively repetitious, interpersonal vicious cycle of projection and counterprojection which has kept such patients fixated in their state of developmental arrest.

Once the supervisee learns to value the feelings that are aroused in the therapeutic interaction, he will be in a better position to understand something about their meaning and function in the context of the ongoing therapeutic interaction and to formulate what he might do with such feelings in order to benefit his patient. Should he contain them and protect his patient from them, should he convey them in tones of speech? Should he use them to formulate questions or interpretations?

I shall illustrate this approach presenting three clinical vignettes.

VIGNETTE ONE

A supervisee, with considerable discomfort, presented a male patient whom he was treating. He described his own experience in the treatment as alternating between "being lost and being found." Occasionally there were moments or possibly a whole session in which he felt he understood the patient and felt comfortable in interacting with him. For the most part, however, he felt lost, confused, stupid and very inadequate.

He made this presentation at a moment of crisis. The patient had just informed him that he was quitting therapy because he had become addicted to cocaine. He had concealed this addiction throughout the course of treatment. He had just applied to a drug program, but this was not why he wanted to leave the therapy. He wanted to leave the therapy because he felt he had ruined it. He had agreed to come back for another session to discuss the matter further. The therapist said he had no idea what to do with this patient, and he felt like a total failure.

I asked the therapist if he thought there might be some way in which his feelings were related to the patient's feelings. The therapist said yes and elaborated on how the patient probably felt lost, confused, like a failure, but that he covered this up with a "macho" manner. The supervisee also suspected that the patient needed to use cocaine in order to enable him to maintain this "macho" exterior and to contain himself, because he was probably terrified of falling apart or going crazy.

The supervisee remembered that the patient grew up in a household dominated by a "macho" father who often lost control and went into terrifying rages. In reflecting on the way the patient behaved in the sessions with him, he realized that there were many cues that the patient was internally very agitated. He would, for instance, hit himself very hard on the knee for emphasis while talking.

After very little discussion the supervisee was able to understand that the patient probably needed his therapist to contain and ride out the emotional turbulence induced by the therapeutic interaction. The supervisee found himself able to do this the next time that he was with the patient, and he reported that it had an immediate soothing effect.

In this example the therapist's countertransference resistance, or more accurately, his resistance to his countertransference, was mainly based on a lack of understanding as to how he might use this experience to understand the therapeutic interaction and to gain control of it. Once he reached this understanding, he was able to implement it successfully, indicating the relative absence of subjective factors that might have interfered with his capability of using such understanding.

VIGNETTE TWO

This vignette involves a therapist who was quite capable of tolerating her induced feelings and was quite sophisticated in understanding how they might be used therapeutically. In the situation presented for supervision, however, subjective factors had to be dealt with before she could be relieved of her countertransference resistance and be enabled to use the countertransference experience to work effectively with this therapeutic situation. The therapist presented the situation in two stages. It involved a couple which consisted of her primary patient, and her patient's husband. The patient married this man after two years of therapy, knowing that he was very immature and a heavy cocaine user. The marriage soon began to deteriorate. Each partner felt abused and misunderstood and uncared for by the other. The husband was referred by the supervisee to a number of competent therapists, all of whom he rejected. He agreed to attend couple sessions, but only with the supervisee.

Under pressure from the wife, the supervisee began

couple sessions. They turned out to be chaotic. Both husband and wife persistently made destructive communications to each other. The husband frequently would disrupt the sessions by walking out.

The supervisee felt both hopeless and helpless. In supervision she began to feel all the more so by the fact that she had already tried almost every intervention that I had suggested.

The supervisee was asked how she would feel if she were able to stop seeing the couple. She said she would feel very relieved. She was then asked if there was any reason why she should not inform the couple that she was discontinuing couple sessions because she found herself incapable of getting them to behave themselves and to communicate constructively. The supervisee found this suggestion agreeable, and she decided to follow it. She also decided to continue to see the husband individually as well as the wife. She was afraid of the consequences for the marriage should she abandon him totally. Although she had found his behavior intolerable in the couple sessions, she now found him more tolerable, sometimes even likeable, in the individual sessions.

In the next supervisory session, she reported that while she continued to feel relieved at not having to suffer through conjoint sessions, she still felt greatly stressed and under a great deal of pressure to help these people, to save their marriage. She felt hopeless about succeeding. She was also very afraid of the husband's potential violence to his wife.

She was helped in supervision to elaborate her hateful feelings toward both these patients, to the husband for being what she called an infantile creep, and to the wife for marrying him and messing up the good work that she was doing before the marriage. The therapist was then asked why she found it necessary to save this marriage?

Why not let the marriage break up? She might then have the patient back in treatment by herself, like in the good-old-days. In response to this question, the therapist had the recognition that vis-à-vis this couple she found herself in the same terrible emotional situation that she experienced growing up in her family. Her younger brother, she said, almost from the time he was born, was a source of great trouble and conflict within the family. He was constantly upsetting her parents, and they were incapable of coping with him. It was her role to be the family peacemaker from the time she was a small child. She was frequently terrified that her family would break up and often felt helpless and hopeless. She realized that there were many times that she hated her brother and wished that she could get rid of him so that peace and harmony could be restored to her family life.

The supervisee was asked if she were able to give up the project of trying to save the marriage. She was also asked if, whenever she felt impotent in response to pressure from either the wife or the husband to improve the marriage, she would be able, matter-of-factly, to communicate her impotence to be of any help. The supervisee said that she found these suggestions agreeable and that she now understood that the couple, in all likelihood, had made her the depository of all mature concern and responsibility for making the marriage work. It was as if they had split off and externalized their unwanted superego and activated it in the therapist. This freed them of all internal conflict and enabled them to give full range to their infantile destructive impulses, which included defeating her every effort to help them. In succumbing to the pressure to save their marriage, the therapist understood that she was unwittingly preventing the couple from feeling any internal pressure to control their behavior toward each other.

VIGNETTE THREE

A supervisee reported that he was feeling very frustrated and abused by a female patient. She had bounced two checks and had not, as yet, made good on them. In addition, she refused to cooperate in changing her appointment time, which had been given to her at the start of the summer with the understanding that it was temporary and that she was expected to resume her regular appointment in September. The current schedule was preventing the supervisee from attending the supervisory sessions on time. It was now December and the patient continued to refuse to cooperate.

I asked the supervisee, "Why can't you tell the patient that you will discontinue treatment with her until she pays her bill? And why can't you tell her that you can no longer see her until she is ready and willing to change her appointment time as she originally agreed?" The supervisee responded as follows, "She starts to argue with me and it becomes too difficult. I feel frustrated and I begin to feel sadistic. When I get angry the patient gets terribly upset and I feel like a terrible person. I can't stand these feelings."

I commented that the supervisee seemed to be capable with other patients of setting limits and, if necessary, tolerating bad feelings.

He said there was something else. There was the matter of the referral source. The referral source is a senior colleague. The patient was a nurse who worked in the same hospital as the referral source. The supervisee was afraid to lose both the respect of the referral source and future referrals.

I asked the supervisee, "Why would the referral source lose respect for you and not send you any more patients?"

He responded, "This patient will complain that I am

mercenary and that I am sadistic and that I mistreat her. She will ruin my reputation."

At this point I was feeling a rising frustration and some annoyance, and I recognized that I was impotent to help the supervisee overcome his resistance to setting some limits that would stop his patient from torturing and bullying him. I also recognized that something of a parallel process was being created with me. I opted not to communicate my understanding of this situation to the supervisee because I had no confidence that he would experience it as helpful. I thought that at best he might find such information mildly interesting. At worst, I expected that he would feel criticized and feel worse about himself for unwittingly inducing this parallel process. I did not think that aggravating his bad feelings would enable him to function more effectively with his patient.

I decided, instead, to extricate myself from the parallel process by matter-of-factly and comfortably signifying my acceptance of my failure to have any direct influence on him. By disengaging myself in this way, I hoped that I might indirectly enable the supervisee to take appropriate action vis-à-vis his patient. I said the following: "Since you are unwilling to upset the patient because you can't stand feeling like a bad person and since you can't take a chance on having the patient ruin your reputation and your referral source, the situation seems hopeless to me. I can see no alternative, for the time being, to your continuing to be abused and frustrated by this patient."

The supervisee later reported that in the next session with his patient he informed her that he was discontinuing further sessions until she paid him what she owed him and until she agreed to come at an alternative time. The patient, not at all upset, said that it made sense to her that therapy sessions should be discontinued until she was able to catch up financially. She said that she would pay her bill as soon as possible so that she could resume her sessions. The supervisee said he was very satisfied with this solution and he was confident that the patient would soon be returning to treatment at a more agreeable appointment time.

CONCLUDING DISCUSSION

I would summarize the main features that differentiate the approach put forth in this paper from the traditional tutorial method of supervision as follows:

The supervisor works to enable the supervisee to contact and put into words, with a minimal accompanying sense of risk, the widest possible range of negative thoughts and feelings vis-à-vis the supervisor, the supervision, and his patient. In this way the development of tacit collusion between supervisor and supervisee to ignore indications of the supervisor's possible negative impact, either on the supervisee or on his work with the patient under supervision, is limited, and, the supervisee is helped to protect his patient from toxic countertransference feelings.

The supervisor's attentiveness to the supervisee's needs and feelings, along with his practice of active-participant-observation, constitute a paradigm of interpersonal relatedness that the supervisee may be expected to internalize and carry over to his work with his patients with good effect. The relational aspect of this supervisory approach, then, is no less, and possibly more, a fundamental source of learning than are the more straightforward didactic communications of the supervisor.

I would expect that this model of supervision is less compatible than is the traditional tutorial model with the aims and practices of the training committees of most psychoanalytic institutes. The primary concern of training committees is, typically, to oversee and evaluate the candidate's assimilation of supervision. Its aim is to keep itself and the supervisee informed about those of his limitations which may be retarding his progress toward becoming a competent enough analyst to be certified as such and graduated by the institute. It is generally considered to be the supervisee's responsibility to correct his deficiencies.

In the model put forth in this paper, the supervisor monitors and evaluates the supervisee's assimilation of the supervision, but with a different purpose: namely, to ascertain the effectiveness of his own conduct of the supervisory relationship. If he notes that the supervision is not taking, before ascribing fault to the supervisee, the supervisor assumes responsibility for investigating and determining how his conduct of the supervision might be contributing to the supervisee's difficulties. He then attempts to revise his approach accordingly.

Thus there is no more pressure placed on the supervisee to progress in the supervision than would be placed on a patient in analysis. Here the view taken of progress is essentially a maturational one. Because of this it might be argued that treating the supervisee in this way implies some disrespect for him as a responsible adult. I can only say that in my experience this approach generally successful in facilitating steady progress toward both psychoanalytic competence and mature professionalism. In this interpersonal context, the supervisee seems to experience himself as being more consistently respected as an adult than in the more authoritarian tutorial relationship. In the latter, because he receives a steady flow of communications informing him about his errors and faults, he often finds himself in the emotional position of a bad and deficient child.

The traditional method of psychoanalytic training and supervision, despite its authoritarian tilt, has worked well enough to achieve its main aim, which is to graduate competent analysts. Because it works and because it is subject neither to internal nor external pressure to change, like any ongoing system, it is likely to resist change. For this reason a more maturationally oriented approach can be more freely practiced outside of the setting of formal psychoanalytic training.

Psychoanalytic understanding, however, despite the fact that it continues to be both essentially conservative and highly politicized, seems to be inexorably progressive. New concepts of theory and practice that prove themselves valid seem to be gradually assimilated, in one way or another—sometimes after being discovered anew—into the various schools of psychoanalytic thought. I would expect that the ideas put forth in this paper on supervisory practice will also, to the extent that they are valid, be gradually integrated with the traditional model to soften its evaluative emphasis and to correct its authoritarian tilt.

REFERENCES

Doehrman, M. J. G. (1976). Parallel processes in supervision and psychotherapy. *Bulletin of the Menninger Clinic* 40:3–104.

Epstein, L. (1982). Adapting to the patient's therapeutic need in the psychoanalytic situation. *Contemporary Psychoanalysis* 18:190–217.

Erikson, E. H. (1964). *Insight and Responsibility*. New York: Norton.

Fiscalini, J. (1985). On supervisory parataxis and dialogue. *Contemporary Psychoanalysis* 21:591–608.

Freud, S. (1905). A case of hysteria. *Standard Edition* 7:3–122. London: Hogarth.

Gediman, H. K., and Wolkenfeld, F. (1980). The parallelism phenomenon in psychoanalysis: Its reconsideration as a triadic system. *Psychoanalytic Quarterly* 49:234–255.

Lesser, R. M. (1983). Supervision: Illusions, anxieties, and questions. *Contemporary Psychoanalysis* 19:120–129.

Reich, A. (1951). On countertransference. *International Journal of Psycho-Analysis* 32:25–31.

——— (1960). Further remarks on countertransference. *International Journal of Psycho-Analysis* 41:389–395.

Searles, H. F. (1962). Problems of psychoanalytic supervision. In *Collected Papers on Schizophrenia and Related Subjects*. New York: International Universities Press.

Spotnitz, H. (1969). *Modern Psychoanalysis of the Schizophrenic Patient*. New York: Grune and Stratton.

Stern, D. B. (1983). Unformulated experience. *Contemporary Psychoanalysis* 19:71–99.

Sullivan, H. S. (1940). *Conceptions of Modern Psychiatry*. New York: Norton.

12

Supervision Amidst Abuse: The Supervisee's Perspective*

MARY GAIL FRAWLEY-O'DEA, PH.D.

*Paper presented at the Fifteenth Annual Spring Meeting of the Division of Psychoanalysis (39) of the American Psychological Association, Santa Monica, April 1995.

INTRODUCTION

It is only within the last few years that psychoanalysts began to consider once again the sexual abuse of young children and adolescents as a significant etiological factor in adult psychopathology. While few analysts today would disagree that child abuse occurs and can lead to serious psychopathology, many analysts yet have to integrate what is known about early sexual trauma and its effects into their day-to-day thinking and clinical models. Achieving that integration requires an analyst to create working space for a model of traumatogenic psychopathology in which dissociation, rather than repression, is the linchpin of psychic processes. Often, this represents a new way of conceptualizing that challenges long-held beliefs about psychopathology and treatment.

If psychoanalysis only recently began to reconsider the role of trauma in adult psychopathology and to reformulate treatment models for this group of patients, I do not think we yet have attended at all to the potential impact of trauma on the supervisory process when the supervisee is working with an adult survivor of childhood sexual abuse. If we believe that, at least to some extent, central relational configurations and themes at play between the analyst and patient are enacted in complementary or concordant (Racker 1968) patterns between supervisor and supervisee, it behooves us to consider the ways in which transference and countertransference constellations paradigmatic of work with trauma survivors come to infuse the supervisory space.

In the hope of stimulating reflection on and dialogue about this aspect of psychoanalytic work, Irwin Hirsch and I present in these chapters elements of his supervision of my analysis of a woman who had been abused sexually as a child. Over the course of the supervision and, even more clearly during subsequent discussions between us, it became increasingly evident to Irwin and me that the supervisory process had been disappointing and disorienting in ways that remained inchoate and thus unspeakable for a long time. Further, this unarticulated morass of relational reactions and enactments seemed somehow impervious to the potentially moderating effects of mutual respect, admiration, and even affection that grew between us. Irwin and I disagree, I think, as to the extent to which transference and countertransference patterns between patient and analyst generally are transmitted one way or another into the supervisory process—I say they usually are, and Irwin, I believe, is more hesitant about this—but we have come to accordance that, in this case, our supervisory relationship reflected key aspects of my work with the patient.

Before discussing the vicissitudes of my supervision with Irwin, I provide some detailed case material for you to keep in mind as you consider what Irwin and I have to say about our work together. After presenting the case data, I offer some reflections on my supervision with Irwin, suggesting ways in which I think relational configurations and themes central to the analysis were enacted within the supervision. Finally, I discuss the possible wider implications of Irwin's and my experience for other supervisory relationships when the supervisee is working with a traumatized patient.

CASE DATA: CHRISTINA

Christina, an attractive 35-year-old woman, began treatment with me 7 months prior to the inception of my supervision with Irwin. The patient had been referred to me by her best friend, who was also in analysis with me at that time.

Christina is the youngest of 4 children; she has an older sister and 2 older brothers. An apparent split appears among the children. Both women are beset by a myriad of psychological problems and functional deficits while both men seem to have extremely successful careers and warm family lives.

Christina has had almost no relationship with her sister. The sister is perceived to have been chronically depressed and withdrawn as long as Christina can remember; she is obese and, now in her late forties, has lived an isolated life with no romance and not many friends. At one point, Christina confided in her sister that she more and more suspected that she, Christina, had been abused sexually as a child; at the time the patient felt the perpetrator probably had been their father. Having lived all her adult life residing less than 1 mile from her parents' home, the sister accepted a business transfer to Hong Kong within a few months of receiving this news. Christina has not heard from her sister since the latter moved to the Far East. As for her brothers, Christina has superficial relationships with both of them.

This patient presented to treatment with no memories of her mother prior to 7 years of age. Until quite recently, Christina's mother was described as presenting two personas during the patient's childhood. On the one hand, she was a socially active volunteer with many friends who ran the household with efficiency. On the other hand,

Christina also remembered her mother as dramatically unavailable. Early in treatment, for instance, she reported a screen memory in which she banged at the door after school for what seemed to be an interminable length of time while her mother slept upstairs; the patient waited so long and was so upset that she urinated on the garage floor. Christina also recalled her mother sitting in a rocking chair in the livingroom for what seemed like hours on end simply staring into space. When the patient embarked on an adolescence marked by drug and alcohol abuse, shoplifting, stealing money from her parents, and truancy, she perceived her mother as utterly denying any problems in order to maintain an image of a perfect family. Christina, in turn, felt totally unseen.

Two very early dreams relate to Christina's mother. In the first, a child steals frozen cookies from a cupboard in her mother's kitchen then sits behind a chair in the living room eating them. In another dream, Christina is going to take a bath. There is a cupboard in which are stored frozen cookies, money, baubles. The patient thinks about stealing the cookies but does not. She gets into the tub and her mother comes bursting into the bathroom. The patient is upset and asks her mother to leave but she will not. Christina pushes and hits her mother, who says that the patient can have what is in the cupboard if the mother stays in the bathroom.

Long after supervision with Irwin ended, Christina recovered in treatment long-dissociated memories of her mother's incredibly sadistic physical and sexual torture, all of which seemed to have occurred prior to age 7. It is a dilemma for me to convey this mother's—I want to say madness—without gratuitously sensationalizing this material. Let it suffice to share one memory of an apparently recurring scene in which Christina's mother tied her in a chair and then teased her vagina, nipples, and eyeballs with the tip of a sharp kitchen knife.

Christina's father was a busy and successful internist. The patient has clear and pleasant memories of him up to age 7, no memories of him between ages 7 and 13, and, then, unhappy memories of him after age 13. The patient has a screen memory of dancing with her father in the livingroom as a very little girl, happily standing on his feet as he twirled her around the room. After age 13, she primarily recalls her father retiring to his library each evening with a bottle of Scotch and angrily rebuffing any requests for interaction with family members. While for a long time Christina believed that it was her father who had abused her sexually, it is now not clear to her what her father's role in all of this was.

In her early twenties, after years of heavy drinking, Christina moved to New York, got a job, enrolled in college, and stopped drinking. She used AA well and has remained sober and drug free for over a decade. In the late 1980s, she obtained a B.A. in history and entered an M.S.W. program. At the time of the supervision in question, Christina was a full-time social work student and she waitressed to support herself.

Throughout her life, Christina's relationships with girls and women have been problematic. She perceives that she formed "you and me against the world" friendships with one girl or woman at a time; these tended to end suddenly for reasons that remained a mystery to her. As an adult, she also forged a number of mentoree relationships with intelligent, strong, often lesbian or bisexual women. Christina typically initially reacted with an idealized, erotically-tinged transference to these women. Inevitably at some point, boundaries were crossed and Christina and the women became friends. Later, Christina became disillusioned and ended the relationships, blaming the women for not maintaining appropriate boundaries with her.

This patient's relationships with men have been equally chaotic. She did not date at all in high school and, given her baseline acting out during that period, it was initially surprising to me that she did not have intercourse for the first time until she was 19 years old. Her first lover was a man who himself was in the process of coming out of the closet as a homosexual; Christina felt that she loved him and that she was in a "desperate, unrequited, begging place" with him for a long time. In New York, Christina had sequential relationships with a man and his roommate; the first is described as purely sexual while, in the second, she seemed to pursue again an essentially unavailable man. Next, Christina lived with and became engaged to a man who regularly beat her and entered with her into sexual practices she described as bizarre; these included bondage with both of them being tied up at various times, Christina urinating in the bed to excite her fiance, and then penetrating the man with a penis-like apparatus she strapped on. She ended the engagement after a particularly brutal beating during which her fiancé broke dinnerware and then forced Christina onto the floor to clean up the broken dishes.

At the time of my supervision with Irwin, Christina was involved with a social worker. Christina initially chose this man as a supervisor because of his reputed expertise in working with sexually abused children. During the course of supervision, the supervisor began to function as a quasi therapist for Christina and then, eventually, they began an affair. After Christina broke off the affair, the man asked his wife for a divorce and moved out of the marital home. He then contacted Christina and, at the time Irwin was supervising me, they had resumed a relationship; eventually, they were married.

Throughout her life, Christina has engaged in a number of ritualized behaviors. She frequently worries her anus with a cotton swab or a finger until her anus bleeds; she experiences this as both painful and sexually stimulating. She has compulsions about urination. Particularly before going to bed, she often returns to the bathroom several times to "make sure that every drop is out" and, in the past, she has urinated in seemingly strange places such as the garbage, the kitty litter, or the hall outside her bedroom. From time to time she has injured herself as when, in a dissociated state, she banged her knee against the wall, badly damaging the knee. Finally, she sometimes finds herself "mumbling, hissing, spitting" in rage, out loud in a voice that she does not recognize as her own. Over the course of treatment, we have identified the voice as belonging to a dissociated, feisty adolescent self state. While Christina is not a true multiple personality, she is profoundly dissociated with identifiable self states, like the adolescent and 2 very little girls, that alternate in consciousness.

Christina had been in therapy several times before working with me. She felt her previous therapies had helped her to construct a better functioning persona and to cease some of the worst self-destructive behaviors. At the same time, she perceived that the "core" of her problems had yet been touched and she began thrice weekly treatment with me to try to reach these issues. At the commencement of this supervision, Christina had been in treatment 7 months. Interestingly, I had presented this case history to a previous supervisor several months before repeating it to Irwin. Although that supervisor and Irwin are markedly different men, both responded to the intake material with the same interpretation, which was that this woman had grown up in a situation analagous to that portrayed in *Blue Velvet*, a movie in which a conservative, white picket-fenced, well-gardened Southern town hides an unspeakable, bizarre, and vicious underbelly. That certainly turned out to be true.

THE SUPERVISEE'S PERSPECTIVE ON THE SUPERVISION

There are an almost unlimited number of thematic threads to follow through my treatment with Christina and my supervision with Irwin. Here, I will focus on two relational configurations enacted by Irwin and me that, in complementary and concordant ways (Racker 1968), expressed aspects of the analytic work with Christina.

Frozen Cookies: A Complementary Paradigm

Two of Christina's early dreams included frozen cookies. Perhaps the penultimate symbol of an idealized American mom is one who has warm, freshly baked chocolate chip cookies ready to serve her child when she runs in the door from school. For Christina, however, frozen cookies symbolically represented the unavailable, unseeing, but post-abuse mother—the mother rocking in a rocking chair, dissociatively staring off into space. As an adolescent, this patient often joined her mother by sitting in the same room with her in silence, seemingly for hours, also staring off disconnectedly. Neither spoke nor moved other than to rock. The alternative, however, to this frozen maternal presence was a terrifyingly dangerous mother whose liveliness or heat turned to viciously sadistic abuse.

In her treatment, Christina has, at various times, enacted both her attachment to and identification with the hot, abusive mother and with the frozen, almost catatonic mother. Of note, however, was that during my supervision with Irwin, the ambiance of my work with Christina was neither chaotically hot nor frozen. Rather, we seemed to engage easily and playfully. In retrospect, it seems to me that a primary transference to me then was as the father with whom, as a little girl, Christina comfortably and securely twirled around the living-room, dancing on his feet.

Where, then, were the frozen cookies?

Looking back from this vantage point, I suggest that, in a complementary relational configuration, Irwin and I enacted the frozenness that was missing then from the treatment with Christina. In his chapter, Irwin examines aspects of the relationship between the two of us—specifically his discomfort with my initial idealization of him and our discussion of my discovery about a week prior to beginning supervision with him that, several years before, he had supervised my analyst's work with me—that created space for and evoked frozenness. It is my belief now, however, that the relational paradigm of frozenness co-constructed by Irwin and me reflected not only our responses to each other but also bespoke a central relational theme for my patient that, at the time, was projected out of the treatment and into the supervision.

During the months that I presented Christina to Irwin, a predictable pattern emerged. As I entered the office building in which Irwin and I met, I began to feel anxious, and the anxiety increased as I sat in the waiting room. This was not the mild to moderate anxiety I might feel during any supervision but was rather, an intense, paralyzing level of anxiety which left me experiencing myself as frozen. Even at that time, I used the word frozen to describe my subjective state during the supervisory hours, although I did not make the connection then to Christina and the frozen cookies.

As the months went on and my experience of supervision continued unabated, I began to entertain a persistent fantasy in which I would rise from my chair, cross over to Irwin, place my hands on his shoulders and say, "Irwin, let's dance." The fantasy in part bespoke my own desire to enliven the supervisory relationship with a more libidinal flavor. It occurs to me now, however, that this fantasy also represented an identification with Christina's yearning to reconnect with the alive, playful, safe father of her early childhood, a relational striving she may have experienced during those afternoons of silent, frozen rocking with her mother.

That the frozenness at play between Irwin and me at least in part reflected a relational constellation complementary to that being enacted in the consultation room is supported by changes that occurred in both dyads when I changed the case being supervised. After several months, my subjective experience of supervision became so intolerable to me that I found a way to present another patient to Irwin. While, at the time, I had not found Irwin's supervision of my work with Christina to be particularly helpful, I felt that he greatly assisted me in working with the second patient. In addition, I became measurably less tense and more at ease prior to and during the supervisory hours.

What I never considered until I sat down to write this chapter and, in so doing, reviewed my process notes of Christina's treatment, was that almost immediately after I changed cases in supervision, the transference/countertransference paradigm between Christina and me shifted dramatically. In my notes, I comment on how sudden this movement seemed to me and how unprepared I was for it. Specifically, the "hot," abusive mother and the confused, abused child entered the analytic work. Christina, experiencing herself as my victim, in fact enacted her mother's vicious devaluation of her, vituperatively castigating me for weeks as being self-involved, amazingly inept, and wanting more than anything to shame her by having her need me. In turn, I countertransferentially identified with Christina as a child. I experienced myself as shocked and unfairly abused but obviously responsible for somehow transforming my patient into a crazy woman.

Well, what can we make of all this? Fairbairn's (1943) model of endopsychic structures provides one way of conceptualizing what was happening in my work with Christina and in my supervision with Irwin. It is my contention now that the relational configuration of frozenness between Irwin and me represented the dissociation from the treatment of the repressed anti-libidinal ego attached to the repressed rejecting object, in this case, Christina's attachment to and identification with the frozen, unavailable mother. Further, during these months of supervision, Christina was involved in a mentoree relationship with a female professor in which she felt an eroticized attraction to the woman while, at the same time, experiencing her as self-centered and exploitative. This relationship, I believe, represented enactment of the repressed libidinal ego attached to the repressed exciting object, or Christina in relationship to her alluring but abusive mother. The dissociation and enactment outside the consultation room of both bad object relationships left Christina and me free for several months to relate in a paradigm involving her central ego cathected to me as an external, idealized object. The ambiance of the treatment during this period was playful, safe, and warm. We enjoyed each other's company and both of us looked forward to the sessions. Although both of us were aware intellectually that our relationship would not be always so carefree, each of us seemed determined to preserve for the time being the mutually idealizing relational configuration at play between us.

In reviewing the case now, it seems to me that it may have been helpful for Christina and me to engage in a protracted period of smooth sailing in order to develop a relationship sturdy enough to weather the *Sturm und Drang* that ensued when previously dissociated relational constellations entered the analytic space. To the extent that Irwin and I enacted and contained for Christina the relationship between the anti-libidinal ego and the rejecting object, we may have enabled a vital sense of going on being (Winnicott 1962) within her treatment. It also seems possible that, when I changed cases in supervision, the container for the relational paradigm of fro-zenness was removed, subjecting the analytic dyad to the infusion of bad object relationships previously held at bay and encapsulated outside the treatment.

ARTICULATED IDEALIZATION, ACTED OUT DEVALUATION: A CONCORDANT CONSTELLATION

While the relational paradigm of frozenness was complemen-tary to that in play between me and the patient, at least one concordant (Racker 1968) relational constellation also was enacted within both dyads.

Christina began treatment consciously idealizing me. Her perception was that her friend had been changed profoundly in her work with me and Christina was sure that she would be equally transformed. She was intrigued by the idea that she was in psychoanalysis and found my willingness to discuss the relationship between us quite wonderful.

Similarly, I entered supervision with Irwin with an idealized transference. Several years before, as a doctoral student, I had heard Irwin give a paper on the participant observer model of treatment, and I still remember sitting in the audience excit-edly thinking, "This man really knows what analysis should be about!" And, although I knew that I was disturbed to learn that Irwin had at one time supervised my analyst in our work together, I was quite sure that I recalled my analyst measurably improving during what I calculated must have been the supervision with Irwin. Like Christina expecting to be as transformed by me as she assessed her friend to have been, I anticipated making at least as impressive strides in supervision with Irwin as I decided my analyst had. Since Irwin's paper had emphasized the importance of making explicit enactments occurring between analyst and patient, I looked forward particularly to a parallel process unfolding within the supervisory relationship.

That Christina's conscious idealization of me was offset by unconscious fear that I would betray her was depicted in an early dream. In the dream, Christina is running through streets in an area of her hometown that is not very nice. People are chasing her. She knows that, if she can reach the water, she will be all right. She gets to the water. A blonde, blue-eyed man is standing there. He appears to want to help her but she knows that he is an evil, Aryan type.

In discussing the dream, I suggested to Christina that she knew that I (blond, blue-eyed) was not what I seemed to be to her and that, eventually, I would betray her. Things and people not being what they appeared to be was, by then, a recurrent theme in the treatment. Christina acknowledged that it made sense to her that I was not as all good as I seemed to her then but stated that it did not *feel* that way; she consciously experienced only warm, admiring feelings.

Before Christmas, Christina and I discussed at length my upcoming vacation. She acknowledged that she would miss me but disclaimed any anger or sense of betrayal that I was leaving her during the first Christmas in her life that she would not spend with her parents. On her way back from her boyfriend's home after Christmas, Christina dozed at the wheel and ran off the road, an accident from which she was extremely lucky to escape uninjured. She had been required to leave her boyfriend's home because his children were arriving for visitation; they had not been told yet about their father's relationship with Christina. I persistently interpreted her fury at both her boyfriend and me for abandoning her and putting other relationships ahead of ours with her at such a crucial time. Again, I was met with intellectual assent but not with affective resonance.

Over the next weeks, there were no further incidents like the accident and, moreover, some of her other self-destructive behaviors like stimulating her anus until it bled abated in frequency. However, Christina reported that, after many of our sessions, to which she ostensibly looked forward with unambivalent pleasure, she drove directly to a donut shop, where she consumed up to a half-dozen donuts.

Irwin's supervision regarding the donuts brought to an apex my own disappointment in him. While I recognized that the donut consumption was a concretized, externalized expression of dissociated feelings about me and my treatment of Christina, I also felt that eating donuts was significantly less damaging than car accidents, a bleeding anus, or a bruised and banged-up body. Further, it was my assessment that Christina simply was not capable yet of directly experiencing disruptive reactions to me and that, therefore, I should not push too hard about the donuts as long as more seriously self-mutilative acts remained in abeyance. Irwin, on the other hand, suggested that I be insistent and persistent in pursuing the meaning of the donut eating. I felt trapped. On the one hand, I wanted to comply with Irwin's supervision. On the other hand, when I did, I experienced myself as unnecessarily abusing the patient. It was at about this time that I changed the case.

The donut situation brought to a head what had been growing disappointment in Irwin who, to my mind, had turned out not to be what *he* seemed. The parallel process of examining and making explicit the supervisory relationship as I was supervised to do with the patient never unfolded. To the contrary, in part due to the frozenness that pervaded the supervisory space, Irwin and I, during his supervision of my work with Christina, never addressed our own developing relationship. Concurrent with his advice that I tenaciously pursue Christina's split-off reactions to me, Irwin seemingly ignored what I perceived as clear signs of my own unspoken anger and sense of betrayal.

While Christina claimed to be unaware affectively of anything but highly positive feelings about me, I was conscious of my disappointment in Irwin. Like my patient, however, I acted out rather than directly articulated my experience of disillusionment. For instance, I was quite erratic in paying Irwin; often I had a check in my wallet for weeks before I gave it to him. Most significantly, I changed the case I was presenting. Although the reason I offered to Irwin was plausible, I actually expected to be found out and confronted. My anger was increased by the contradiction I perceived between Irwin's unyielding stance on the donuts and his apparent utter lack of awareness of my own acting out. I was frustrated and experienced myself as unseen and neglected.

As in the complementary relational configuration of frozenness between Irwin and me, there were aspects of our relationship alone, some of which Irwin will discuss, that contributed to my disappointment in Irwin and to his inattention to my acting out. I would suggest that, in addition however, this relational paradigm represented a concordance with a central transference and countertransference theme in the treatment with Christina. To the extent that this is true, Irwin enacted Christina's unseeing, neglectful mother while I identified with Christina as an enraged but silent, unseen, acting out adolescent.

WIDER IMPLICATIONS FOR THE SUPERVISORY PROCESS

Moving beyond the specifics of this case and this supervision, there are two foci of my supervisory experience with Irwin which have more general implications for supervisory dyads in which the supervisee is presenting work with an adult survivor of childhood sexual abuse. One involves the role of dissociation both in the treatment and in the supervision. The other pertains to the secondary traumatization of the analyst treating a sexually abused patient.

Dissociation

Dissociation is the hallmark of trauma. It is a process of severing connections between events that seem irreconcilably different, between events and their affective significance, between events and cognitive awareness of their meaning, or between events and their symbolic representation. Unlike repression, which is a horizontal division of conscious and unconscious mental contents, dissociation involves a vertical split of the ego which results in two or more self states that are more or less organized and independently functioning. Such dissociative states are unavailable to the rest of the personality and, therefore, are not subject to psychic operations of elaboration. Rather, they are likely to make their presence known via the emergence of recurrent intrusive images, violent or symbolic enactments, inexplicable somatic sensations, repetitive nightmares, anxiety reactions, and psychosomatic conditions.

The analyst working with a patient for whom dissociation is a primary psychic mechanism is immersed in rapidly shifting, often wildly chaotic transference and countertransference paradigms. For protracted periods of time, much that occurs in the consultation room is nonverbally enacted rather than verbally represented. It is inevitable, I think, that, like the patient, the analyst is subjected to dissociative experiences in which symbolized representations of the analytic process are submerged in more inchoate feelings, fantasies, and sensorimotor impressions. Further, it seems entirely possible that the ambiance of dissociation with which the treatment is imbued may infiltrate the supervisory process in ways that are confusing and disorganizing for both supervisor and supervisee.

Jody Davies and I (1994) suggest that successful analytic work with an adult survivor of childhood sexual abuse requires the analyst to fully enter into the dissociative world of the patient. Here I offer the hypothesis that successful supervision of the analyst treating an adult survivor may well require the supervisor to enter into the dissociative experiences of the supervisee in ways that invite symbolization and elaboration of the currently formless and unspeakable. An example illustrates the point.

About midway through the supervision with Irwin, I began to have a recurrent countertransference experience related to Christina and her mother. At times, when the patient was talking about apparently innocuous or nonconflictual aspects of her relationship with her mother, I was overcome by stark, gripping, nameless terror. So intense was my fear that I had trouble breathing and I felt as if I might faint. When asked by me about her own affective state, Christina reported feeling quite fine. Irwin interpreted this experience as signifying the patient's rage at me and wish to hurt me. I judged that I was projectively identified with a dissociated self representation of Christina and that I was containing feelings of unbearable terror that the patient once experienced in relationship with her mother.

Correct content interpretation aside, the countertransference state was overwhelming to me and remained unsymbolized for years. I suggest now that it might have been helpful had Irwin invited me to try to enter that experience during supervision where I might be able to put into words—to symbolically organize—what it was that I was feeling. The result would have been, at least in part, my own fantasies regarding what had occurred between Christina and her mother. Whether or not these fantasies accurately reflected reality, the process of entering into the dissociative experience of my patient, now located within me, might have relieved some of my own anxiety by anticipating the speaking of the unspeakable that was to come much later when Christina recovered the memories of her mother's abuse.

If supervisors *expect* that their relationship with a supervisee working with a patient whose history includes significant trauma will be marked by some degree of dissociation, they and their supervisees more likely will be attuned to those dissociative processes as they unfold within the supervision. This not only would assist the analyst in better grasping all the relational constellations pertinent to the treatment but would also intervene in the secondary traumatization of the therapist engaged in this work.

Secondary Traumatization of the Analyst

The sexual abuse and trauma literatures (Courtois 1988, Herman 1992) make clear that therapists treating adult survivors of trauma are secondarily traumatized by the work. Chaotic and kaleidoscopically shifting transference and countertransference paradigms at play within the analytic space, combined with the powerfully intense, often unsymbolized affects engendered by the work, threaten to overwhelm and, often, do overwhelm the therapist. Further, the narratives shared by these patients as they reclaim long dissociated memories and affects associated with their abuse frequently are horrifying to hear and quite literally assault the therapist with evidence of our fellow human beings' debasement and capacity for evil. Finally, the inchoate but affectively riveting fantasies and self states evoked in the analyst as she struggles to contain the patient's dissociated mental contents are disturbing, disorganizing, and, over time, take their toll on the clinician. Often, the analyst manifests symptoms of traumatization like intrusive thoughts about a patient's abuse, nightmares, exaggerated startle responses, and states of hyperarousal and psychic numbing, all secondary traumatic responses to the analytic work.

During my supervision with Irwin, I think that I was traumatized by the work with Christina. The recurrent projective identificatory experience of terror; confrontation with her chronic self-destructive behaviors like banging up her body; metabolizing dreams filled with images of betrayal, bizarre sadism, and fear; and even listening to the part of her life story that she did remember at the time, like her engagement to a batterer, often left me cognitively and emotionally overwhelmed. At the time, however, I was not aware of being secondarily traumatized. Rather, I conclude in retrospect that my own traumatization and my concurrent need for holding was expressed in supervision in an ongoing debate with Irwin about Donald Winnicott.

I had entered supervision idealizing Winnicott almost as much as I idealized Irwin! Early on, however, Irwin let me know that he disagreed fundamentally with Winnicott's conceptualizations of pathology and treatment and, further, was annoyed that Winnicott somehow seemed to escape real criticism in the literature. I was crushed beyond what was called for or what would have been characteristic for me in this kind of situation. I recall feeling very near despair about Irwin's antagonism towards Winnicott. As supervision went on, I continued to refer to a Winnicottian treatment model as one I considered most approriate for this patient. Looking back now, I wonder if, in part, I was in fact expressing my own yearning to be able to fold into a supervisory holding environment as I contended with powerfully disorganizing aspects of the analysis with Christina.

My work with Irwin suggests that, like the patient, the analyst working with an adult trauma survivor may need a reliable holding environment within which he can, in Winnicott's (1962) terms, safely go on being while he tames and slowly integrates the disruptive precipitates of analytic work with a trauma survivor. A supervisor who is aware of the potential secondary traumatization of the analyst can help the supervisee assess his own degree of traumatization, co-creating with him, when necessary, a supervisory space that includes holding and containment.

Psychoanalytic work with an adult survivor of childhood sexual abuse is disruptive, traumatizing, and immensely rewarding. The recent reawakening within psychoanalysis to the all-too-frequent occurrence and consequences of childhood sexual trauma has provided treatment models that guide the analyst through the hidden shoals of work with this population. Similar attention to the vicissitudes of supervision when the supervisee is working amidst abuse may enhance and further clarify analytic treatment of adult sexual abuse survivors while, at the same time, enriching the experience of supervision for both members of the supervisory dyad.

REFERENCES

Courtois, C. A. (1988). *Healing the Incest Wound*. New York: Norton.

Davies, J. M., and Frawley, M. G. (1994). *Treating the Adult Survivor of Childhood Sexual Abuse*. New York: Basic Books.

Fairbairn, W. R. D. (1943). The repression and return of bad objects. In *Psychoanalytic Studies of the Personality*, pp. 59–81. London: Tavistock/Routledge, 1990.

Herman, J. L. (1992). *Trauma and Recovery*. New York: Basic Books.

Racker, H. (1968). *Transference and Countertransference*. Madison, CT: International Universities Press.

Winnicott, D. W. (1962). Ego integration in child development. In *The Maturational Processes and the Facilitating Environment*. Madison, CT: International Universities Press, 1965.

13

Supervision Amidst Abuse: A Supervisor's Perspective*

IRWIN HIRSCH, PH.D.

*Paper presented at the Fifteenth Annual Spring Meeting of the Division of Psychoanalysis (39) of the American Psychological Association, Santa Monica, April 1995, and at The Manhattan Institute for Psychoanalysis, January 26, 1996.

INTRODUCTION

This is a disquieting theme to write about. I imagine that everyone's thoughts immediately relate to the theme of a male supervisor abusing a female supervisee and her female patient. Since I am retrospectively aware of some confirming data that this may have occurred in some form, my anxiety about a public presentation is underscored. Also, some of the abuse that the patient, Christina, has suffered is clearly of a sexual nature and the material pulls for possible parallels of sexuality in the supervisory relationship. Though this, indeed, may be so, Dr. Frawley and I have decided not to explore or address the specifics of such possible fantasies or the subtle manifestations of them. This does not quiet my concern that readers will enjoy speculation and view less than total disclosure as cowardly at best and destructive at worst. It is also troublesome to present a supervision experience that did not go particularly well and that left the supervisee disappointed. This is so despite the productive healing that this joint paper does represent. On the other hand, this considerable discomfort is worth enduring, perhaps, because the experience raises some significant questions about supervision. I have always felt that I have learned more from work that was not entirely successful than from relationships that seemed productive throughout.

In order, I will discuss my view of the patient–analyst dyad; the patient–analyst–supervisor triad; and some questions or issues that all of this raises about the supervisory process.

THE SUPERVISOR'S PERCEPTION OF THE PATIENT–ANALYST DYAD

I will write mostly from how I recall viewing the analysis at the time of supervision while knowing that later input considerably influences my viewpoint.

My view of supervision in general is that it is most rich when the focus is primarily upon the patient–analyst interaction. I believe that the heart of analysis lies in the examination of the transference-countertransference matrix and that despite the central place of transference in the theory of therapy, it is most commonly relatively overlooked (Gill 1982). My supervisory efforts emphasize less the understanding of the patient as a single entity than the patient and analyst in interaction and how that reflects the patient as a unitary being. I see the analytic dyad as a playground where the central themes of the patient's life are lived out, with the unwittingly participating analyst enacting these key themes with the patient (Levenson 1983). Countertransference is inevitable and both a function of the unique analyst and the pull of the patient to use the analyst as an object of both repetition and potential new experience (Hirsch 1995, Racker 1968, Searles 1979). Ergo, productive analysis cannot occur without countertransference enactment, usually examined most meaningfully after it has been enacted (Aron 1992, Ehrenberg 1992, Hirsch 1995, Hoffman 1983, Renik 1993, Wolstein 1975). I am in basic agreement with Gill's (1982) contention that analysis usually works best when the analytic interaction is made explicit at whatever time the analyst becomes aware of such experience.

With this background, the treatment theme that struck me first was the enactment of a boundary violation between patient and analyst. Dr. Frawley was therapist to Christina's best friend, a situation that some analysts avoid because of the complications involved in learning things about one patient from another. Christina's life, indeed, is highlighted by intrusion of boundary. There is ample evidence in the data that points to overt sexual abuse—the ultimate in disrespect of boundary. She has taken this trauma and tried to get control over it (she is also identified with it) by repeating this theme throughout her life. There does not appear to be a single relationship in her life that is not characterized by a blurring of the normally accepted boundaries. It is likely that this is the only way that Christina has been able to significantly attach to another.

Dr. Frawley and I initially differed about my interpretation that there was a fair measure of hostility and destructiveness in Christina's violation of boundaries and that this should be part of the immediate understanding of the transference-countertransference matrix. Though Dr. Frawley generally agreed with the view of Christina as, among other things, destructively angry, she felt that her patient was not ready to address this in the transference without risk of harming the analytic bond. With regard to themes of intrusion and aggressive violation in general (this theme was rampant in her dreams), I believe that Dr. Frawley was more inclined to connect with Christina, at the time, as the victim of such experience while I was more attuned to her, in her contemporary adult life, as the aggressor or perpetrator.

The theme of the patient's anger in general and how to address it (containment vs. here-and-now making explicit[1]) continued to be a point of significant difference between Dr.

---

1. At this writing, Mitchell (1995) has suggested that a combination of the contemporary Kleinian concept of containment and the contem-

Frawley and myself throughout our discussion of Christina. I perceived this affect as spilling over into virtually every aspect of the patient's life, whereas Dr. Frawley saw such feelings as more circumscribed. For example, I was more skeptical than was Dr. Frawley about Christina's feelings for her lover as well as about her commitment to social work. I viewed the patient, in identification with her parents, as presenting a surface and hypocritical do-gooder respectability that currently disguised her destructive sadomasochistic rage.

Like Christina's mentor/therapist/lover, Dr. Frawley was idealized yet she was viewed as a deceptive enemy in the patient's dream-life. Following her sessions where her fear of being destroyed by Dr. Frawley as well as her own destructiveness were split-off, the patient binged on chocolate junk food. This had a clear childhood referent to harmful parenting. She had experiences where she scratched, hissed, spit, mumbled, stole, urinated on others' property, and hit in undirected rage. I believed that though she had not integrated these experiences, they were within her awareness sufficiently not to be considered dissociated. I believe she was asking for Dr. Frawley to help her integrate this rage. On the surface, as in her family (captured in the theme of the film *Blue Velvet*), she was a helper of abused children, involved with a venerable lover and an ideal analyst. On the other hand, her expectation was that her idealized lover *and* her idealized analyst would both eventually defile her as her parents defiled her. I further believed that she both identified with the defilers and the defiled, struggling with the temptation to destroy before she was once again the victim. My supervisory urgings worked toward making every subtle or indirect expression of rage or aggression expressed toward Dr. Frawley as explicit as possible.

---

porary interpersonal emphasis on immediate experience might be the most salubrious combination of mutative analytic action.

Dr. Frawley and I agreed about Christine's fears and expectations but disagreed as to how available her profound anger and destructiveness was to her. Dr. Frawley believed that Christina's anger was expressed in dissociated states, almost in the form of a multiple personality configuration. Therefore, efforts at integration of the terror of the victim and the rage of the perpetrator were not yet warranted. I do not believe in the entity of multiple personality[2] and was inclined to articulate these internal opposites as I saw them in the transference–countertransference interaction and Christina's outside life. I continued to make such recommendations, and Dr. Frawley respectfully demurred until she stopped presenting Christina and began with another patient. My failure to address this change, of course, represented a major shortcoming in my supervisory effort and leads into discussion of the patient–analyst-supervisor triad.

Prior to Dr. Frawley's decision to no longer present Christina, I had two explanations that accounted for our differences. The first related to what had emerged as a somewhat different psychoanalytic perspective. I saw her approach as emphasizing the holding of a wounded child whereas mine underscored the patient as active repeater of earlier configurations. My conscious supervisory tact was to present what I thought was best but to respect Dr. Frawley's point of view. My second explanation reflected my uncertainty, about which I will speak further in the following section. Fundamentally, I began to suspect that my supervisee had so much experience with sexual abuse that perhaps my own approach to analysis in this case was questionable. It seemed inauthentic to retreat from what I still

---

2. I believe that a therapist's view of dissociated states within an individual, to the point of thorough and radical unintegration-multiple personality, actually enhances the degree of hysterical split. This, in my mind, makes multiple personality a co-creation of patient and therapist and works against personality integration.

thought best, but I did not feel comfortable in directly addressing our differences.

THE PATIENT-ANALYST-SUPERVISOR TRIAD

It is now widely accepted that the interactional features of the
patient-analyst relationship are more important to therapeutic outcome than is the accuracy of the therapist's interpreta-
tive comments. Indeed, "accurate" interpretations generally
reflect an interpersonal cohesion between analyst and patient,
making interpretation at least as much of an interpersonal
event as a cognitive one (Greenberg 1991, Mitchell 1993). One
can, perhaps, say similar things about the supervisory relationship. I do not believe that my supervisory shortcomings
with Dr. Frawley were primarily related to my observations
about the patient or Dr. Frawley's relationship with the patient. My problems were a function of my failure to attend to
the relationship between Dr. Frawley and myself. This situation
is analogous to the therapist who makes interpretations that
have only an intellectualized effect because the transference-
countertransference matrix is not included. This is especially
noteworthy since transference-countertransference themes are
so central to my point of view as an analyst and, indeed, is
one reason why Dr. Frawley had chosen me as a supervisor in
the first place. I was suggesting to Dr. Frawley that she
address the rage of negative transference themes with her
patient while I ignored the anger and disappointment Dr.
Frawley felt toward me in our own relationship.

   As Dr. Frawley describes, she abruptly stopped presenting
Christina because she experienced me as relentlessly intrud-
ing into their relationship. I became to her the invasive abuser
in their relationship and I did not recognize that Dr. Frawley
perceived me as such. I also did not recognize Dr. Frawley's
beginning to present another patient as a way to fend off my

intrusions and protect her and Christina's relationship. Though it is not unusual for analytic candidates to present more than one case, I did not at all consciously perceive Dr. Frawley's motive for so doing and she did not inform me of her motive. As it turned out, the second patient presented apparently flourished with my supervisory help. I was evidently content to lose myself in that satisfaction.

Learning from my post-supervision discussions with Dr. Frawley, there were many other interactional elements that were unattended by me and were not verbally articulated by her. Dr. Frawley highlights the fearful look in her eyes that I did not notice as distinct from her normal ocular expressiveness. She refers to missed sessions for which I did not ask for payment and some instances of late payment. While this does not deviate from my usual policies, this fact is secondary to my non-recognition of the meaning of these expressions to Dr. Frawley and to their significance in our particular relationship. As Dr. Frawley also notes, there was a considerable stiffness and reserve to our relationship. She feels that I was the initiator of this tenseness. At the time, I did notice that Dr. Frawley was tense and anxious and I chose to respect that boundary and to not address it. In retrospect, my reluctance to address either her excessive reserve or my own reflects another split between my instruction about what analysts are supposed to do with their patients and how I proceeded as a supervisor. The medium was decidedly *not* the message.

There are a variety of idiosyncratic reasons that may account for my relational blindness. Some of these understandings are related to unique interactional features between myself and Dr. Frawley and others may reflect possible parallels between the supervisory and the analytic relationship.

The most strikingly dramatic and unique feature of the supervisory relationship was that I had supervised Dr. Frawley's analyst some 4 or 5 years prior when he was a candidate in the very same analytic training program. Dr. Frawley knew this as well as being aware that she was, at least, one of his training cases that was presented to me. My strongest experience at the time of beginning supervision with Dr. Frawley was my wish that I had not known her through the report of her analyst. Though I had forgotten most of the details of her life and life history, there were, of course, some memories and I wished there were none. I felt a strong sense of intrusion by virtue of knowing certain things that I could not address. Though we discussed this briefly at the start of supervision, I minimized the effect this had upon me. I proceeded with Dr. Frawley as if I really knew nothing about her, denying that my intrusion into her life was, in fact, central to our relationship. In retrospect, it seems that I tried to forget anything that I recalled about Dr. Frawley. This hysterical forgetting probably spread to my disease of hysterical blindness: a failure to recognize so much of Dr. Frawley's interaction with me. I was so ill at ease with my fundamental invasion of Dr. Frawley's privacy that I believe I became far more removed, cautious and disconnected than is usual for me. I reinforced the broken boundary by constructing an excessive boundary in the supervisory relationship.

A second and related initial feature to our relationship was Dr. Frawley's idealization of me, largely a function of my supervision of her analyst. I attributed her reserve with me to this feature. Her initial idealization was, indeed, so strong that she viewed my basic theoretical orientation as far more similar to hers (British object relational) than it actually was, despite her familiarity with my writing. Dr. Frawley had no way of knowing that I am excruciatingly uneasy with being in an idealized position. My personal conflict between the enjoyment of being idealized and my extreme discomfort with it reflects one of my own neurotic themes. I have a history of destroying idealizations and I believe that served as one my unintended motives in disappointing Dr. Frawley. Once again, the failure to address this theme in the supervision directly led to it being acted out in the supervisory relationship.

Another significant element of the supervisory relationship was Dr. Frawley's stature as an expert in the area of sexual abuse and my own relative lack of experience in this area. Dr. Frawley was in the midst of co-authoring a major book on this subject and had just completed an excellent article on the same theme. I have had, in contrast, very few patients with such a background nor was I especially familiar with the literature on the subject. Under the circumstances, I often felt woefully ill-equipped to supervise Dr. Frawley on a sexually-abused patient. This was further accented by my gender: I was a male supervisor supervising a female analyst, on a sexually abused female. At other times, however, I had the grandiose notion that Dr. Frawley's expertise in this area meant nothing in comparison to my ability to tune in to their analytic interaction. It was partly my own sense of inadequacy that led to my defensive insistence on Dr. Frawley dealing with negative transference themes, while ignoring her own perception of the patient's primary affect of terror and her own terror of me.

A number of parallels exist between the supervisory relationship and the analytic relationship. The question of whether the analytic relationship evokes a "parallel process" in the supervision is a major theoretical point of contention and I will attempt briefly to address this in the subsequent and final section. Regardless of how common or patterned parallels are in general, a number of them are evident in this particular situation. The most glaring and obvious parallel is the theme of intrusion, invasion, breech of boundaries, and abuse. Christina's whole interpersonal life is characterized by her initially being the victim of abusive intrusions and subsequently perpetrating that theme as both the victim and the perpetrator. The supervisory relationship was, indeed, highlighted by the severe intrusion of my having supervised Dr. Frawley's analyst. In my relationship with Dr. Frawley I attempted to be extremely cautious and reserved in light of this, but nonetheless enacted intrusion by my repeated efforts to get Dr. Frawley to deal with her patient in a way contrary to what she believed to be best.

The theme of empty idealization reflects a second parallel. Until her period of self-destructiveness and rebellion, Christina had an inordinate desire to perceive her violent parents as respectable pillars of society. Despite their sordid private world, it was Christina's job to keep them nice and clean. After a period in her life of dirtiness and ugliness, Christina once again found cleanliness in the form of a return to social consciousness (as a profession). More recently, she has developed a romance with a man who himself was a pillar of society. In defiling or being defiled by her mentor/therapist, a revered leader in her social work community, she has once again exposed the sordidness that she believes lies beyond all idealization and respectability. Further, in her effort to make this relationship clean and respectable, she is struggling to forge a love affair characterized by repair.

Dr. Frawley and Christina are in active pursuit of redeeming their relationship. Largely in indirect form, Christina lived out rageful destructiveness while simultaneously idealizing her analyst. If she has been able to address the hate and rage in the transference-countertransference matrix, she may indeed resurrect Dr. Frawley, not as an unrealistically idealized figure, but perhaps as a flawed but helpful one. This evolution would reflect a stronger internal integration of hate and love for Christina. In initiating a post-supervisory panel discussion and a joint article on our work together, Dr. Frawley has helped redeem our supervisory experience. She and I jointly exposed her empty idealization of me during our work with Christina. The ugly truth behind this idealization became evident, preceded by joint efforts toward a reintegration of my capabilities and my shortcomings as a supervisor.

Still another closely related parallel is the theme of people not being what they seem to be. Christina's parents, her mentor/therapist/advisor, and Christina herself are all quite opposite to what they appear. Indeed, Christina is a helper of abused children, while seducing a venerable older man, spitting, hissing, publicly urinating, and biting. Dr. Frawley is a wonderful and decent analyst to Christina while simultaneously destroying Christina's life, symbolized by post-session chocolate junk food. I am an esteemed object-relational supervisor who is actually interpersonal in orientation and a washout in supervision. Everything that I preach in my writing about the value of explicit transference–countertransference dialogue I ignore in my supervision with Dr. Frawley.

The theme of "not-seeing" may be yet another parallel. The unfortunate alternative to not seeing is often the acting out of what is not seen. At the time of supervision, Christina had not yet articulated the nature of sexual abuse and sexual perversion within her family—she did not fully see what was there. In the transference, she saw only the wonderful Dr. Frawley, yet she acted out the destructive elements of her relationship with her analyst. In supervision, I repeatedly did not see Dr. Frawley. I did not read the meaning in her eyes, her reserve, her late payments and her ceasing to present Christina to me. I tried not to see that she was the subject of my supervision of her analyst. It is only obvious to say that when blindness is pervasive in an interpersonal configuration, there is some part of both parties that is served by it. At some point, one of the two individuals must begin to see in order for progress to be made. In the supervisory relationship it was Dr. Frawley who broke through in this regard.

An additional parallel is the similarity between Dr. Frawley and myself in not wishing to be the "bad object." Dr. Frawley was reluctant to address the negative transference perceptions of her patient and I did not want to see how I was hurting Dr. Frawley and her patient in my omissions and commissions. Dr. Frawley's posture with her patient was to step back from anything but overtly benign engagement, to be the good object to someone whose life was filled with bad ones. I, in turn, wanted to be benign with Dr. Frawley. I wished to assure her that I was not using my prior knowledge of her to intrude or to take advantage. In my conscious effort to be a good object, so many vital interactional themes were lost that I become more of a disappearing or neglectful object.

REFLECTIONS ON THE SUPERVISORY PROCESS

It should be perfectly clear by now that the biggest problem in my supervision of Dr. Frawley was my failure to see and/or address a variety of key issues in our relationship. The accuracy or lack thereof of my supervisory comments and recommendations were largely irrelevant because our own interaction was ignored. As I have stated many times as a teacher, my severest therapeutic failures have come when I was too uneasy to deal with transference–countertransference themes that had emerged. In my experience, sins of omission have caused far greater damage than sins of commission (see Singer 1970). Patients of mine who have terminated treatment prematurely have rarely done so because of things I said that were hurtful, off-target or premature. They left treatment because they sensed that I was unprepared to address themes that made me often more anxious than it did them. Looking back at supervisory experience, I can draw clear parallels. Those times when I did not wish to get into an important something with a particular supervisee, and instead, stayed exclusively with the clinical content, were the least rewarding experiences for both myself and my supervisee. In this respect, a clear parallel between supervision and analysis may be made. In supervision, just as in therapy, it is often the anxiety of the analyst/supervisor more so than the patient/supervisee that leads to serious omissions. There is, however, a very significant difference in the two processes. In the analytic relationship I believe that transference material takes priority to all others. When transference is visible, unless other content is at the point of urgency, it should generally be addressed. A primary aim of the analytic enterprise is, indeed, making explicit the key internalized interpersonal configurations as they emerge in the here and now of the analytic dyad. This is what I attempt to teach students when they present patients to me. The aim of the supervisory relationship is, of course, quite different from that of therapy. The latter is not designed to change personality and thus, the making explicit of all inter-actional themes *whenever* they appear is not warranted.

I believe that the supervisory relationship works best when the idea of making the relationship explicit is considerably modified. If the learning process subjectively appears to the supervisor to be effective and there is no awareness of anxiety about any particular interactional theme, it may be best to stay with the clinical content and the therapeutic interaction. There are three reasons I can think of to shift the focus to the supervisory relationship. The first is a sense that the supervision is not going well and the supervisee is not learning or is ill at ease. The second is a feeling of inhibition on the part of the supervisor—an anxiety that leads to a holding back in dealing with either process or content. The third is when a parallel (parallel process) is seen between the analytic relationship and the supervisory relationship. Failure to address the supervisory relationship explicitly in these instances will more than likely lead to a thwarted supervisory experience.

In one respect, this makes the supervisory relationship more complex than the analytic relationship. In the latter, the analyst may be set to address *any* transference–countertransference theme as it emerges into the analyst's awareness. In the supervisory relationship, there are always interactional themes but in my view they are not to be addressed much of the time. As noted, I believe these themes should become explicit when they reflect problems, inhibitions, anxieties, and parallels. The supervisor must, therefore, be more discerning than the analyst. Since this is primarily an educational experience, many feelings and observations are best left alone. In the analytic relationship, I believe that nothing should be left alone. The primary focus of the supervisory relationship, for me, is the relationship between the patient and the analyst (see Fiscalini 1985). This aspect is what makes supervision relatively easy for supervisors, since although the supervisor inevitably becomes part of that patient–therapist mix to a degree, the supervisor is often an observer. Participant-observation dictates that the supervisor, by definition, is part of all patient–therapist data. Nonetheless, the strongest role of the supervisor is that of observer. In this context, the observer is an educator who must analyze the teacher–student relationship only when the forces in that relationship are in sharper relief than that of the patient–therapist interaction. It is often difficult to discern when those forces take priority to the patient–analyst clinical content. I believe that the ability to make such distinctions is the hardest part of supervision for the supervisor.

Perhaps the most troublesome aspect of supervision is the difficulty in resolving problems in the supervisory relationship within the prescribed time period of the relationship. Most supervisions in the context of training experience last one year or so. It may sometimes only be clear toward the end of that period that all is not well in the experience. This, of course, could and should be addressed but there is little time to resolve the problems and to initiate a more productive mode of engagement. In analysis, there is *always* destructive interaction. If repetition and enactment of bad early experience does not occur, there can be no effective outcome. This destructive engagement may be lived out over a long time period before anything new or corrective develops. The beauty of analysis is that there is time to do this; it is open-ended. This makes it imperative for supervisors to be acutely aware that time cannot pass before problematic interactional themes are examined. There is less luxury of time and margin for error than in the analytic process.

Regarding the thorny concept of parallel process, Caligor, Bromberg and Meltzer (1984), in their volume on supervision, conclude that parallel process is universal in the supervisory interaction. Their primary hypothesis is that it occurs through an empathic process wherein one party, usually the supervisee, unconsciously enacts aspects of the patient's personality for the supervisor to see and to address. If this data is not visible to the supervisor, valuable material is lost. Indeed, there were a number of significant examples of possible parallel process enacted between Dr. Frawley and myself in our work together. For the most part, I did not attend to them and if I had, the experience would probably have been a richer one. On the other hand, the concept of parallel process need not have been evoked in order for me to see these very same issues. For instance, there was a breach of boundary in Dr. Frawley seeing Christina's best friend as a patient and there was a breach of boundary in my having supervised Dr. Frawley's analyst. In a second example, Christina "cleaned up" Dr. Frawley, idealizing her to a point where she saw none of her badness. This was not addressed sufficiently in the transference and the destructive elements in the relationship were, instead, acted out. Dr. Frawley initially idealized me and my lack of attention to this was one of the features that lead to her eventual disappointment and a certain amount of acting-out in relation to it. In my role as supervisor, I could have seen these themes in causal sequence or as independent yet similar in form. Looking for parallels may have assisted me in seeing more in the supervisory relationship but that was not the only way for me to see what could have been seen.

While it is always best to use all potential sources of data, the concept of parallel process suggests a certain inevitability of parallel. It implies a causality. With regard to Dr. Frawley and myself it is not clear that our mutual breach of boundary could be viewed in this cause-effect manner. Similarly, it is plausible that the idealization that occurred in both relationships was parallel but quite independent from causal connection. They may have had nothing to do with one another—a coincidental parallel. The term "coincidental" may indeed reflect considerable naiveté on my part but I am troubled by an *assumption* of causal parallel process. Caligor and his colleagues view parallel process as inevitable and I am more prone to view it as one of many possible interactions that may occur in a supervisory relationship. In my view, parallels may be evident by virtue of an empathic process and there may be a cause-and-effect relationship. This is valuable data for a supervisor to address. On the other hand, parallels often do not exist. And belief in the concept may lead the data to fit the concept. Upon reflection, I do not believe it is generally a good idea to rely on universals because universals always run the risk of becoming formulaic. A supervisor should use all data but ought to avoid squeezing the data into an expected formula. It is, indeed, possible that parallel processes occur in great frequency in the supervisory process, yet I believe that it is best not to rely too much on them to inform the process.

My final point relates to the same theme: the risk of invoking universal principles in human relationships that are characterized by uniqueness and idiosyncracy. Those who argue that diagnosis has great value point to the amount of data lost when clinicians do not apply all that is known about aggregates to an individual who is one of that group. In some ways, it is like a self-imposed ignorance to not do so. Yet, this is the very point that Levenson (1983), Stern (1990), Hirsch (1995) and others argue: the value of ignorance, surprise, and naiveté in the psychoanalytic enterprise. On one hand there is the risk of ignoring key information and on the other of fitting patients into categories because of neatness of fit. I believe it is less dangerous to lose information by ignoring diagnostic and aggregate material than it is to assume something about a patient because he or she fits into a particular entity. Obviously, there are many who see the greater danger in the other direction.

Is there "supervision amidst abuse"? In this instance there was a parallel, indeed, many parallels. I did abuse figuratively Dr. Frawley (and her patient) by repeatedly suggesting that she address certain themes in the analysis that she believed would be hurtful to the therapy relationship. I did not see Dr. Frawley's reaction to this and, further, did not see her acting-out by protecting Christina from me and presenting a different patient who I might treat better. I did not carefully address basic supervisory boundaries that were broken by virtue of my having supervised Dr. Frawley's analyst. The abused patient is usually victimized by a perpetrator and by another family member who chooses not to see what is happening. These themes will inevitably be repeated in the transference–countertransference interaction, a point that Dr. Frawley addresses as the center-piece in her excellent volume on the subject (Davies and Frawley 1994). She and her co-author make it clear that every key historical interaction will be repeated in the analysis and that these interactions will be enacted from both sides and in every possible configuration. I am in agreement with that principle, yet I am concerned about expecting it. I worry that if these expectancies are looked for in advance, they may be found in a forced or non-spontaneous manner. I think there best could be a sense of paradox between being an informed professional and a naive observer. We can be too informed so that nothing is a surprise and the data always fit the theory. We can never be too naive but true naivete is impossible and we cannot make believe that we are theory- and expectancy-free. This too is not authentic because no analyst is truly free of theory or expectancy.

I am uncomfortable going beyond Dr. Frawley's and my own idiosyncratic experience and agreeing that there is "supervision amidst abuse" or that parallel process is inevitable with any particular type of patient. I prefer to believe that there is not such a generality while also expecting that in many instances there are interactions in the analytic and the supervisory relationship that are expectable. I believe that both analysis and supervision are most facilitated when the analyst and supervisor are optimally willing to be used as servants of the process and to examine any or all of the data, particularly the interactional data, as fully as possible. In order to do this optimally, each analytic and supervisory interaction is best viewed as unique and idiosyncratic. The freedom to raise and examine any issue that seems relevant in each unique configuration is likely to evolve into a relationship characterized by generosity rather than abuse. I am grateful to Dr. Frawley for constructing a post-supervisory situation where I can do this very thing.

REFERENCES

Aron, L. (1992). Interpretation as expression of the analyst's subjectivity. *Psychoanalytic Dialogues* 2: 475–507.

Caligor, L., Bromberg, P. and Meltzer, J. (1984). *Clinical Perspectives on the Supervision of Psychoanalysis and Psychotherapy*. New York: Plenum.

Davies, J. and Frawley, M. (1994). *Treating the Adult Survivor of Childhood Sexual Abuse*. New York: Basic Books.

Ehrenberg, D. (1992) *The Intimate Edge*. New York: Norton.

Fiscalini, J. (1985). On supervisory parataxis and dialogue. *Contemporary Psychoanalysis* 21:591–608.

Gill, M. (1982). *The Analysis of Transference, Volume I*. New York: International Universities Press.

Greenberg, J. (1991). *Oedipus and Beyond*. Cambridge, MA: Harvard University Press.

Hirsch, I. (1995). Therapeutic uses of countertransference. In *Handbook of Interpersonal Psychoanalysis*, M. Lionells, J.

Fiscalini, C. Mann & D. B. Stern, eds. Hillsdale, NJ: Analytic Press.

Hirsch, I. (in press). Observing-participation, mutual enactment, and the new classical models. *Contemporary Psychoanalysis.*

Hoffman, I. (1983). The patient as interpreter of the analyst's experience. *Contemporary Psychoanalysis* 19: 389–422.

Levenson, E. (1983). *The Ambiguity of Change.* New York: Basic Books.

Mitchell, S. (1993). *Hope and Dread in Psychoanalysis.* New York: Basic Books.

Mitchell, S. (1995). Interaction in the Kleinian and interpersonal traditions. *Contemporary Psychoanalysis* 31: 65–91.

Racker, H. (1968). *Transference and Countertransference.* New York: International Universities Press.

Renik, O. (1993). Analytic interaction: Conceptualizing technique in the light of the analyst's irreducible subjectivity. *Psychoanalytic Quarterly* 62: 553–571.

Searles, H. (1979). *Countertransference and Related Subjects.* New York: International Universities Press.

Singer, E. (1970). *Key Concepts in Psychotherapy.* New York: Basic Books.

Stern, D. B. (1990). Courting surprise. *Contemporary Psychoanalysis* 26: 452–478.

Wolstein, B. (1975). Countertransference: The psychoanalyst's shared experience and intimacy with his patient. *Journal of the American Academy of Psychoanalysis* 3: 77–89.

14

Resolving Impasses: Including Patients and Supervisees in Consultations

SUE N. ELKIND, PH.D.

Supervision and consultation to therapists are integral parts of the profession of psychotherapy. Like electricians and plumbers, musicians and artists, poets and novelists, we learn our art and craft largely through practice and apprenticeship to master craftspersons. Our apprenticeship is never complete: Psychodynamic psychotherapy is an ever-evolving specialty that we keep striving to understand and define. As part of this process of evolution, most of us continue to rely on and learn from some form of consultation throughout our professional careers to help us define ourselves and our work. In particular, we rely on consultation for help when serious impasses arise.

Yet an invisible paradox regarding consultation operates. Despite the broad reach of our explorations and despite our recognition of the invaluable contribution that another person's perspective on a therapeutic relationship can provide, we do not actively include patients in consultation when serious impasses occur. We do not actively recommend to patients consultation in which we would participate, nor do we wholeheartedly encourage patients who want consultation on their therapy with us to seek it. While we implicitly trust our own motives in seeking an outside perspective, we tend toward mistrust of the motives of our patients should they request a consultation: we assume they are acting out, diluting the transference, breaking the frame, or being resistant to the process. We tend toward an omnipotent stance, expecting more of ourselves than is humanly possible, attempting to handle every dilemma on our own or assuming we can avoid abandoning or failing our patients. As a result, we have preserved the sanctity of the therapeutic dyad, with the exception of consultation for the therapist, overlooking the possibility that safeguarding the dyad can, at times of extreme difficulty, isolate the participants and worsen their dilemma.

For the past 8 years, I have been responding to a wide range of requests from patients for consultation when they are in a serious impasse with their therapists or after their therapy has ended in a rupture. As I respond to these requests, I am providing a new service and simultaneously developing a model for it relying on intuition, a variety of theoretical perspectives, and leaning on colleagues for consultation and discussion. I have discovered that consultation that actively involves the participation of patients or supervisees, usually in separate meetings, not only provides a sometimes urgently needed service, but also serves as a way of seeing into the broader issues of depth psychotherapy. A consultant is uniquely positioned at a vantage point outside the therapeutic or supervisory relationship, yet is linked, directly or indirectly, to both participants.

In this chapter, I will provide 3 vignettes that illustrate the range of dilemmas that I have confronted in my position as consultant to patient, supervisees, and therapists. Through the vignettes, I hope to convey the anxieties, frustrations, uncertainties, and rewards of being a consultant to patients *and* therapists (or supervisees and supervisors). With their permission, I have also included the perspective of the individuals whose stories are recounted in the vignettes. They have enriched the vignettes with their accounts of the consultation. Their contributions affirm that each participant experiences the consultation differently, perhaps concurring in the overall outcome but focusing on different aspects as significant. As relational perspectives of psychotherapy abound, we are giving increasing credence to the validity of multiple subjectivities, regarding therapeutic relationships from the vantage point of a two-person rather than one-person psychology. As we do so, the importance of giving patients a separate voice in professional articles comes to the fore.

Two central theoretical concepts that I rely on—primary vulnerabilities and relational modes—have evolved from my clinical work providing consultations. I will define them briefly here, but they are addressed in detail in my book *Resolving Impasses in Therapeutic Relationships* (Elkind 1992). I prefer to define these concepts intuitively, rather than precisely, through linking them to a cluster of existing theoretical concepts. I believe that such definition helps our conceptual language remain vital and fluid rather than becoming deadened and reified.

The most useful concept, not only for consultations but for psychotherapy, has been the conception of an area of *primary vulnerability*. By primary vulnerability, I refer to a central area of psychological sensitivity that we defend ourselves from experiencing. When areas of primary vulnerability are activated, our connection to ourselves or to significant others is threatened. Our energy and attention is then channeled primarily into protecting and preserving our sense of self. When we collapse into our areas of primary vulnerability, we are unable to see ourselves or others with clarity.

Each of us, therapist or patient alike, inevitably has areas of primary vulnerability that are usually shaped early in life as a consequence of our temperament or innate attributes and our interactions with our caretakers. Examples that each of us has undoubtedly experienced or encountered in others include, among others, fears of being abandoned, betrayed, misperceived, or deprived. I have found that serious impasses are apt to occur when the primary vulnerabilities of both patient and therapist are activated, or in jeopardy of being activated, in the therapeutic relationship. Their defenses and primary vulnerabilities intersect problematically, giving rise to a stalemate in the transference–countertransference matrix.

The second concept which I have found useful is that of the quality of the *relational mode* that the therapist and patient have established (Elkind 1992). For example, when therapists must function in a problematically constricted way in order to preserve the patients' coherent self-state, they are functioning as *coerced relational partners*. In many of the impasses I have encountered, patient and therapist have become deadlocked in *entrenched relational modes*. Consultation can sometimes lead to a loosening in unyielding and problematic relational modes.

Areas of primary vulnerability and the quality of the relational mode can be understood in terms of the present or "real" interaction between therapist and patient and in terms of the historically influenced transference-countertransference matrix in which the therapist and patient are operating. A significant aspect of my role as consultant has been to facilitate this understanding by providing a safe psychological space in which exploration can occur. Within a psychological space outside the troubled therapeutic relationship, patient and therapists often have the capacity to reflect on the transference and countertransference dynamics, areas of primary vulnerability, and the particular quality of relational mode.

CONSULTATION WITH A PATIENT AND THERAPIST IN AN IMPASSE

I am going to begin with an example of a consultation that involved the active and voluntary ongoing participation of both therapist and patient because this kind of direct intervention is without formal precedent. Most often, the request for consul-

tation comes from patients who tell me they are in an unresolvable, serious impasse with their therapists. Sometimes
they contact me at the suggestion of the therapist, but more
often they have heard of my special interest on their own.
Following the ground rules I have established, I recommend
that they let their therapist know that they are seeking
consultation. I ask if their therapist would be willing to
participate in the consultation through a separate individual
contact with me. Most patients who contact me on their own
have already raised the idea of consultation with their therapists, who have acquiesced with varying degrees of enthusiasm
and willingness to participate. Whether or not therapists want
to participate, patients find that actively seeking an outside
perspective is empowering and satisfying regardless of the
outcome.

Less frequently, the request for consultation is initiated by
the therapist, who is more likely to rely on private consultation, peer support, or personal resources. As therapists have
become familiar with my work locally through my practice, and
nationally as a result of the publication of my book (Elkind
1992), an increasing number have been raising the possibility
of consultation with their patients and offering to be involved.

Contacting the therapist and patient to ask for permission to
write this vignette was not easy. I was concerned about calling
them unexpectedly after the two years that had elapsed since
our consultation, not knowing what the effect of my contact
might be. Digressing from their current explorations in therapy
to revisit the impasse might jeopardize or interfere with the
ongoing therapeutic process. I was also concerned that they
might not feel free to withhold permission out of a sense of
obligation. In fact, the first therapist and patient I contacted
for permission gave careful thought to my invitation. With
some regret, they ultimately decided that they might want
to seek consultation from me in the future. They wanted to

protect this possibility without having had another role in relation to me.

For the patient and therapist in this vignette, deciding to give permission was complicated. They had to confront what it would be like to relive their impasse, with its attendant difficult affect states, when they read my summary of it and added their comments. After careful consideration, they chose to take on the challenge of revisiting the impasse and to regard it as an opportunity.

In describing the consultation, I will use the present tense in order to convey more directly what the experience of living through the consultation was like.

> The patient, whom I will call Ms. A, is a 30-year-old woman employed in a medical research laboratory. She heard me talk about my book, *Resolving Impasses in Therapeutic Relationships*, at a presentation open to the public and decided to contact me. In the telephone contact in which we make an initial appointment, Ms. A tells me that her therapist, a woman I will call Dr. R, is familiar with my work and feels that consultation on the impasse they are in might help them. They endured a prolonged period of misattunement and anger anticipating Dr. R's 3-month maternity leave. Dr. R has now returned to work, but their stalemate has only worsened.
>
> In our initial session of an hour and a half, Ms. A conveys a wealth of information about her therapy and her early history in an articulate, competent manner. She begins with a summary of her experience in psychotherapy. Prior to beginning therapy with Dr. R, she worked with a male therapist who also did body work. This relationship ended badly after a year and a half. The therapist failed to maintain professional boundaries throughout the therapy, for example by having social contact with Ms. A. He also did not have expertise in early

trauma, which emerged during the therapy as a crucial aspect of Ms. A's childhood. The body work elicited memories of physical abuse with concomitant strong feelings which the therapist was unable to work with constructively. His inadequacy caused problems both in the therapy and in Ms. A's life. As the therapeutic relationship deteriorated, Ms. A became increasingly immobilized and depressed. Eventually she could no longer function effectively at her job and had to take a leave of absence. She could see that the therapy was having a harmful effect, but she was also attached to the therapist, who kept promising that he would try to help her and believed he could. She was having difficulty deciding whether to terminate.

During her time away from her job and over the course of a summer, Ms. A consulted several times with Dr. R about her therapy. Ms. A found the consultation to be extremely helpful. She felt that Dr. R was invaluable in framing questions about the work with the male therapist that focused Ms. A's thoughts and feelings about what was wrong. Ms. A made good use of the consultation and was able to leave the therapy with a clear sense that her decision was a good one. A few months later, she called Dr. R and asked if they could meet for therapy. Dr. R agreed to work with her.

In the first year of the therapy, Ms. A recovered from the devastating impact of the prior therapy and picked up the pieces of her life. With Dr. R's encouragement she was able to return to work and resume evening classes toward a Masters degree in a scientific field. As time went on, Ms. A came to appreciate more clearly how damaging the previous therapy had been. Ms. A then began to have difficulty trusting Dr. R and accessing her feelings, which seemed increasingly out of control. The more Dr. R helped her contact her feelings, the more Ms. A felt threatened and dissociative.

About 3 months before Dr. R's maternity leave, Ms. A began to feel completely unsafe in the room with Dr. R. Dr. R's pregnancy and psychological involvement with her unborn child, as well as the reality of an impending extended interruption, constituted an overwhelming abandonment. As if the abandonment were not enough, Ms. A felt then, and continues to feel now, that Dr. R judges her harshly and actually dislikes her. In the face of Dr. R's negative feelings, Ms. A tends to dissociate or withdraw into silence. Her withdrawal and retreat compound the problem in the relationship because Dr. R's responses to her withdrawal have not seemed helpful and have worsened Ms. A's feelings of being unsafe. From Ms. A's perspective, Dr. R has insisted that their problems are related solely to transference, to the revival of early experiences around abandonment caused by the maternity leave. But Ms. A is uncertain. She cannot tell what is related to transference and what is related to the current interactions they are having. Perhaps her impulse to leave therapy is healthy. After all, it was difficult to disengage from the male therapist, who was clearly not good for her. Maybe she is once again remaining too long in a relationship that is no longer good for her.

Ms. A summarizes her early history to provide me with a context for the impasse. She is the youngest of 4 children, the result of an unplanned pregnancy late in her mother's childbearing years. Her siblings are more than 10 years older and she has as little contact with them as an adult as she did growing up. During her childhood, Ms. A was cared for by a series of babysitters, none of whom stayed with her family for more than a year. Ms. A was left behind when her parents traveled. They would often take her older siblings with them on vacation and leave her with a babysitter, usually a new one that she did not meet until the vacation began.

Ms. A felt actively disliked by her mother, even though to the rest of the world, and within the family unit, her mother was considered a warm, loving mother. Ironically, Ms. A was regarded by her family as cold and overly sensitive. But, Ms. A wondered, how could a mother leave a 1-year old baby with a new babysitter for 6 weeks and go off with the rest of the family? Or leave a baby with babysitters who were at best neglectful and were at times cruel and abusive?

As Ms. A's stories of abandonment and neglect during her childhood multiply, I focus on the precariousness of her ties to her parents and siblings. Her family apparently could rid themselves of her at any time, leaving her with no experiential framework for being in a relationship that endures through negative feelings. Her needs and her positive sense of self were sacrificed to preserve the family's image as a happy family. The dissonance between her experience of abandonment and the family's sense of itself as close and loving have left Ms. A doubting her capacity to perceive reality accurately. The starkness of the absence of a bond with her mother highlights the significance of the persisting breach with Dr. R.

Ms. A clearly recognizes the correspondence between her experiences with her mother and family and the current context of therapy. Dr. R's pregnancy and extended maternity leave have re-created Ms. A's experience of being left behind by her family when they went on trips. The maternity leave has heightened Ms. A's sense of being unsafe in the relationship. Her feelings of anger, hurt, and endangerment seem to elicit feelings of frustration, annoyance, and impatience in Dr. R that only worsen the negative cycle. When Dr. R seems critical of her or frustrated, the positive connection between them is eradicated. When Dr. R tells Ms. A the equivalent of "Your perceptions of me are wrong," her experience in her family of having her view of reality negated is re-created. In the therapeutic relationship, as in her family, Ms. A feels that she is receiving judgment rather than empathy, being disliked rather than cared about, and that her cries for love and acceptance are once again dissipating in the wind.

By the end of our session, Ms. A and I are both left with the same unanswered questions. To what extent is Ms. A experiencing a reenactment of early issues that offers an opportunity to work through early trauma? Does the abandonment by Dr. R for her maternity leave and the subsequent unbridgeable disconnections represent an irreparable recreation of the trauma? Would it be healthy assertiveness to leave the therapy, or would leaving mean a missed opportunity? We agree that I will contact Dr. R and Ms. A gives me a signed release to communicate with her. We plan to meet again after I have heard Dr. R's perspective on the impasse.

In the session with Dr. R, I begin by summarizing the information that Ms. A has given me about the therapy and her early history. As is usually the case, there is no significant disagreement in the events that Dr. R and Ms. A report. Patients and therapists are understandably anxious about how the other will represent them. But I have consistently found that patients and therapists are careful to be accurate and fair in describing each other and the events that have transpired.

Dr. R tells me how difficult the work with Ms. A has been for her ever since the impasse worsened in the weeks before her maternity leave. The problems go beyond the adjustments that would normally accompany the birth of a baby. Dr. R experiences intense hostility from Ms. A, even though Ms. A regards herself as benign. Dr. R discloses with impressive honesty how difficult a time she has been having withstanding Ms. A's anger at her, and the struggle she has had tolerating her feelings of dislike for Ms. A. We talk about the feelings of dislike as projective identifications, the taking inside herself of the hatred that was a significant part of Ms. A's early experience.

Ms. A was a child who felt hated by her mother. She has carried that hatred inside her, just as Dr. R is now having to carry it within the crucible of the therapeutic relationship. Ms. A's responses—feeling confused, endangered, victimized, and disliked—intensify Dr. R's struggle, which in turn worsens Ms. A's plight. At this moment in the consultation, neither Dr. R nor I know whether naming the dislike and hate as a powerful state that has been constellated in the relationship—and that is an essential part of the therapeutic process—will enable the feelings to be tolerated and worked with constructively.

Dr. R and I agree that I will meet again with Ms. A and try to talk about projective identification and the constellation of the state of dislike. But neither of us knows precisely how to effect a shift in the relationship that will restore a positive alliance so the negative state can be worked with constructively. Perhaps my presence as a third person to whom both Dr. R and Ms. A have communicated their experience is in itself an intervention that will effect a change in the therapeutic relationship even if no interpretations or other interventions occur.

Ms. A and I meet several days after the session with Dr. R. Ms. A has just come from what she describes as a terrible session with Dr. R and is clearly not in a frame of mind to discuss projective identification. She tells me that after meeting with me, she felt anxious and fearful, as if she had betrayed Dr. R. In the session, Dr. R had been quiet, which heightened her anxiety. Knowing that Dr. R and I had met, she asked Dr. R what we had talked about. Dr. R responded and eventually mentioned that Ms. A had difficulty remembering the positive aspects of the therapeutic relationship before their impasse. Ms. A reacted to this statement with confusion. They tried unsuccessfully to trace the beginning of Ms. A's confusion. Ms. A then perceived Dr. R to be irritated with her and frustrated at being misunderstood. The harder they tried to figure out what was going wrong in order to make things better, the worse everything got. Finally Dr. R asked Ms. A if she thought it would be possible for them both to have anger and hatred and yet be together in the office? Ms. A thought this might be difficult, too much like her mother, who tried to keep up the outer appearance of harmony and rein in her dislike of Ms. A. The session was uncomfortable and anxiety-producing and there was no relief in sight.

In listening to Ms. A, I experience moments of feeling confused, helpless, and extraordinarily pessimistic about the viability of the relationship. These feelings reflect the extent to which I have become part of the process in which the patient and therapist are engaged. I have the challenge of holding these feelings without acting on them (for example, by recommending that the therapy be terminated). Clearly the initial positive alliance between Ms. A and Dr. R has been obliterated by the feelings of anger, betrayal, and abandonment triggered by Dr. R's pregnancy and maternity leave. Their experiences of each other are not reducible to transference, fantasy, or projection. They are living through a powerful reality-based experience superimposed over similar experiences Ms. A endured in childhood. But acknowledging this reality is not enough to bring about a shift. Because a substantial part of the consultant's role is one of psychologically holding the relationship, I suggest that Ms. A continue to meet with Dr. R and meet with me again in two weeks. I will contact Dr. R to let her know about this plan.

When Dr. R and I talk, I share my pessimism. I acknowledge the reality that wounding in areas of primary vulnerability can be severe enough to overwhelm the therapeutic alliance (Elkind 1992). Dr. R's vulnerability in relation to her pregnancy and the impact of the pregnancy on Ms. A may constitute this intolerable degree of wounding for both of them. Ms. A is yearning for an empathic, loving connection to Dr. R which, in view of the real impact of the pregnancy and maternity leave and Dr. R's feelings, seems beyond reach. Perhaps we will need to think about a referral to another therapist. If so, I will be in place as a transitional or bridge therapist for Ms. A.

Before the next session with Ms. A, I am worried that their relationship has gotten even worse. I am unprepared for what occurs next. Ms. A enters my office with a completely different physical demeanor. She seems cheerful, bright, and energized, a vast contrast to the pale, depressed, withdrawn person who had been in my office only two weeks before. She announces that something shifted in the therapeutic relationship almost right away. "Things were spiraling out of control. Now they're spiraling back into control." From Ms. A's point of view, the main problem—feeling uncared for by Dr. R—has changed. Even Dr. R's voice is different.

When I ask Ms. A what happened, she recounts with considerable vitality how she went into the session with Dr. R after meeting with me and described her distress and pain at the disconnection. Surprisingly, Dr. R asked her how it would be if she sat next to her. Without hesitating, Ms. A said, "Yes!" She adds, "That made her *literally* on my side."

From that pivotal moment, their interactions continued on a new positive course. Even when it seemed in a subsequent session as if they might slide back into one of their worst misattunements, Dr. R was able to stop the downward spiral, examine what had transpired, and the interaction shifted onto a positive track. According to Ms. A, Dr. R has learned that rhetorical questions are not helpful and has stopped asking them. When Ms. A feels confused, Dr. R helps her regard the confusion as a protective mechanism that she relied on as a child to cope with a reality that was too painful. Dr. R is clearly recognizing how wounded Ms. A is rather than pressing her to be stronger.

From my perspective, Dr. R's spontaneous act of sitting next to Ms. A, and Ms. A's readiness to allow a change, has enabled a shift in the entrenched relational mode to occur. A change has occurred not only in their behavior, but in the unconscious meaning each has to the other. When Dr. R sat next to Ms. A, she altered the previous experience of dislike and hate. Ms. A and I wonder what enabled Dr. R to move closer to Ms. A and to be more expressive of her positive feelings. Had she been more reserved in an effort to avoid the boundary breaches of the prior male therapist? Did the fact that I was able to express my caring for Ms. A permit her to do so as well? Perhaps the consultative relationship served as a bridge from one relational mode to another, metaphorically serving as a way station for a leap that would otherwise have been too great.

Ms. A then shares with me how difficult it is for her to feel angry at another person. The anger gets intercepted and turned against herself even before she recognizes it. Our consultation has helped affirm that her needs are reasonable, that she doesn't need to feel ashamed or that the situation is hopeless. In the past, she would have retreated, unable to advocate for herself, becoming quieter and quieter, muting her feelings, believing she had to accept passively how things were, "like playing possum until things got better."

In a follow-up conversation with Dr. R, I ask what happened to bring about a change. Dr. R explains that the consultation helped her make an internal shift. She was aware of the risk involved in exposing the relationship to me when they were at a rock-bottom place, not knowing if Ms. A could remain in therapy after the maternity leave or if she could access her caring feelings for Ms. A. Dr. R feels that she and Ms. A learned in the process a great deal about trauma and its replication and about the importance of looking at the present interaction in the context of transference. Her outlook about the sanctity of the therapeutic dyad has been altered.

At this point I would like to include comments from Ms. A and Dr. R written two years after the consultation took place. Dr. R writes, "I really feel strongly that this is Ms. A's story and I'd like to not interfere. I do think you have really captured her, her story, and all the sadness her history holds. That has been a powerful reminder for both of us." Dr. R experienced the consultation as immensely helpful during a time of hopelessness about the therapy. She adds, "I was determined to persevere." Her comment reminds us of the importance of qualities, often overlooked, that are essential resources for therapists during critical phases of the work. Tenacity and perseverance are, at pivotal junctures, as valuable as knowledge and experience. In this case, tenacity and perseverance served to protect against a permanent collapse into states of hate and dislike.

I will include a significant portion of Ms. A's feedback because patients so rarely have a voice in our books and journals. Ms. A first describes her reaction to reading about herself in the vignette. "It was a very powerful experience for me. I was moved that in the very short time we worked together you were able to perceive the reality of my experience so clearly. It occurred to me as I was reading it that this is one of the important reasons I entered therapy in the first place; to be seen and mirrored in this way. Thank you."

With respect to the consultation, Ms. A writes:

> It was really important for me to have a third party affirm that I was not solely responsible for the deterioration of our relationship and that the responsibility did not lie entirely with me to repair it. You validated for me that therapy was a relationship with another person in which both of us had a set of vulnerabilities and responsibilities.

> There is something insulting about the assumption that clients will inevitably try to "triangulate" if a third party enters the therapy. It presumes that clients have more interest in acting out their neuroses than in repairing a foundering relationship with their therapist . . . There is a safety in knowing that the consultant is creating a safe place in which to air your differences, and who won't stand with you *against* the other person, won't take sides, blame, or judge, but will be a fair witness, who is able to provide an impartial perspective and mirror the central dilemmas causing the impasse.

> There was something else which may sound small, but was crucial to me. At one point during our consultation, I was sitting in your office and was telling you about how much I felt Dr. R disliked me. Before I left, you validated my perceptions, acknowledged how painful it must be, *and* you told me that in the very short time we had worked together, you

found me likeable. I can't tell you how powerful it was to me to hear you tell me you liked me. Coming from a family in which I felt like a pariah, it was what I always longed to hear. Of course this longing played itself out in my therapy. I was quick to interpret every gesture as a sign of disapproval and needed desperately to hear explicitly that I was likable and liked. You gave me that and it gave me a certain strength to go back to my relationship with Dr. R and believe that this was something I could reasonably expect from her.

I think the experience of working with you on this chapter will be positive for me. Since things have improved between us, I have been afraid of conflict with Dr. R, of "rocking the boat," I think, partly because we've had such difficulties in the past, and partly because I always assume relationships are extremely fragile and precarious. I think this work will enable us to go back to some of this painful material and realize that our relationship actually has enormous resilience.

PONDERING THE CONSULTATION TWO YEARS LATER

In this consultation, I—a female consultant—functioned as an overarching Godmother/Grand-Mother/Good-Mother for the patient and therapist, who were entrapped in a maternal transference complex of hate, envy, rage, and intense fears of abandonment and deprivation in the face of limited supplies. As long as the therapeutic dyad remained isolated, functioning in a vacuum without a relational support network to hold it, both individuals felt trapped in a stifling situation of hatred and dislike, caught in entrenched relational modes vis-à-vis one another. The dyadic structure of psychoanalytic psychotherapy, which we ordinarily and without question presume to be helpful and which we scrupulously protect, became a hellish crucible for both participants.

The positive outcome of consultation to patient and therapist in this case, and in other cases with a similar dynamic, indicates to me that the isolated dyadic structure itself can constitute a particular transference enactment that cannot be worked with symbolically within the dyad. The structure of the dyad, even with the best intention of patient and therapist and often in spite of their individual psychological makeup, contributes to a collapse of the psychological or symbolic realm that is essential for psychological work. Patient and therapist become focused on psychological self-preservation and there is literally no psychological room available for mutual empathy when in each other's presence. As a result, there is a shared experience of deprivation, limited supplies, and the constellation of a self-experience of being unlovable, bad, disliked, hated, and worthless which can only be located in oneself or in the other, with neither position providing relief.

The mere presence of a consultant to each member of the therapeutic dyad in such a situation is in itself a powerful direct intervention, particularly if the patient has empowered herself to choose the consultant and initiate the consultation. Certain patients have had the childhood experience of being trapped with a careperson upon whom they were dependent yet by whom they were primarily and often traumatically used as objects in the service of the careperson's psychological needs. They either lacked, or could not adequately use, an empathic protective other. When this experience of helplessness is re-created in the therapeutic relationship, an enactment is created simply by the dyadic structure, and this *structural enactment* can overpower and defeat all the well-intentioned efforts of therapist and patient. The presence of the consultant disrupts the structural enactment.

When I first began doing consultations, my attention was focused primarily on the relational dynamics and the intersecting defenses and primary vulnerabilities of patient and therapist. As a result, I was not able to see the impact of the dyadic relational structure on the therapeutic relationship. Although I understood that consultation altered this dyadic structure, I did not yet recognize the dyadic structure itself as constituting an enactment of early trauma. I believe that I had a resistance to this awareness related to the breaking of a taboo through tampering with the sanctity of the therapeutic dyad.

Beyond constituting a direct *structural intervention*, the consultant also has the potential to alter the therapeutic relationship through specific nonverbal functions and conceptual interpretations, which in addition to the intervention in the structure can open up other exits from an entrapped state. In this particular case, because both patient and therapist were willing to allow me to have an impact, I could serve certain specific functions for each of them.

For the patient, initiating a consultation was an empowering act which offset the experience of helplessness and dependency on a dangerous other. My liking and acceptance of her, and my concern and empathy for her, served as *nonverbal or functional interventions* that each had a powerful positive impact, enabling the patient to have a different experience of herself. She was able to move out of a self-experience as unlovable, despicable, and worthless, which had been occurring in the therapeutic relationship for some time, to a more positive self-experience as a good-enough person. She was then able to bring this different experience of herself into the therapeutic relationship, which, like domino theory in reverse, enabled her to behave as well as to feel different in relation to her therapist.

In addition to this nonverbal or functional intervention, the consultation provided the patient with a conceptual, narrative understanding of her primary vulnerabilities and their activation. This conceptualization, a *verbal intervention*, provided an objective mirror that reflected back a broader picture of herself than the one she had resigned herself to, namely as an unlovable and unwanted burden. Reading the vignette I wrote about her 2 years later served the same therapeutic function. The simple fact of my connection to her therapist also opened up the hope that I could have an impact on her therapist on her behalf, thereby enabling her therapist to restore the functions that had previously helped her.

For the therapist, I provided a reflection of the hopelessness and futility that she had been feeling. Suggesting that she consider transferring the patient to another therapist with my help mobilized her tenacity and energy for the therapeutic work. I am convinced that the relief provided by my involvement, so that she no longer felt trapped and alone with a difficult patient, reduced her need to defensively distance from her patient. In keeping with the metaphor of mothering and pregnancy, prior to the consultation the therapist had been in the position of a mother entrapped with a colicky infant who could not be soothed. Continuing within this metaphor, the consultant, in the position of a Grand-Mother/ God-Mother/ Good-Mother, provided a symbolic soothing balm for the Patient/ Baby and provided a much-needed respite for the depleted Therapist/Mother. After her intervention, a rested, restored, and renewed Therapist/Mother could resume her work with a once-again calm, responsive patient.

What was the impact of this consultation on the negative maternal transference complex? (I believe that a similar impact could occur in a case involving a negative paternal transference complex.) In optimal development, mother and daughter live through and survive many discrete states in relation to each other, including extreme negative states, loving states, indifferent states, states of mutual harmony and gratification, and states of profound disappointment and disillusionment. Survival of these diverse self- and other-experiences enables mother and daughter to develop a capacity to hold in a manageable tension the complicated and discontinuous mixture of positive and negative, gratifying and disappointing, pleasant and unpleasant experiences. When the mother–daughter relationship is disrupted psychologically by traumatic abandonment, neglect, or abuse, as it was in this case, these states remain discrete. For mother or daughter, a negative state can become the fixed and only real nature of the self and/or other in childhood, and this state may be reactivated in the therapeutic relationship, where it remains entrenched. As with Ms. A and Dr. R, an entrenched relational mode and frozen psychological experience of self and other becomes established.

As a result of this consultation, the intrapsychic and interpersonal experience of being unlovable and depleted—and of being unloving and angry—did not have to be frozen in consciousness or split-off, repressed, or denied. Because it was shared and witnessed by a consultant, the negative constellation of a maternal transference complex was detoxified and could be held in consciousness. New self, other, and relational experiences could then begin to occur for both patient and therapist. As we know, such an expansion of conscious experience can also occur in successful therapies that remain within the structure of a dyad. But when the therapeutic relationship is in dire jeopardy, the intervention of a consultant can be experienced as life-saving for both individuals. A rupture in this case would have reinforced the preexisting entrenched negative relational mode and self-experience that the patient hoped to alter in therapy. The loss of hope and reinforcement of negative self experience would have resulted in the felt experience of having been harmed by the therapy and a resistance to trying again.

CONSULTATION WHEN THE PATIENT COMES ALONE

Although I receive many requests to help patients and therapists in serious impasses, I have also responded to other requests. These requests have caused me to take a closer look at the assumptions that operate implicitly about the proper role of a therapist. For example, I sometimes receive calls from patients requesting consultation to evaluate their ongoing, long-term therapy. I suspect that many therapists respond to requests from patients who want help evaluating how their therapy is proceeding. Some patients simply want to step outside the therapeutic relationship in order to take a look at it. Because the therapist is embedded in the system, the therapist necessarily cannot provide an outside vantage point. A consultant can often facilitate the process of grappling with these questions, even though conventional thinking in the profession is tilted toward exploration exclusively with the therapist. If we assume that an experience can occur in consultation that cannot take place within the therapeutic relationship, rather than assume that the therapeutic relationship must contain everything, we are in a better position to expand our comprehension of the process of therapy. The case vignette of Ms. S affirms this position.

> In seeking consultation, Ms. S wants an outside perspective on her therapy. She does not intend to let her therapist know about the consultation beforehand. She regards herself as doing something constructive and healthy on her own behalf and does not feel that she is being destructive to her therapy. Her therapeutic relationship has been long and intense—10 years at 3 times a week—and she wants a separate space, all her own, to sort out where she has been and where she is going. Ms. S is not considering leaving her therapist, but she does

have a specific question having to do with whether or not she should reduce the number of sessions from 3 to 2 times per week. The question of cutting back has come up for her because she is in the midst of changing professions and will have less income to allot to therapy. But she does not want to alter the nature of the important therapeutic relationship solely because of money or a change in direction in her external life.

At first I feel a pull to question Ms. S's certainty about excluding her therapist from knowing about the consultation. I have been trained, with valid reason, to be aware of the possibility that patients might take action outside the therapeutic relationship fueled by feelings in relation to their therapists. If this occurs and patients are made aware of what is occurring, they might choose instead to bring their feelings, and the psychological issues embedded within them, back to therapy. I have been trained to suggest that patients raise questions about altering the number of sessions or terminating directly with the therapist—not with an outside consultant. Their wish to exclude the therapist is meaningful and should be explored with the therapist.

On the other hand, I also believe that patients not only have the right to seek consultation but can have positive and constructive reasons for doing so. The psychological meaning of the choice can be explored both in ongoing therapy and in consultation. In this case, Ms. S clearly wants to provide herself with a separate vantage point from which to regard the accomplishments of her psychological work in long-term therapy. I can see no reason to judge her wish in advance as destructive or to assume that the effect of consultation on the therapy would be detrimental. Consultation with me would not preclude exploration in the therapeutic relationship. I schedule an appointment of a session and a half in length with Ms. S.

Ms. S spends her time with me reviewing the course of what has clearly been a long and vitally important therapeutic relationship. I listen and ask questions as they arise. Somewhere in the middle of the session, she stops talking and is silent for a moment. "You know," she says, "I didn't realize it when I asked for this appointment, but I've actually given myself a chance to think about my therapy and organize what it has meant to me. Hearing myself talk about it with someone outside the experience is surprisingly powerful."

At this moment, an unanticipated and spontaneous benefit of the consultation occurs. Ms. S is having a profound experience of the transformative change that has occurred as a result of her therapy. For a significant and moving moment, Ms. S and I share the experience of appreciating the fruits of all her work in years of therapy. Listening to Ms. S, I find myself feeling privileged to be included in her account of the struggles with her therapist and with herself. The psychological shifts that can occur in psychotherapy—elusive and mysterious, so difficult to convey in words—are directly conveyed as Ms. S speaks. Both of us are left with a clear affirmation of the value of her therapy that will undoubtedly find its way back into her ongoing work. The question she has brought to me—whether to leave the therapy in view of her decreased income—resolves itself. Ms. S decides to continue in therapy at the same frequency and to alter her involvement independently of changes in her professional life or her income.

In retrospect, my anxiety about providing this consultation was related to my concern about excluding the therapist and to the negative feelings I imagined the therapist might have toward me, not to the question with which the patient was struggling. I have no doubt about the value of the separate and independent space for Ms.

S. In this case, Ms. S's certainty about the value of the consultation helped me manage my initial uncertainty.

When I contacted Ms. S for permission to include the vignette, she offered the following comments. As with Ms. A, I include them in order to represent the patient's point of view, not only as I imagine it but in her own words. Ms. S writes:

> Something I knew I wanted for myself in life was the ability to feel, think, and articulate clearly and effectively. Before the consultation, I somewhat narrowly saw this as the ability to speak a professional language . . . About halfway through the consultation, in the process of explaining myself to Dr. E, I suddenly realized I was doing just that: Feeling, thinking, and articulating clearly. It was a profound moment for me and one fully shared with Dr. E. It has left us with a special bond that I will carry with me. My moment of integration! It was a strong, healthy experience and one I have been able to build on in all aspects of my life.

The notion that patients in-depth psychotherapy can receive something of value from a consultant is a simple idea that has broad implications. By insisting on the exclusivity of the therapeutic dyad, we may implicitly and unnecessarily reinforce patients' feeling of dependency on their therapists. While an experience of dependence can be important in facilitating a regression, the experience of dependence can also be problematic when it persists. Patients may locate needed capacities in therapists and have difficulty claiming these capacities as their own, making it difficult to separate from therapists and move on in their lives. The reminder that psychological resources are located not only in oneself but also in other relationships can be invaluable.

HOLDING A SUPERVISORY COUPLE

Another experimental and perhaps unusual consultation request to which I responded came from a supervisor and her supervisee who asked me to meet with both of them. I would like to describe our consultation in some detail because most difficulties in supervisory relationships are handled within the dyad. If problems cannot be resolved, the supervisee may choose to work with another supervisor. In this consultation, both the supervisor and supervisee chose to see a consultant, thereby creating a separate space within which they could get help with a specific difficult case and perhaps establish a new way of working together.

> Dr. L, a therapist who is participating in a post-graduate training program, asks if I would be willing to meet conjointly with her and her supervisor, Dr. T, to talk about a particularly difficult patient that Dr. L has been seeing. Dr. L (supervisee) and Dr. T are basically working well together, but the patient is challenging Dr. L (supervisee) in areas of personal vulnerability, giving rise to anxiety about Dr. L's adequacy and raising the question for Dr. L of whether she can continue working with this patient. She and her supervisor, Dr. T, both feel that an outside perspective will help them by offering another perspective on the difficult therapeutic relationship and insuring that they are not sharing a blind spot that might be making the therapeutic relationship unnecessarily difficult.
>
> When we schedule a time, Dr. T (supervisor) comments on one of her aims for the conjoint session. She hopes to model for Dr. L (supervisee) the reality that therapists at every level of experience need the holding environment and outside vantage point that consultation provides, particularly for patients who challenge us the most.

When the three of us meet in my office, Dr. L (super-visee) presents her work with Mr. B, a man in his thirties who survived an early childhood of neglect and chaos, while Dr. T and I listen attentively. Dr. L succinctly conveys basic elements of Mr. B's history. After being relinquished by his birth mother because of her intractable drug addiction, he lived in multiple foster homes. At age 21, he was reunited with the only accessible member of his biological family, a great-aunt on his mother's side, who has recently died. Currently alone, without a family of his own, and without siblings or other relatives or a connection to any of the foster families he lived with, Mr. B struggles to support himself as an installer for the telephone company. He came to the clinic at which Dr. L is doing postgraduate training so that he could receive help with recurrent bouts of immobilizing depression. He informed Dr. L in their first session that he has attempted therapy many times before and never with any success.

Dr. L, a warm and caring individual as well as the mother of young children, understands the depth of his life-long deprivation and the resulting despair and need. She has bravely planted herself at the border between his overwhelming hopelessness and the glimmer of surviving hope that has enabled him to come for help.

Mr. B's combination of a desperate need to find a reason to keep struggling to live, and equally powerful hostile challenges to any attempt on Dr. L's part to help him "keep on keeping on," would push any therapist to the brink of defeat. As his stories about his former therapists reveal, Mr. B is able to hone in on a therapist's particular personal vulnerability with unerring precision. Not surprisingly, he was repeatedly defeated in just this way by the mother who took care of him in the foster-care situation that lasted the longest amount of time.

Mr. B has a knack for immobilizing Dr. L, as he has

other therapists, until she literally cannot find words to speak. After many sessions, she is left with agonizing worry about his safety and obsessive doubts about her capacities. Her worry and self-doubt has escalated to the point where she is considering transferring him, not only because of the feelings he is eliciting but because she wonders if he deserves a different therapist since she is being rendered ineffectual. However she knows a transfer would be disastrous for him, akin to repeating the imagined and real rejections from parents in one foster-care situation after another. In the worst of the despair he evokes, she doubts the value of psychotherapy much as he doubts the value of being alive. Yet she can also appreciate Mr. B's growing attachment to her and understand that he is expressing positive feelings and gratitude nonverbally as best he can. For example, he never misses a session and he has even begun to arrive early.

The transference matrix of this relationship is readily apparent to the three of us. Mr. B has engendered in Dr. L a despair about her ability to be effectual that parallels the despair he suffers on a broader scale about life not being worth living. She can barely stand to feel for brief periods of time what is a persisting, familiar state for him. But merely identifying the transference matrix, which Dr. T (supervisor) has already done, does not make the feelings easier for Dr. L to tolerate. Anxiety and doubt have clearly become part of the supervisory relationship as well. Now the anxiety and doubt is being presented to me in this unusual consultation.

I offer comments on the dynamics of the therapeutic relationship and the option of transferring Mr. B to a different therapist. I can see from Dr. T's (supervisor) nods that I am touching on fundamental ideas that she has already raised with Dr. L. But brilliant cognitive insights about projective identification, the enactment of

early nonverbal experiences in the therapeutic relationship, and all our combined wisdom about receiving and
bearing suffering related to individual fate and the human condition seem at the moment like the flimsiest of
protection in the emotionally charged sessions that Dr. L
and Mr. B are living through.

After Dr. T and Dr. L leave, I find that I continue to
ruminate about the case, searching for ways to help Dr. L
withstand the onslaught of her internal experience. Having taken inside me the problem in the case—part of
what makes the role of consultant both challenging and
difficult—I wait for her follow-up call to learn how our
consultation affected the therapy.

Dr. L's message sounds optimistic. Meeting with Dr. T
and with me has en-*couraged* her, she reports. Consequently she felt internally stronger when in the office
with Mr. B in their subsequent session. Her confidence
apparently made a difference to Mr. B, because he seemed
to settle down and disengage from the polarized conflict
with her in which the forces of death, carried by the
patient, challenged the endurance of the spirit of life,
represented by Dr. L.

As I ponder our three-way consultation, I wonder
whether one source of the positive impact came from the
fact that the *three* of us met together, bearing the suffering of Mr. B on all our shoulders, creating a human
container strong enough to hold it. In the consultation,
the three of us were psychologically containing an un-
mothered man. Two of us, the consultant and supervisor,
constitute a maternal matrix, to hold the therapist/
daughter/mother so that she can withstand the assault
on her adequacy by the neglected, abandoned patient/
boy who is filled with rage and hurt. Perhaps I, the
consultant/father, helped the maternal dyad of supervisor
and supervisee withstand this assault. The consultation

may make the most significant contribution in this non-verbal dimension.

Four months later Dr. L (supervisee) calls me to request another conjoint supervision session, which we schedule. Once again, Dr. L has been pushed to the edge of her endurance and is considering transferring Mr. B despite the progress he has made both in his life and in understanding himself. Once again the three of us sit together in my consulting room and cover the same territory. I am more aware in this second meeting of a visceral sense that Dr. L (supervisee) is like a sponge soaking up courage and strength. Her fear of reentering the office with Mr. B is palpable. His cynical, sarcastic comments are incredibly wounding. They immobilize her, render her speechless, knock her off center, strip her of authority. My predominant memory of the consultation is, once again, not carried in words. Rather, I recall the experience of us sitting together, shaking our heads in sorrow, appreciating the patient's struggle to find meaning in life, to find meaning that will make the struggle to live worthwhile.

Once again, I receive a follow-up message from Dr. L indicating that the next session went well. She felt centered, in charge of herself, as if, in her words, "I found my courage after the consultation."

The positive effect of this consultation suggests that some therapeutic relationships can be most effective when, rather than an individual or dyad, there is a "basket" of healers to establish a useful conceptual frame and hold the enormity of human suffering. Peer consultation groups undoubtedly serve this function, as can small group supervision within training programs. But these groups, which meet over time and are designed to address the needs of each member, are more complex. For example, envy and competition can operate consciously and unconsciously. A consultant to the supervisory dyad has a unique and specific function in relation to the particular case.

In our structured conjoint consultation of a consultant, supervisor, and supervisee, the focus of the consultation was exclusively on the supervisee and her patient, and the consultation was finite in scope. Within this unconventional structure we created an atmosphere of mutual respect and support. Both therapist and supervisor were in accord in wanting my help on behalf of Mr. B and Dr. L. One step removed from the anxiety generated by Mr. B, yet the recipient of Dr. L's and Dr. T's concerns and doubts, I was in a good position to appreciate the problematic impact of Dr. L's anxiety on her ability to feel effective, or, in the language of primary vulnerability, the problematic intersection of Mr. B's and Dr. L's primary vulnerabilities. Keeping my focus on Dr. L's strengths, suggesting ways of thinking about the therapeutic relationship and of intervening, functioned to pull Dr. L and Dr. T out of the depotentiating state of vulnerability.

When I contacted Dr. L and Dr. T for permission to include this vignette, they offered their perspectives on what was useful about the consultation. I had not attributed special significance to the aspects of the consultation that they focused on as valuable, underscoring once again the importance of including, when possible, everyone's point of view. Their comments led me to appreciate, rather than minimize, the significant role I played.

Dr. T (supervisor) writes that the vignette "captures the flavor of the consultation well." She notes that I omitted from the vignette a significant fact: she had previously worked with a male patient who was similar to Dr. L's patient and who had terminated the therapy without feeling helped by her. I in fact chose to omit this information from the vignette because I was concerned about including more information about Dr. T than she would feel comfortable with. Her response serves as yet another reminder to me that we cannot always know either what will help or what will hurt, not only in the actual work of psychotherapy and supervision/consultation, but even in the reflecting and writing about it. Attempts to simplify or reduce the complexity can result in the loss of significant information. She writes,

> Maybe you deleted this deliberately, but in the first consultation especially, I was still feeling a bit vulnerable about my work with Mr. S [her male patient], and Dr. L's client reminded me of him in many ways. So rather than just a general concern about a blind spot, I had the particular concern about my own vulnerabilities re Mr. S—especially my feelings of failure, hopelessness, and inadequacy. The parallel with Dr. L's feelings is obvious. And the first consultation on Mr. B was actually directly helpful to me in working through some of my remaining feelings about Mr. S.

> Although the notion of a "basket of healers" is lovely, and accurate, I also think there were specific things you said which were helpful to me as a supervisor. First, you encouraged Dr. L to be more honest, more authentic with Mr. B. Although I had done this with Mr. S, I felt more constrained in encouraging Dr. L to do this. In other words, I felt it easier to take a risk myself, to step outside the usual boundaries of therapeutic appropriateness, than I did encouraging Dr. L to do that. Your "permission" to Dr. L to do that enabled me to support her in being more honest.

In the second consultation, you took the issues from the purely psychological to the existential—by shifting discussion to Mr. B's search for meaning, hope, purpose in life, and then to Dr. L's inability, or any therapist's inability, to "solve" this dilemma for him. Again you encouraged me, as well as Dr. L, to move beyond usual therapeutic boundaries, which enabled Dr. L to respond in more down-to-earth, authentic ways, that helped considerably.

Dr. L (supervisee) reminded me that I had also omitted a significant piece of information about her, once again in an effort to protect her privacy. Prior to beginning supervision with Dr. T, the supervisor, Dr. L had worked with a supervisor with whom she discussed Mr. B. The perspective of the previous supervisor had seemed restrictive and had heightened Dr. L's feelings of inadequacy. Dr. L hoped and expected that she would work more effectively with Dr. T than with her previous supervisor.

Dr. T and Dr. L had been focusing on tapes of the therapy sessions. But this "micro-perspective" of looking at what she had said and could have said had been counterproductive, heightening her feelings of inadequacy. In our three-way consultation, we took a broader "macro-perspective," which brought about a shift in Dr. L's feelings of effectiveness and confidence and a shift in the relationship with Mr. B. Dr. L writes:

Our first three-way meeting produced several steps forward. Preparing for the meeting, I integrated the material and my feelings about the case and presented well, I felt, on a broad-stroke level. Dr. Elkind's responses were primarily supportive and confirming that this case would be very difficult, even for a seasoned professional. I also felt encouraged to be very honest and direct, more myself. This helped me discard more of the shackles I felt as a less-experienced clinician trying to remain "professional" in a threatening situation that didn't call for a traditional approach. In part, these "shackles" were the "neutrality" that I tried to hide behind when I felt most threatened. Erring in this direction was retraumatizing in its reminiscence of the detached caregivers in Mr. B's life. I left the meeting feeling more confident and courageous, and the improvement in the work reinforced the shift . . . The very unconventionality in which I was participating felt somehow closer to the arena I was in with Mr. B.

After the set-back described by Dr. Elkind, and before our second meeting, I said to myself after a session with Mr. B, "This feels bigger than me, but also bigger than Mr. B. Something comes over him that consumes us both." Then, in response to my descriptions, Dr. Elkind drew the discussion to the level of archetype and existential conceptualization. I felt a deep surge of relief as I found her giving language to what I had understood, though was unable to articulate. I will never forget her saying, "You know, you could talk to him exactly as we are talking now, even consider telling him of our meeting. We could even discuss possibly having him meet with us, all four together." I was happily astonished as the field holding Mr. B and myself seemed to expand finally to dimensions that could embrace and acknowledge the profound breadth and depth of pain this man had endured for a lifetime. I was deeply moved, and our ensuing work has reflected my greater ability to stand beyond my small personal, now rather petty-feeling concerns. The image

I have of this experience is those nested Russian dolls—many layers of containers that expand from inside out to hold us.

CONSULTATION: LIMITS AND POSSIBILITIES

As I reflect on the unconventional consultations I have been providing that include the active participation of both patients and therapists, and on the complicated process of describing them both from my point of view and from the perspectives of the individuals involved, I am struck by the risks each of us have taken. Ms. A and Dr. R, the patient and therapist caught in a seemingly unresolvable impasse, made themselves especially vulnerable in meeting with me while in the depths of a shared experience of hopelessness and despair. They had no assurance that the consultation would help, that I would offer them something that they could make use of to bring about a shift.

Ms. S, the patient who sought an independent consultation to evaluate her long-term intensive psychotherapy, was confident in the value and importance of seeking consultation without including her therapist. But during the sessions with me she also risked allowing something unexpected and spontaneous to occur, bringing about a shared special moment that has had lasting influence.

Dr. T, the supervisor, took a risk in acknowledging that Dr. L, her supervisee, might profit from more than Dr. T could offer in finding a way to work effectively with Mr. B, Dr. L's difficult patient. Dr. L took a risk not only in exposing the overwhelming sense of inadequacy constellated in the therapy with Mr. B, but also in allowing herself to be so deeply affected by her patient.

Working on the vignettes together presented each of us with the challenge of coming to terms with old and new knots in the various relationships. In working on each consultation with the individuals involved, I found that we had to address together some aspect of our present interaction. To give one example, in a preliminary draft of the vignette of Drs. L, the supervisee, and T, the supervisor, I initially referred to Dr. L without the title "Dr.," continuing without thinking the convention I had initially established of distinguishing therapists from patients by the title "Dr." In calling Dr. L, "Ms. L," I not only stripped Dr. L of her status and authority but gave her the challenge of letting me know what I had done. I had to think about the meaning of my unconsciousness, noticing how I, too, had been drawn into the anxiety and self-doubt constellated in the case. Dr. L was able to extricate us, this time functioning as consultant to me. Both of us had to incorporate this new experience into our relationship. Analogous challenging new experiences occurred with each of the individuals I contacted, so that we not only reworked previous interactions, but grappled with new encounters. Everyone involved had to tolerate being both disappointed and disappointing, wounded and wounding, eliciting the best and worst in each other.

I have offered vignettes of essentially positive consultations both to suggest the possibilities that are opened up by including patients and supervisees in consultation and to encourage myself in the sometimes daunting task of expanding available resources in a formally uncharted direction. But there are also limits, dilemmas, and pitfalls in entering into the shadow realm of our profession.

While I have not had an experience of a failed consultation in the sense of making matters worse, in some cases I have had the experience of being unable to effect a change in an entrenched impasse. Patient and therapist have remained at odds in an unyielding deadlock. Other patients continued to experience painful misattunement and wounding from their therapists. With consultation, the patients struggled to change themselves, their therapists, and their understanding of what was occurring in the relationship, but to no avail. Eventually they left the therapy, feeling injured and defeated because they were not able to influence the therapy in a positive way. I am not sure whether I functioned to prolong an unproductive therapy or whether I enabled the patients to dissolve profound transference attachments and leave when they were able. I do not know with certainty whether or how the impasse would have resolved if I had not been on the scene. But I find myself returning to the basic conviction that patients are not easily able to disengage from an unproductive therapy. Unconscious transference ties, the investment in the therapeutic relationship, coupled with a reluctance to have a failure experience with a therapist they selected, make terminating difficult. Going through this difficult process with someone who recognizes the difficulty is in itself useful.

Working at the edge of these limitations, both in what can occur in individual psychological development and in human relationships, is indeed sobering. Acting as a consultant has meant living with self-doubt and unanswerable questions, while striving to shift from judgment to compassion. Put in these terms, the role of a consultant is not altogether different from that of a therapist, or from the challenge facing any of us who attempts to live our life as consciously as we can.

REFERENCES

Elkind, S. (1992). *Resolving Impasses in Therapeutic Relationships*. New York: Guilford.

———(1994) The consultant's role in resolving impasses in therapeutic relationships. *The American Journal of Psychoanalysis* Vol 54, (1):3–13.

———(1995). Consultation when the therapist terminates therapy. *The American Journal of Psychoanalysis*, Vol 55, (4):331–346.

Ogden, T. (1982). *Projective Identification and Psychotherapeutic Technique*. New York: Jason Aronson.
———(1994). *Subjects of Analysis*. Northvale, NJ: Jason Aronson.
Winnicott, D. W. (1980). *The Maturational Processes and the Facilitating Environment*. New York: International Universities Press.

Index

Credits

The editor gratefully acknowledges permission to reprint material from the following sources:

"Towards Autonomy: Some Thoughts on Psychoanalytic Supervision," by Patrick Casement, in *Journal of Clinical Psychoanalysis*, 2:389–403. © 1993.

"And Now for Something Completely Different," by Nina Coltart, in *The Baby and the Bathwater*. London: Karnac Books. © 1996.

"Being Too Good," by Michael Eigen, in *Psychic Deadness*. Northvale, NJ: Jason Aronson. © 1996.

"Collusive Selective Inattention to the Negative Impact of the Supervisory Interaction," by Lawrence Epstein, in *Contemporary Psychoanalysis*, 22:389–409. © 1986.

"On Supervisory Parataxis and Dialogue," by John Fiscalini, in *Contemporary Psychoanalysis*, 21:591–607. © 1985.

"A Proposal to Enlarge the Individual Model of Psychoanalytic Supervision," by Benjamin Wolstein, in *Contemporary Psychoanalysis*, 20:131–145. © 1984.